city
weekends

The Greatest Escapes and Weekend Getaways
In and Around New York City

Alison Lowenstein

universe publishing

Dedication

For Peter, Lucy, and Max, my favorite traveling companions.

This edition first published in 2009 by
UNIVERSE PUBLISHING
A division of Rizzoli International Publications Inc.
300 Park Avenue South
New York, NY 10010
www.rizzoliusa.com

© 2009 by Alison Lowenstein
Cover Illustration by Sujean Rim
Design by Headcase Design

2009 2010 2011 2012 / 10 9 8 7 6 5 4 3 2 1
First Edition
Printed in the United States of America

ISBN-13: 978-0-7893-1857-2
Library of Congress Control Number: 2008910553

Publisher's Note: Neither Universe Publishing nor the authors have any interest, financial or personal, in the locations listed in this book. No fees were paid or services rendered for inclusion in these pages.

contents

acknowledgments

I'd like to give a special thanks to the following people for their support in writing this book:

My wonderful husband, Peter, who went on almost every trip—always driving so I could see the sights—and whose everlasting patience and support truly made this book. My children, Lucy and Max, for their good spirits throughout the many excursions around the New York area and who are now kid-experts on the best hotel rooms and where to find a good kid's meal. My parents, Michael and Eileen Lowenstein, who were extremely helpful and supportive to me and also babysat whenever it was needed. My in-laws, Fred and Melinda Isaacs, who always made time to watch the kids on the numerous outings when the children weren't invited or when I needed time to write. Without all of you guys, this book wouldn't be possible.

I'd also like to thank Matt and Kate Berger, Alison Burke Griffiths, Jenny Isaacs, Debbie and Peter Johnson, Leslie Kaufman, Dina Kutcher, Robin Muskin, Aimee Nadler, Allison Prete, Carla Sosenko, Emma Star, Dave Tauber, Kristin Williams, Amy Widman, and Valerie Walsh. A big thanks to the many folks who helped me with this book, whether you gave me information on your hometowns and favorite vacation destinations, or accompanied me on various excursions. Most of all, thanks to all of you for putting up with me as I talked incessantly about the book and traveling around the New York area.

I'd like to give special thanks to Caitlin Leffel for signing up the book and always standing behind the project, and to my editor, Claire Gierczak, for her exceptional editing skills, patience, and enthusiasm. I'd also like to thank Elizabeth Smith for her fine eye to detail as she copyedited the manuscript, as well as give a special thanks to my agent, Kirsten Manges for her dedication.

About the Author

Alison Lowenstein is the author of *City Baby Brooklyn: The Ultimate Guide for Parents From Pregnancy to Preschool*. A native New Yorker and writer, she is a regular contributor to New York area magazines. She lives in Brooklyn with her family and is currently at work on another New York guidebook.

introduction

New York City is a vacation destination for people across the globe, so it's a wonder why so many New Yorkers find themselves at a loss for good weekend plans. You don't need tons of cash or celebrity status to enjoy an amazing weekend in this great city and its surrounding areas. It's not even necessary to travel halfway across the world to have a fabulous escape.

City Weekends is filled with fun getaways in and around New York City. If you don't have time to leave the city, it's no problem: Simply indulge in a weekend enjoying what NYC has to offer—from free hikes through scenic woods to seeing a Bollywood movie in a theater that sells samosas from their concession stand. Discovering and visiting all the places while researching for the book made me appreciate the unknown treasures of a city in which I've lived in my entire life.

If you're aching to head out of the urban landscape on a weekend road trip, check out the fifteen trips listed in this book—all less than two and a half hours from the city. There's something for everyone. Spend the weekend at an authentic rodeo in New Jersey or get in touch with your spiritual side at an ashram in upstate New York. Fans of spas can spend their weekends heading to the many peaceful retreats featured throughout the book. Outdoors types will find the best places around New York to fly-fish or ski.

In Weekends Away, I've included an extra section of suggested activities for either a day or weekend trip. Fans of kitsch will enjoy a retro weekend sampling drive-in restaurants in the metro area—where a carhop brings you familiar favorites like hamburgers and old-fashioned root beer floats. Then, top off your nostalgic weekend at a drive-in movie theater by checking out the list of the remaining drive-ins surrounding the city.

With a huge selection of plans for inside and outside NYC—within any budget—you can recharge as you discover the area's hidden gems. There were countless times while touring historic homes tucked away in parks or hiking on nature trails, when I felt as if I had removed myself from the stress of urban living without having left the city limits.

If you're dreaming about running off to St. Petersburg, instead jump on the train to Brighton Beach and eat borscht on the deck at M & I International. If you want to feel as if you're in Tokyo, shop in neighboring New Jersey at Mitsuwa Marketplace, a mall that sells only Japanese merchandise and amazing Japanese food. In the New York City area you can travel the world and experience so many new things without ever stepping on a plane. Those who feel they can't get all their vacationing in during their allotted two-week vacation time need never worry again.

New York City is filled with many treasures beyond the typical tourist attractions. You can tour the house of the great jazz legend Louis Armstrong or try your hand at archery—both of which can be done in Queens. You can also gallery-hop around the boroughs or kayak for free off the waters of Manhattan. From the hip to the historic—enjoy all NYC has to offer on your weekend jaunts.

You don't have to live in the city to enjoy *City Weekends* since all locations are easily accessible from the surrounding areas. Spend the weekend following the fun itineraries to make the most out of your NYC visit. Visit a working farm in Queens or a wigwam in the Bronx. Spend a weekend at the beach or on the slopes—it's all nearby.

I had a blast trying out all of the activities in the book so I know you'll enjoy them, too. Whenever possible I've included the Web site for each activity, so that you can check on the admission fees and hours, which often change seasonally. I've carefully researched restaurants near the locations, so you won't ever be too far from food if hunger strikes. Also, it's important to remember many of the destinations are accessible by bus or train if you don't own a car.

Go grab your Metrocard or pick up a Zipcar and enjoy a weekend getaway.

part one

weekends in the city

Chapter One

Traveling the World without Leaving the City:

International Weekends in NYC

They call New York City a melting pot for a reason. In the city you can travel the five of the seven continents and never have to deal with filling out customs forms. From a night at a Russian dinner theater that seems more like Vegas than Brooklyn, to a day at a Korean spa, you can explore some of the world in a NYC weekend. Try eating dinner with your hands at a hip Ethiopian restaurant or spend the afternoon window-shopping at a Chinese mall; it's all a walk or subway ride away.

Follow these easy itineraries that are divided by country to get a flavor for the various ethnicities throughout the five boroughs.

Japan

Head to the east side of Manhattan on the 4, 5, or 6 train to Grand Central Station or take the E or V train to Lexington Avenue and 53rd Street to take a stroll through the galleries and indoor gardens of the **Japan Society** *(333 East 47th Street; 212-832-1155; www.japansociety.org)*. The Japan Society exhibits Japanese artistic work like bamboo sculptures, textiles, and other forms of arts and crafts. You can also sign up for one of their popular programs like the Japanese film series or family-friendly festivals.

After perusing the serene gallery with indoor fountains, head to Fifth Avenue and 54th Street to purchase high-end Japanese goods at **Takashimaya** *(693 5th Avenue; 212-350-0100 / 800-228-1810; www.ny-takashimaya.com)*, where you can get everything from baby items to gorgeous home goods. I especially enjoy browsing there since the store has a sleek design and many hard-to-find items. Don't miss having lunch or afternoon tea in the **Teabox Restaurant**, located on the store's basement level, where you can get a traditional Japanese tea service with a yummy assortment of cookies. This excursion is best planned for a Saturday since the restaurant is closed on Sundays.

After lunch walk west on 42nd Street to 6th Avenue to visit the **Kinokuniya Bookstore** *(1073 Avenue of the Americas; 212-869-1700; www.kinokuniya.co.jp)*. The three floors of this shop are filled with a large collection of Japanese and Asian books in English and Japanese, tons of anime, and a basement filled with an amazing assortment of Japanese school supplies. They also sell cool Japanese toys and T-shirts with fun phrases like I LOVE TOFU. Grab a tea or bento box at **Café Zaiya** on the second floor and sit near the large windows overlooking vibrant Bryant Park or get your order to go and eat in the park.

If the visit to Kinokuniya whets your appetite for more Japanese goodies and yummy eats, spend the afternoon at a Japanese mall in New Jersey. Walk or take the subway to the Port Authority and then get on the #51 shuttle to **Mitsuwa Marketplace** *(595 River Road, Edgewater; 201-941-9113; www.mitsuwanj.com)*. The shuttle is for customers and employees of the mall only and will drop you off at the marketplace in about a half an hour. The shuttle leaves every half hour starting from 8:15 a.m. until 7:45 p.m. and costs $3 each way. If you're in search of Hello Kitty paraphernalia you won't be disappointed.

Korea

You don't have to head to Korea to spend a luxurious day at a real Korean spa. Just head to **Spa Castle** *(131-10 11th Avenue, College Point; 718-939-6300; www.nyspacastle.com)* in Queens. Take the 7 train to the last stop at Main Street in Flushing and jump on a shuttle bus to the spa. If you drive, you will get the rock star treatment, as the valet parking at the spa is free.

Here you can easily spend a day relaxing and enjoying the medicinal effects of Spa Castle's seven sauna rooms, and its lounges, sleep areas, and pools, because for a single fee, you have free range over its facilities. An appealing aspect of the spa is that you don't have to carry cash around. Upon entering the spa you are given a bracelet that is similar to a credit card as it is used to track all your purchases. When your visit is complete, you are billed accordingly.

You are also given two lockers when you check in—one for your shoes and another for your clothing and belongings—as well as a uniform to wear during your stay. Make sure to pack a bathing suit, because the roof of the spa houses indoor pools, which are open year-round. The pool features also include a waterfall and a kiddie pool if you are visiting with your family. If you're like me, you will want to spend the whole day relaxing in the Japanese Hinoki bath built with ancient pinewoods.

It's good to note that Spa Castle has two restaurants on-site, so that you'll never go hungry. If you're in need of a spa service, head to the various treatment centers throughout the spa, but make sure to stop by the rooms early as they tend to book up quickly. (I had to wait an hour for a foot massage.) Another notable treatment they offer is a traditional body scrub, which is the perfect remedy for dry winter skin. If you'd like to continue the spa treatments at home, Spa Castle sells Korean beauty and spa products in the changing area. I left with a hydrating facial mask that only cost me a dollar.

After a day at the spa, spend a fun night out in Manhattan's Koreatown by grabbing some unbelievably tasty mandoo, or Korean dumplings, at the **Mandoo Bar** (2 West 32nd Street; 212-279-3075), where the waitstaff seems to be the friendliest and happiest in the city. Your enthusiastic waiter will bring you good-sized portions of these incredible dumplings and some pints of Korean beer. After dinner, you might want to stroll down 32nd Street, stopping in at the various Korean shops and karaoke bars. If you plan on having Saturday lunch at Mandoo, it would be worthwhile to check out the **Lee Young Hee Museum of Korean Culture** (2 West 32nd Street; 212-560-0722; www.lyhkm.org). This small museum is located on the third floor of the same building as the Mandoo Bar and pays tribute to Korean culture and heritage. The museum is open weekdays and Saturdays from 11 a.m. to 5 p.m.

China

There are three vibrant Chinatowns in New York City so you can definitely spend the entire weekend touring all these colorful communities in Manhattan, Queens, and Brooklyn while sampling amazing Chinese food.

Start your escape on Mott Street in Manhattan's Chinatown, grabbing a meal at one of the many restaurants on a street lined with numerous shops spilling over with tables of fresh fish and trinkets. Good eats can be found at the **Peking Duck House** (28 Mott Street; 212-227-1810; www.pekingduck-housenyc.com). Although a majority of the restaurants in Chinatown prominently display dead ducks among other animals, in the windows, vegetarians will be happy to find **Buddha Bodai** (5 Mott Street; 212-566-8388; www.chinatown-vegetarian.com). This kosher vegetarian restaurant serves family-sized portions of classic Chinese dishes, but uses substitutes for meat. They also have a large location in the Chinatown in Queens.

You don't have to head to neighboring Little Italy for dessert, just stop by the **Chinatown Ice Cream Factory** (65 Bayard Street; 212-608-4170; www.chinatownicecreamfactory.com) for some green-tea ice cream or fill your bags with the buckets of candy offered at popular Asian candy shop chain from Hong Kong, **Aji Ichiban** (37 Mott Street; 212-233-7650; www.ajiichiban.com.hk).

After feasting on sweets, learn about Chinese culture and history at the **Museum of Chinese in America** (215 Centre Street; 212-619-4785, www.mocanyc.org). Once housed in a public school, the museum opened its doors on Centre Street in the fall of 2008, and features exhibits on the history of the Chinese in America and also offers various cultural programs.

From the heart of Chinatown, walk along Canal Street and check out the crowded streets filled with shops. Soak in the atmosphere of folks bargaining and buying everything from pocketbooks to watches, then head down uptown on Broadway to the **Pearl River Market** (477 Broadway; 212-431-4770; www.pearlriver.com), where you can pick up tea sets, kimonos, and authentic Chinese goods. If you are in search of Chinese herbs, stop by **Lin Sister Herb Shop** (4 Bowery; 212-962-5417; www.linsister.com) where they also offer acupuncture treatments.

Film fans should visit the **ImaginAsian Theater** (239 East 59th Street; 212-371-6682; www.theimaginasian.com). This Upper East Side movie theater shows Asian films with subtitles and hosts various film festivals throughout the year. Check out a Chinese flick or the occasional Bollywood film at this unique theater.

Leave Manhattan for Queens, by jumping on the 7 train and taking it to the last stop in Flushing. There you'll exit onto Main Street to find its storefronts written in Chinese—this is a thriving Chinese community. Head to the **Flushing Mall** located just a few blocks from Main Street (133-31 39th Avenue; 718-888-1234; www.888flushingmall.com). Unlike other malls, this one doesn't have the typical American chain stores but instead is filled with shops selling Chinese toys, clothes, and a large assortment of dumplings from various vendors. Touring this mall, with no signs of American products, might make you feel as if you are at a shopping plaza in China.

For a more luxurious Chinese shopping experience, visit the newly opened **Queens Crossing** (136-17 39th Avenue; 718-888-1234; www.queenscrossing.com), located one block from Main Street. This mall houses up-market shops like **Liuligongfang** and the **Shanghai Museum of Art Shop**, which both sell Asian art. The mall has a few restaurants to choose from, including some contemporary high-end Asian fare as well as some Korean food.

Brooklyn's Chinatown, located in Sunset Park on 8th Avenue from around 42nd Street to 62nd Street, houses Chinese shops, a large Chinese supermarket, and tons of great eats. Just take the R train to 53rd Street and you'll reach this bustling neighborhood. Make sure to dine on dim sum at **Pacificana** *(813 55th Street, Brooklyn; 718-871-2880)*. The neighborhood is always growing, so enjoy exploring new shops and restaurants as they appear in this area of Brooklyn. Unlike other Chinatowns, which have become a little touristy, there is a strong sense of a Chinese-American neighborhood community here, so the trinket shops are few and far between.

India

Hop on almost any Queens-bound subway line and you'll find that it stops at Roosevelt Avenue in Jackson Heights. Upon exiting the train, you'll be in the center of an Indian community. Located right next to the subway entrance on 37th Road is the **Eagle Movie Theater** *(73-07 37th Road; 718-205-2800; www.eaglemovietheater.com)*, plastered with Bollywood movie posters. Here you can watch new Bollywood films with English subtitles for only $8. Films are shown in the evenings. If you haven't seen a Bollywood film, this is definitely the place to see one. Watch the elaborate dance scenes on the big screen while chowing down on a two-dollar samosa from the concession stand. The colorful coming attractions for the new releases will have you coming back to see more flicks at this one-of-a-kind Queens movie theater.

Outside the theater is the heart of Little India; walk one block down to 74th Street, where the street is filled with sari shops and a large Patel Brothers—an Indian supermarket chain. This is the perfect place to pick up the spices necessary to cook your own Indian food at home. On 74th Street you'll also see folks shopping for jewelry and traditional Indian wedding dresses. This main shopping drag is also known to entice foodies the city over with delicious Indian fare, the most popular being the **Jackson Diner** *(37-47 74th Street; 718-672-1232; www.jacksondiner.com)*, which serves tasty food from northern India. This is one of my favorite restaurants in the city and I actually had my thirtieth birthday party in their back room. The large open space provides a nice atmosphere for dining and on weekends they serve a buffet lunch.

If you're inspired to dance after seeing a Bollywood movie—and admittedly I was—sign up for Bollywood dance classes in Manhattan. Two popular Bollywood dance schools are in the Chelsea area; **Bollywood Axion Dance Studio** *(257 West 39th Street; 646-373-2555; www.bollywoodaxion.com)* offers weekend classes for beginners, with the choice of Absolute Beginners Bollywood or just Beginners Bollywood. You can also take classes at **Bollywood Funk NYC Dance School** *(West 26th Street; 212-502-7997; www.bollywoodfunknyc.com)*, where they have classes for beginners every Saturday afternoon.

If your Indian escape includes spending an afternoon eating good Indian food, there are two areas of Manhattan to check out. On 6th Street between 1st and 2nd Avenues in the East Village, you have your choice of Indian restaurants. I had a friend who used to joke that they all share the same kitchen, but the food on the menus does vary in taste and price. Restaurant hosts stand outside, trying to entice you to dine at their restaurants, but don't feel intimated; check the menu. Although many of the restaurants on 6th Street have closed in the past few years, there are still a few good ones on 2nd Avenue between 4th and 6th Streets. You can also visit Lexington Avenue between 27th and 29th Streets, often referred to as **Curry Hill**, where you can dine in one of many Indian restaurants ranging from vegan kosher to takeout.

Russia

Take the B or Q train to Brighton Beach and underneath the elevated train tracks lies Brighton Beach Avenue, filled with Russian shops and restaurants. Often referred to as Little Odessa, this Russian beach community will make you think you're in a town along the Black Sea—shop signs are in Russian, and English is hardly ever spoken on the street. From here you can walk a block toward the water to take a stroll on the boardwalk.

If you want to spend the day at the beach, don't bother packing a picnic. You can have lunch at **Café Tatiana Restaurant** *(3152 Brighton 6th Street; 718-891-5151; www.tatianarestaurant.com)* on the boardwalk for authentic Russian food. Or you can just stop by a personal favorite, **M & I International Foods, Inc.** *(249 Brighton Beach Avenue; 718-615-1011)* and pick up some great Russian takeout on the second-floor café, located past the enormous candy area and bakery. For less than $10, you can feast on all sorts of Russian stews, meats, and potato dishes in this cafeteria-style restaurant. The main floor sells a variety of Russian imported food—from cheese to meat.

Spend the afternoon window-shopping at the fur shops and Russian bookshops that line Brighton Beach Avenue. Peruse the posters for the Russian entertainment in the area, because if you're a fan of a good theatrical

Vegas-style performance, you must spend an evening out in Brighton Beach. Book a table at the **National Nightclub** (273 Brighton Beach Avenue; 718-646-1225; www.come2national.com) and remember, the more folks you invite, the better. In fact, if you bring eight people, you get a free bottle of both vodka and wine. Just call ahead to reserve a table since the place gets crowded and is occasionally closed for private events.

Upon your arrival at the National, you are seated at a large banquet table where there are appetizers covered with plastic wrap. Although dinner starts between 7:30 p.m. and 8 p.m., the over-the-top floorshow starts at 9 p.m. and throughout the show, food is served and drinks are poured in this extremely festive atmosphere. The floorshow opens with Russian performers playing the keyboard as they sing renditions of "The Lady in Red" and performing elaborate dance numbers that rival any Vegas show. The dance floor in front of the stage is crowded with folks of all ages dancing to the music. During intermission, the host for the evening calls people to the stage who are celebrating everything from a fiftieth anniversary to a Sweet Sixteen—everything is in Russian with the exception of a few English songs.

Although there isn't an enforced dress code, folks get decked out to come to the National. In fact, half of the fun of the evening is getting ready for a night out at this club. If possible, bring your own vodka or drinks because a bottle is quite costly at this club.

What could be a better way of recovering from a vodka hangover than at Russian bathhouse? There are many bathhouses throughout the city. You can head to the Russian sauna at the **Russian and Turkish Bathhouses** (268 East 10th Street; 212-473-8806; www.russianturkishbaths.com) in the East Village, which have been around since the turn of the century. For a modern Russian spa experience, tucked away on Fulton Street near the South Street Seaport is the **Wall Street Bath and Spa 88** (88 Fulton Street; 212-766-8600; www.wallstreetbath.com). When I went, I was greeted by a woman behind the counter who was wearing an I LOVE KAZAKHSTAN T-shirt. The spa has a nice pool, a Turkish steam room, two saunas: one, a classic style "Old American Schvitz," and the other a traditional Russian sauna where you can opt for a fifteen-minute massage as you sweat out your impurities. If you are hungry, stop by the restaurant on the premises, which sells various Russian foods like borscht and other tasty Russian dishes.

Some fun ethnic restaurants:

In NYC you can enjoy dining at ethnic restaurants all over town, but here are a few particularly atmospheric restaurants that might make you feel as if you're dining abroad.

Sammy's Roumanian Steak House *(157 Chrystie Street, Manhattan; 212-673-0330)* Old-school Jewish food served in a festive atmosphere.

Ghenet *(284 Mulberry Street, Manhattan; 212-343-1888; 348 Douglass Street, Brooklyn; 718-230-4475; www.ghenet.com)* Eat with your hands at either location of this exceptional Ethiopian restaurant.

Tacis Beyti Restaurant *(1955 Coney Island Avenue, Brooklyn; 718-627-5750)* Experience authentic Turkish food at this Brooklyn favorite.

Brazil Brazil Restaurant *(330 West 46th Street, Man-hattan; 212-957-4300; www.brazilbrazilrestaurant.com)* Dine on Brazilian specialties at this local favorite in the theater district.

Cambodian Cuisine *(1664 3rd Avenue, Manhattan; 212-348-9100; www.cambodiancuisinenyc.com)* Enjoy some Cambodian food in one of the few Cambodian restaurants in the city.

Bohemian Hall *(2919 24th Avenue, Astoria; 718-274-4925; www.bohemianhall.com)* Grab a beer and some Czech food at this Czech beer garden. Get there early since it tends to fill up fast.

Ayvavti *(19-06 Ditmars Boulevard, Astoria; 718-545-4554; 78-02 5th Avenue, Brooklyn; 718-833-7033; www.agnantimeze.com)* Indulge in delicious Greek dishes at this popular restaurant with locations in both Queens and Brooklyn.

Mulberry Street, Little Italy, and Arthur Avenue, the Bronx Choose from the myriad of restaurants and Italian specialty shops that line Mulberry Street and Arthur Avenue.

Ethnic museums in Manhattan:

National Museum of the American Indian *(1 Bowling Green; 212-514-3700; www.nmai.si.edu)* Learn about the history and culture of the Native Americans who lived in what would become New York City at this downtown museum. It's free and open daily from 10 a.m. to 5 p.m.

Jewish Museum *(1109 5th Avenue; 212-423-3200; www.jewishmuseum.org)* Peruse the exhibits on Jewish heritage or attend one of their many events and programs ranging from a lecture series to film festivals.

El Museo del Barrio *(1230 5th Avenue; 212-831-7272; www.elmuseo.org)* Learn about Latino culture at this uptown museum, which hosts various events throughout the year.

Scandinavia House *(58 Park Avenue; 212-879-9779; www.scandinavia-house.org)* The Scandinavia House is the headquarters for the American-Scandinavian Foundation and has galleries with art and artifacts from the region. They also host events and have many kid-friendly activities in their Heimbold Family Children's Center.

Ukrainian Museum *(222 East 6th Street; 212-228-0110; www.ukrainianmuseum.org)* This East Village museum has exhibits on the history and culture of the Ukraine including collections of traditional clothing from the region's past.

A Few Notable Cultural Events in NYC

JANUARY/FEBRUARY
Chinese New Year Parade
Chinatown, Manhattan
917-660-2402
www.betterchinatown.com

MAY
Cinco de Mayo
Flushing Meadows Park,
Queens
311
www.nycgovparks.org

JUNE
Egg Rolls & Egg Creams Festival
Lower East Side, Manhattan
212-219-0888
www.eldridgestreet.org

JULY
Festa del Giglio
Williamsburg, Brooklyn
718-384-0223
www.olmcfeast.com

Bastille Day at Bar Tabac
Boerum Hill, Brooklyn
718-923-0918
www.bartabacny.com

AUGUST
The Hong Kong Dragon Boat Festival in New York
Flushing Meadows Park,
Queens
718-767-1776
www.hkdbf-ny.org

Chapter Two

Open House:

Tour Elegant Homes of NYC (They Aren't For Sale)

Most New Yorkers are obsessed with real estate, so wouldn't it be fun to spend a weekend looking at other people's homes? From the Manhattan brownstone where Theodore Roosevelt was born to the Queens house where jazz great Louis Armstrong lived with his wife—spend a weekend peeking into the lives of others. From posh pads to tenements—put the Sunday *Times* Real Estate section aside and go on a weekend house tour throughout the five boroughs. If you believe in ghosts, you should be happy to know that many of these historic homes are said to be haunted.

Manhattan

Even though many city dwellers would pay top dollar to call these digs home, they are not for sale. The homes you'll be touring are all historic landmarks that pay tribute to New York's vast cultural history.

Start your excursion downtown in the East Village: Take the F or B train to Broadway/Lafayette Street or the N or R train to 8th Street and head to the **Merchant's House Museum** *(29 East 4th Street; 212-777-1089; www.merchantshouse.org)*. On your self-guided tour, you'll be handed a binder filled with interesting facts about the lifestyle of a successful merchant in the 1800s and the family tree of the Tredwell family, the only family to ever occupy the home. Walk through the three floors and a garden and take notice of the decorative arts, clothing, and other home furnishings from the time period. Some say that the Tredwells, a wealthy family that imported hardware, still haunt the house and in the information area they have pictures of ghosts that have been spotted in the rooms.

The museum is located in the now-trendy Noho area, across the street from the B Bar, so it's hard to imagine what life was like back then, but the interior of the home will transport you to a quieter time. The folks at the museum are very friendly and encourage you to relax and read in the garden, which is truly an urban oasis. The museum is open Thursdays through Mondays from 12 noon to 5 p.m. They also host events, including lectures on fortune-telling and the art of flirting in the 19th century.

After your visit, walk down Houston Street to the Lower East Side. At the turn of the century, this area was filled with pushcarts and immigrants in search of the American Dream. In 1888 a Russian immigrant opened Katz's Deli. Still in its original location on Houston Street, this deli has been serving up salami and other deli treats for over a century. Grab some lunch at **Katz's Deli** *(205 East Houston Street; 212-254-2246; www.katzdeli.com)* and dine on scrumptious food like stuffed derma and corned beef.

Before heading into our next open house, grab a pickle at **Guss's Pickles** *(85 Orchard Street; 212-569-0909)*. Started in 1910 by immigrant Izzy Guss, the pickle stand was originally housed on Essex Street but is now located near the Tenement Museum on Orchard Street. Guss's Pickles offers a tasty assortment of fresh pickles from the barrel.

You already learned how a wealthy merchant from the 1800s lived; now see the apartments in a turn-of-the-century tenement at the **Lower East Side Tenement Museum** *(108 Orchard Street; 212-431-0233; www.tenement.org)*. Here you can tour the apartments of 97 Orchard Street, which an estimated seven thousand people called home between 1863 and 1935. The museum offers various tours of the restored apartments, where you can learn about the past tenants. From an immigrant family that ran a garment business out of their apartment to a family in mourning—catch a glimpse of the immigrant experience on the Lower East Side. The museum even has a tour geared for kids where a teenage guide, dressed in period clothing, tells the story of her family's life in the tenement.

Each apartment tour is roughly an hour and must be purchased separately. They do offer discounts, however, if you purchase tickets for multiple apartment tours. Although the visitor center is open on Mondays, apartment tours are only available Tuesdays through Sundays. The tours are given at scheduled intervals throughout the day, but check the schedule on the Web site, where you can also purchase tickets. I recommend buying tickets in advance since the museum gets quite crowded on weekends and there is a maximum of fifteen people for each tour. The museum also offers fascinating walking tours of the Lower East Side on weekends. If you get to the museum and the tours are sold out, you can look around the interesting visitor center or watch a free video about the museum. The tenement shop has a great selection of books on the immigrant experience in New York City.

Staying on the east side of Manhattan, take a trip back in presidential history and head to the **Theodore Roosevelt's Birthplace National Historic Site** (28 East 20th Street; 212-260-1616; www.nps.gov/thrb) in the Flatiron District. This isn't the original four-story brownstone where Teddy was born in 1858, and I promise that there wasn't a Jennifer's Convertibles on the corner when Teddy lived here, but the building has been reconstructed as an example of homes of the era. Operated by the National Park Service, the brownstone offers tons of information and exhibits on the early life of this legendary president. The museum is closed on Sundays and Mondays, but you may visit Tuesdays through Saturdays between 9 a.m. and 5 p.m., with the last tour given at 4 p.m. The five period-styled rooms can only been seen on a guided tour, although you can tour the exhibit located on the ground level on your own. The exhibit includes interesting memorabilia like Theodore Roosevelt's bible and christening gown. There is also a small gift area where you can purchase stuffed teddy bears and even a plush version of Teddy Roosevelt.

Next, head uptown to visit what was once George Washington's Manhattan headquarters at the **Morris-Jumel Mansion** *(65 Jumel Terrace; 212-923-8008; www.morrisjumel.org)* in Washington Heights. You might think it odd to find a freestanding mansion off the 163rd Street stop on the C train, a block from a C-Town grocery store, but so is Manhattan's diverse history. The mansion, a relic from the neighborhood's grand past, played an interesting role in America's beginnings. For instance, the mansion's parlor was where former vice president Aaron Burr wed Eliza Jumel, a onetime prostitute and wealthy widow. The mansion has served as everything from an inn in the late 1700s to a country home in the 19th century.

Decorated in 18th- and 19th-century décor, the museum is a tribute to the city's past; a time when it wasn't crowded with apartment buildings and was instead considered the countryside. You can take a self-guided tour of the mansion from 10 a.m. to 4 p.m., Wednesdays through Sundays. They also offer guided tours on Saturdays at noon.

Head even further uptown on the A train to 207th Street to visit the **Dyckman Farmhouse Museum** *(4881 Broadway; 212-304-9422; www.dyckman-farmhouse.org)*, where you can explore a restored Dutch Colonial farmhouse that was built in 1754. The Dyckman family restored the house and then donated it, opening it as a public museum in 1916. For almost a century visitors have been touring the colonial home viewing the five rooms decorated with authentic period furnishings including the relic room, which has various artifacts from the area on display.

The farmhouse once had an extensive garden on its grounds, but now only has a half-acre that you can walk around on your visit. In addition to a garden, there is also a smokehouse and a replica of a military hut from the Revolutionary War. It's hard to imagine a farmhouse existing on lively Broadway; especially now that chain restaurants and bodegas surround the area. Visit the farmhouse on Wednesdays through Saturdays between 11 a.m. and 4 p.m. and Sundays between 12 noon and 4 p.m.

If you happen to have a day off midweek, you should visit stunning **Gracie Mansion** *(East End Avenue at 88th Street; 212-570-4751)*, which only offers public tours on Wednesdays with reservations. Although not a weekend activity, you could possibly take a tour during lunchtime since they offer afternoon tours.

The Bronx

When most people think of the Bronx they might imagine an infamous co-op city filled with apartment buildings. But in the Bronx you can also take a break from the city grind and see some greenery beside restored masterpieces of historic architecture.

Take the 1 train to 242nd Street to visit the **Van Cortlandt House Museum** *(246th Street and Broadway; 718-543-3344; www.vancortlandthouse.org)* an 18th-century Georgian-style home that once belonged to the wealthy Van Cortlandt family. The house is located in popular Van Cortlandt Park, which houses both a golf course and an equestrian center. The land was once the Van Cortlandts' successful wheat plantation, complete with a working mill and livestock. You can tour the historic home decorated with period furniture and collections from the Van Cortlandts. There is also a colonial-style herb garden to enjoy. If you are a history buff, stop by the gift shop in the old caretaker's cottage and pick up some books and other history-related paraphernalia. The museum is open Tuesdays through Fridays from 10 a.m. to 3 p.m. and remains open an hour later on the weekend.

Take the 6 train to Pelham Station and hop on the B45 bus to make your way to the gorgeous **Bartow-Pell Mansion Museum** *(895 Shore Road; 718-885-1461; www.bartowpellmansionmuseum.org)* located near City Island. Built in the 1800s, the Greek Revival architecture of the home is stunning. Walk through the mansion, decorated in period furnishings and spend some time daydreaming that you live in this beautiful home. New Yorkers who love a good view will be taken by the Orangery, a room that was originally a conservatory and is now filled with large windows and views of the greenery outside.

The mansion is housed in Pelham Bay Park, so take the opportunity to stroll through the park and visit the wigwam that pays tribute to the original inhabitants of the area, the Siwanoy Indians. The mansion is open Wednesdays, Saturdays, and Sundays from 12 noon to 4 p.m., but the park grounds are open daily from dawn until dusk.

If you'd like to visit a historic home that also doubles as the headquarters for the Bronx Historical Society take the D train to Bainbridge Avenue and 205th Street or the 4 train to Moshulu Parkway and stop by the **Valentine-Varian House** *(3266 Bainbridge Avenue, Bronx; 718-881-8900; www.nycgov-parks.org)*, which was once owned by affluent blacksmith Isaac Valentine. The Georgian-style home is the last of its kind on this stretch of road in the Bronx. Peruse the various exhibits in the house on Bronx history. You can visit the house on Saturdays from 10 a.m. to 4 p.m. and Sundays from 1 p.m. to 5 p.m.

Fans of literature will enjoy a visit to another home run by the Bronx Historical Society on Bainbridge Avenue: the **Edgar Allen Poe Cottage** *(3309 Bainbridge Avenue; 718-881-8900; www.bronxhistoricalsociety.org)*. To think that Poe came to this area of the Bronx to escape from city life is a bit mind-blowing, but this tiny cottage is where Poe wrote many poems, including the famous "Annabel Lee," and it is also the place where Poe lost his beloved wife and cousin, Virginia, to tuberculosis. The cottage houses portraits of Poe as well as some of his furniture. When Poe lived here, he was very poor and so it isn't decorated lavishly, but is an interesting place to visit to see both a cottage from the early 19th century and a literary landmark where a legendary poet suffered heartbreak and composed priceless works. The cottage is currently closed for renovations as they are building a new visitor center opening in August 2009. The cottage itself is slated to reopen in 2010.

Brooklyn

Despite being known as the borough that many up-and-comers call home, Brooklyn is also filled with important American history. Visit the historic homes in the area and see the first Brooklyn trailblazers—and I'm not talking about the folks who were lucky enough to score a brownstone before the word got out that Brooklyn was cool.

Head to Prospect Park and tour the **Lefferts Historic House** *(718-789-2822; www.prospectpark.org)* located near the Prospect Park zoo and the carousel, close to Flatbush Avenue. The house was built in the late 18th century and depicts family life of the period. There are many weekend programs offered at the house for families like learning to churn butter and candle-making.

The Lefferts house is a very welcoming place—unlike many other historic homes with priceless heirlooms on display, it is one to visit if you have kids in tow. They offer interactive exhibits and it's all free. You can tour the home on weekends from 12 noon to 4 p.m. in the fall and winter and from 12 noon to 5 p.m. during the spring and summer.

For a trip that's a bit off the beaten path but worth the excursion, take the A train to Utica Avenue station. At Utica Avenue, (also known as Malcolm X Boulevard), take the B46 Bus to Clarendon Road to visit the oldest residence in New York City—the **Wyckoff House Museum** (5816 Clarendon Road; 718-629-5400; www.wyckoffassociation.org), restored to show American farm life in Brooklyn during the 17th through 19th centuries. Located in an industrial section of a residential neighborhood, there aren't too many dining options aside from a McDonald's, but there are picnic tables on the premises, so I suggest bringing a lunch.

As you enter the farmhouse you will notice the original structure, a one-room house from 1652. Look for the three-hundred-year-old corncobs in the walls that were used for insulation. The house has undergone two major renovations: one extension built in 1742 and another from the 1800s. As you tour the house you will see how the dwelling has transformed in style to include new amenities through the centuries. There are also some Wyckoff heirlooms on display, like china and two bassinets used by the Wyckoff children, dating back over two hundred years.

There are good weekend activities like garden workshops offered at the museum and in the summer they host Fireside Feasts where they cook colonial recipes over an outdoor fire pit on Thursday evenings. All events are free. The museum is closed on Sundays from November through April. From May through October you can stop by on Tuesdays through Saturdays from 10 a.m. to 4 p.m. You can only view the house on a guided tour, which is given three times throughout the day at 11 a.m., 1 p.m., and 3 p.m. A few times a year they also offer an interesting cellar-to-attic tour.

Head to Crown Heights, on the A or C train to Utica Avenue, to see the **Hunterfly Road Houses** in Weeksville (1698 Bergen Street; 718-756-5250; www.weeksvillesociety.org). The town of Weeksville was created by James Weeks, a free man who purchased the land. The town was once a thriving African American community created eleven years after slavery ended in New

York and where many former slaves took refuge. This pre-Civil War black community had its own schools, churches, and black-owned shops. Everything is decorated in period furniture reflecting the customs of the black urban culture of the time. Now all that is left of historic Weeksville are these few homes.

Staten Island

Take the ferry to explore the grand homes of Staten Island. In fact, although it's not open to tour, Staten Island is the only place in the city with a Frank Lloyd Wright house, which is located in the Lighthouse Hill area.

For homes that you can actually peek inside, start your visit close to the ferry. Located on the water with priceless views of the shore, this home with a perfect view makes you wonder if it inspired Alice Austen to become one of America's first female photographers. Take the S51 bus two miles from the ferry terminal to Hylan Boulevard. As you walk toward the water, you will encounter this charming house on priceless New York City real estate. Stepping into the **Alice Austen House Museum** *(2 Hylan Boulevard; 718-816-4506; www.aliceausten.org)* you will see Austen's photographs on display. Her pictures of New Yorkers from the turn of the century are great examples of life in New York during that time.

The house, also known as Clear Comfort, was built in 1690, and Austen moved into the home as a child in the 1860s. She lived there until 1945 when she encountered money troubles and fell ill. The story of Austen, which is on display along the walls of the museum with photographs of Austen and her subjects, is both inspiring and heartbreaking. The home also has old-fashioned cameras on display. I was taken by the unbelievable views of New York harbor and the Verrazano-Narrows Bridge from her front yard. The Alice Austen House plays host to summer concerts on its lawn. Try to attend their 4th of July concert, where you will have a great view of the fireworks. Check the Web site for ongoing events at the house.

After touring the house, head over to Main Street and have lunch at the **Bay Street Luncheonette** *(1189 Bay Street; 718-720-0922)*, which serves up one of the best egg creams this native New Yorker has ever tasted. They have actual fountain soda with different syrup flavors and a good selection of breakfast and lunch treats. The place seems as if it is from another time. You can easily envision the luncheonette in the fifties when kids hung out inside, drinking soda after school.

If you have a car, take a twenty-minute drive, or hop on the S74 bus from the ferry terminal to Richmond Road and St. Patrick's Place to **Historic Richmond Town** *(441 Clarke Avenue; 718-351-1611; www.historicrichmondtown.org)*, where you can tour historic homes and other buildings, including an outhouse and a tavern. The tavern runs a special concert series from January through April, where you can step back in time and listen to music of a bygone era by candlelight, keeping warm by the fireplace, as this 19th-century tavern doesn't use electricity.

When you visit this historic town, be sure to head to the visitor center to gather some info on the exhibits. When we were there they had an interesting exhibit on colonial toys. Besides touring all the homes, you can see an early stone bridge from the 1800s as well as the town general store. As I toured the cottages and homes of various time periods in this village, I couldn't stop thinking of how New York must have looked ages ago and how much it has transformed.

You can join a guided tour from September through June on weekends at 2 p.m. and 3:30 p.m. In the summer months, you can take a self-guided tour between 10 a.m. and 5 p.m. on Saturdays and 1 p.m. and 5 p.m. on Sundays. They host various events throughout the year, many of which are family friendly; just check their Web site for a list of events.

The woman at the gift shop at Richmond Town told me that I must head to the Conference House in the charming town of Tottenville, because it is not only stunning, but it's also known to be haunted. According to a *Staten Island Advance* article, the spirit of a fifteen-year-old girl who died over two hundred and fifty years ago haunts the house. Apparently she looks out from the second-floor window on summer days and is known to tap people on the shoulder.

If you believe in haunted houses, take a peek at the supernatural in the **Conference House** *(7455 Hylan Boulevard; 718-984-0415; www.theconferencehouse.org)*. The house is open for public tours on weekends between 1 p.m. and 4 p.m., from April through mid-December and is easily accessible from the last stop of the Staten Island Railroad, which you can board at the ferry terminal, or take the S78 bus to Craig Avenue. The home is decorated in 17th-century furnishings. It's best known as the building that housed the Revolutionary War's peace conference on September 11, 1776. After the Revolutionary War the home became a private residence.

After you tour the historic home, enjoy a walk through Tottenville, which is also the southernmost point of New York State. The town is filled with old Victorian homes and has the charm of a small New England town. Stop in for ice cream at **Eggers Ice Cream Parlor** *(7437 Amboy Road; 718-605-9335)*, an old-fashioned ice cream parlor from the 1930s that serves up homemade ice cream. For more substantial fare, head to **Dock's Clam Bar & Pasta House** *(240 Page Avenue; 718-227-8500; www.docksclambar.com)* and try their lobster ravioli.

If you want to tour beautiful gardens and a Greek Revival mansion, take the S78 bus to Seguine Avenue and visit the **Seguine Mansion** *(440 Seguine Avenue; 718-667-6042; www.nycgovparks.org)*. The Urban Park Rangers offer guided tours of the museum throughout the year. You must call 311 and ask for the Urban Park Rangers to find out the dates and times of the tours. The mansion is located in Lemon Creek Park, which is known as a good environment for bird watching.

Queens

From historic farmhouses located on an actual working farm to the home of a contemporary jazz legend, there is much to see on your house tour of Queens.

Start your tour by taking the 7 train to 103rd Street/Corona Plaza to tour a jazz legend's home at the **Louis Armstrong House Museum** *(3456 107th Street; 718-478-8274; www.satchmo.net)*. This modest brick home is nestled in a residential area of Corona, Queens located near LaGuardia airport where you can't help but be distracted by the sounds and sights of the low flying planes overhead. The home can be viewed on a guided forty-minute tour. Tours start every hour on the hour with the last tour given at 4 p.m. Tours begin at the visitor center and gift shop located in the Armstrong's former garage. At the gift shop you can pick up books, cd's, and even a pack of Armstrong's favorite laxative Swiss Kris.

Armstrong passed away in the home in 1971 and his wife lived out the rest of her years there. The home opened as a museum in 2003, and you can see where this jazz star lived with his wife Lucille throughout his many years of success and fame in the music world. Nobody has lived in the house after the Armstrongs, so the home and furnishings are original down to the retro aqua blue kitchen with the built in pink blender and custom made six burner range. The den on the second floor, which was more like Armstrong's office, was restored to look the same way it did when Louis, aka Satchmo, was alive with his papers left intact on his desk and a portrait of Armstrong painted by his friend Tony Bennett on the wood paneled walls. Throughout the tour you can hear recordings of conversations with Armstrong since he taped most of the conversations he had with folks in the house.

The house can be toured on Tuesdays through Sundays; weekend tours are given from 12 noon to 4 p.m. They offer free summer concerts so check their Web site for more information. The museum is in the process of building a new visitor center in a lot across from the house, which is slated to open in 2010. The new visitor center will also house all the Louis Armstrong Archives that are currently kept at Queens College.

Head to Jamaica, taking the E, J, or Z train to Jamaica Center, and walk to King Manor Park to tour the **King Manor Museum** *(15003 Jamaica Avenue; 718-206-0545; www.kingmanor.org)*. Once home to Rufus King, a lawyer and congressman who signed the Constitution, the 19th-century farmhouse has an ornate trim and is surrounded by gorgeous apricot trees. The home fits in perfectly with the park's atmosphere, a bit removed from the hustle and bustle of Jamaica Avenue. The house is open for tours from February to December, on weekends from 1 p.m. to 5 p.m., with guided tours given every half hour.

To tour a farmhouse that is still operating and surrounded by animals and farm life, journey to the **Queens County Farm Museum** *(73-50 Little Neck Parkway, Floral Park; 718-347-3276; www.queensfarm.org)* to see the restored Adriance farmhouse on this forty-seven acre farm which is open for free tours on weekends from 10 a.m. to 5 p.m. An enthusiastic tour guide will give you the rundown of the house at this unbelievable farm museum which shows us what agricultural life was like in the city before urban development. Don't forget to feed the goats and to pick up a bottle of wine from the farm's vineyard, which opened in Fall 2008.

Chapter Three

Art History 101:
Galleries, Performance Art, and Much More

You've been to the Met and MoMA, but what about the Chelsea galleries or hidden gems like the Noguchi Museum and the Fisher Landau Center for the Arts in Queens? New York City is filled with top-rate galleries and museums. Some galleries have transformed old neighborhoods filled with warehouses into vibrant artistic centers. So put on some comfortable shoes—make sure they aren't unfashionable, as we are, of course, in New York—and hit the streets to soak in some art.

You can fill many weekends exploring the galleries of New York City, so here are some ideas of how to structure your weekend escape into New York's art world complete with a foray into arty nightlife.

Galleries:

Manhattan

Start your weekend browsing the many galleries of **Chelsea** (www.chelseaart-galleries.com; www.westchelseaarts.com); this area spans from West 17th Street to West 29th Street, from 10th Avenue to the West Side Highway. It might seem strange that a section of the city that is lined with gas stations, car washes, and automotive shops would be transformed into a world of hip galleries, but in recent years there has been an influx of art to West Chelsea. Walk through this stretch of the city and you will easily fill a day checking out cutting-edge artwork ranging from paintings to sculptures.

This is a great rainy day activity since so many of the galleries are housed in the same building and the side streets are just brimming with them. There is also a monthly guide with a map to direct you to openings and events. You can also access a map to the galleries online at www.chelseagallerymap.com. Galleries are closed on Sundays and many close on weekends in the summer or during the holidays, so it's best to call ahead before you go to see if they are open.

If you want to take a break for brunch, you don't have to venture very far, just head to **Trestle on Tenth** (242 Tenth Avenue; 212-645-5659) for a yummy array of afternoon goodies like duck confit hash or simply for a good cup of coffee. Another good spot if you're considering dinner after a day of gallery-hopping or a pre-gallery hopping bite is **Cook Shop** (156 Tenth Avenue; 212-924-4440; www.cookshopny.com). For more casual fare you can stop by the **Chelsea Market** (75 Ninth Avenue; www.chelseamarket.com) for delicious brownies at **Fat Witch** and make sure to wash them down with fresh chocolate milk at the **Ronnybrook Dairy** stand.

Chelsea isn't the only area with an art life; there are galleries throughout the city with a high concentration in SoHo. Although they are housed through-out the area and are not as densely populated as on the streets of West Chelsea, they are certainly worth a look. Stop by the storefront galleries on West Broadway, but note that many galleries on lower Broadway are housed in upper-story lofts in the various buildings. For a listing of the galleries, you can go to the site www.artreach.com or you can stroll down West Broadway from Houston to Canal Street, which is also a gallery hotspot. Be sure to check out the side streets in search of funky art.

On the border of Tribeca and SoHo is **Art in General** (79 Walker Street; 212-219-0473; www.artingeneral.org), a nonprofit arts organization that houses galleries in a six-floor building, including the storefront. Check with the galleries often as exhibitions change frequently. Be sure to ride the elevator to the sixth floor, which is also used as installation space.

For a look at contemporary art that isn't housed in a loft, warehouse, or store-front, head east from SoHo to the **New Museum of Contemporary Art** (235 Bowery; 212-219-1222; www.newmuseum.org) on the Bowery. This sleekly de-signed museum is worth a visit if you are a fan of modern architecture and design. It's the type of place where even the bathroom tile is worthy of a second look.

The café on the ground floor offers light fare and drinks. They also have a large theater in the basement that hosts music and performance art. The museum's art collection changes quite frequently, which gives it a gallery feel. When I was there, they had a diverse collection of sculptures and perform-ance art pieces being shown on large flat screen televisions. The art was eclec-tic and many pieces were quite provocative.

If you'd like to start your weekend early, the museum is open late on Thursdays and there is no charge. There is quite a scene here on Thursday nights when the galleries are crowded with young downtown-types taking a look at the new installations.

Queens

Right across the East River from midtown Manhattan is Long Island City, an industrial part of Queens, which houses many of New York's hidden artistic gems. If you have Mondays off or you are planning a three-day weekend, Long Island City is the place to visit because unlike most museums and galleries, these venues are open Mondays.

The Long Island City Cultural Alliance (www.licarts.org) offers a free guide of LIC's art institutions, events, and neighborhood restaurants. You can download the guide from their Web site or pick up a copy when you get to Long Island City as they are easily found at all of the artistic venues featured in the guide and in various shops and restaurants in the area. So hop on the E, G, 7, or V train to Long Island City and enjoy your afternoon exploring the area.

The first stop is at **P.S. 1 Contemporary Art Center** (22-25 Jackson Avenue at 46th Street; 718-784-2084; www.ps1.org). This art center housed in an old public school building where every space of the school is used to display art, and exhibits change every few months. P.S. 1 has a few long-term installations, which were designed specifically to incorporate the architecture of P.S. 1. Art exhibits range from the Finnish to Feminist. Stroll around the old classrooms and see how the environment enhances the experience of the art. If you're hungry, they have a small café as well as a bookshop with a nice selection of art books. A good tip: if you are a MoMA member, or have a valid admission ticket from MoMA that was issued within the previous thirty days, admission to P.S. 1 is free.

For the last ten years, on Saturdays in July through September, from 9 a.m. to 3 p.m., P.S. 1 hosts Warm Up in the outdoor area of the museum. This annual music series attracts a young hip crowd and fills the courtyard with people eager to dance to music spun by live DJs. The courtyard design changes each summer; each year it is designed by the winners of P.S. 1's Young Architects Program. The summer I visited, the museum was designed like a farm. Afterward, you can grab a drink and a burrito or see some live music in the basement bar at **The Creek** (10-93 Jackson Avenue; 718-706-8783; www.creeklic.com). This joint serves up yummy Mexican with a good selection of beer on tap and is located only a few blocks from P.S. 1.

If you don't want to grab lunch at P.S. 1, the folks there referred me to **Gaw Gai Thai Express** (23-06 Jackson Avenue; 718-706-0999), where you can eat an enormous portion of fresh, delicious Thai food for very little money. The restaurant is directly across the street from the museum and offers casual takeout with a few seats. The only caveat is that it is closed on Sundays.

The closest gallery to P.S. 1 is the **Dorsky Gallery** *(11-03 45th Avenue; 718-937-6317; www.dorsky.org)*, which features ever-changing exhibits of contemporary art. The shows are eclectic, so check their Web site for more information on their current offering. They have shows for all visual art forms from pottery to paintings. Like most galleries, it's not open on weekends during the summer.

Afterward head down Jackson Avenue to the **Sculpture Center** *(44-19 Purves Street; 718-361-1750; www.sculpture-center.org)*, which is housed in an old trolley repair station and tucked away on an industrial side street. Sculptures are displayed outside the center and throughout the interior of this interesting building. The show I saw took me to the basement on a rather ominous walk through tunnels. The sculptures really work within the confines of the building, making this space a great place to see contemporary art.

If you'd like to head away from the Long Island City area, then continue on to a hidden gem a bit farther into Queens. The **Fisher Landau Center for Art** *(38-27 30th Street; 718-937-0727; www.flcart.org)* was transformed from an old parachute-harness factory into a world-class museum displaying contemporary art from the collection of Emily Fisher and her husband, Sheldon Landau. At one time the collection was private, but now you can tour the 25,000-square-foot museum that houses an impressive art collection, including work by Andy Warhol, Jasper Johns, Robert Rauschenberg, among many other famous contemporary artists.

Heading back to Long Island City to a rather desolate industrial section, you can explore the sculptures and furniture design of Isamu Noguchi at the **Noguchi Museum** *(9-01 33rd Road; 718-204-7088; www.noguchi.org)*. This tranquil museum is a must-see on your arty LIC weekend. Tour a museum that is filled with sculptures both indoors and out where the sculptures are set in a pebbled garden. Take a break and relax on the benches outside before heading back in to see Noguchi's furniture designs on the second floor. Need a coffee? Then stop by the café. There is also a small gift shop that offers a great selection of art books and toys. The museum hosts workshops for families and lectures for adults, and a film on view at the museum on Noguchi's life and work that is worth a watch, since it adds to the experience. Although easily accessible by car, the Noguchi Museum is a hike from P.S. 1, so consider calling a car service or driving to the area as parking is abundant.

After the Noguchi Museum, walk a block to the **Socrates Sculpture Park** *(32-01 Vernon Boulevard; 718-956-1819; www.socratessculpturepark.org)* for great views of Manhattan from this four-and-a-half-acre park dotted with sculptures. Kids play and folks walk freely on grounds that are surrounded by art and the waterfront. The park is reflective of the neighborhood as it is a bit industrial, even "rough around the edges," but the landscape changes with the addition of art. The park hosts various events, including a summer film series as well as concerts.

If you have the chance, head to **5 Pointz** *(46-23 Crane Street; www.5ptz.com)* just a block from P.S.1. This large factory decorated in graffiti can be seen from the 7 train, and is representative of the claim that art comes in all forms. Walk around the building to see this outdoor gallery of graffiti art that pays tribute to the urban art form. Presently, the curators are trying to create a museum of graffiti art within the space.

Don't head back to the city for the evening, but instead hang out on Vernon Boulevard, which is filled with hip restaurants and coffee shops—a bustling area with a bustling nightlife. If you want to take in some shopping before you embark on a night of feasting and performance art, stop by the **Art-O-Mat** *(46-46 Vernon Boulevard; www.licweb.com/artomat)*, which is a store that features artisan-made items and also houses a gallery.

For evening entertainment, head to the **Chocolate Factory** *(5-49 49th Avenue; 718-482-7069; www.chocolatefactorytheater.org)*. This venue, housed in a 5,000-square-foot-space that was once a chocolate factory, now hosts dance, music, performance art, and other theatrical performances. The space also functions as a gallery. It has very laid back vibe and the shows usually start around 8 p.m. Check the Web site for a full schedule of upcoming performances and events. They also host the Taste of LIC, for which restaurants from all over the neighborhood participate by letting folks sample their delicacies.

Finally, before you head back to the city, walk toward the water and take a peak at one of the most spectacular works of art—the Manhattan skyline.

Brooklyn

Brooklyn is teeming with galleries from the über-hip Williamsburg neighborhood to super-chic Dumbo. You can enjoy a day both gallery hopping and enjoying the arty nightlife in this borough known for its artistic edge.

To head straight to the heart of hip in Williamsburg, take the L train to Bedford Avenue and look around the independently-owned shops and dine at the eclectic restaurants that make up this colorful stretch of Brooklyn. There are tons of galleries around the area and many are located just a block off Bedford

Avenue; check the Web site *www.freewilliamsburg.com* for a list of galleries in the neighborhood. A famous Williamsburg venue right off Bedford Avenue is **Pierogi 2000** *(177 North 9th Street; 718-599-2144; www.pierogi2000.com)*. This Williamsburg staple was one of the first galleries in the area.

If you want to purchase homemade wares from local artists, stop by **Artists and Fleas** *(129 North 6th Street; www.artistsandfleas.com)*, a weekend market where artists sell everything from handknit items to funky jewelry. After shopping and gallery-hopping, grab a beer and take a tour of the **Brooklyn Brewery** *(79 North 11th Street; 718-486-7422; www.brooklynbrewery.com)*. The brewery operates tours on Saturdays from 12 noon to 5 p.m.

Want to spend the night immersed in cool arty nightlife? Head out for a night at **Supreme Trading** *(213 North 8th Street; 718-599-4224; www.supreme-tradingny.com)*, a gallery/bar/performance space where you can see live music and have a drink while staring at cutting-edge art. An evening at this spacious 7,500-square-foot club/gallery is an adventure in the world of Williamsburg's art scene.

Due to increased rents, one of Williamsburg's famous art spaces/clubs moved out in 2008 and relocated to Dumbo. Dumbo, which stands for "Down Under the Manhattan Bride Overpass," has attracted artists for years because of the abundant loft space available. In recent years it has become more developed and now houses tons of high-end condos. Despite the development, this Brooklyn waterfront area still has an edgy art scene. In the evening, head out to the new eco-friendly **Galapagos Art Space** *(16 Main Street; www.galapagos-artspace.com)* to dance to techno music or see a band or burlesque; you can also explore the area's shops and galleries.

Dumbo is filled with both galleries and studios for working artists. During the month of September, Dumbo artists open their studios for tours (see page 33). As you walk down the cobblestone streets of the area, you can peruse the many storefront galleries like **Smack Mellon's Gallery** *(56 Water Street; 718-834-8761)* or take in a theatrical or musical performance at **St. Ann's Warehouse** *(92 Plymouth Street; 718-254-8779; www.stannsware-house.org)*. If you want to check out some good art books, head to the **PowerHouse Arena** *(37 Main Street; 718-666-3049; www.powerhouse-arena.com)*, a spacious bookstore/gallery that sells books and hosts local art exhibitions, readings, and other arty events.

For a look into the world of local Brooklyn artists see a show at the **Brooklyn Waterfront Artists Coalition Exhibition Space** *(499 Van Brunt Street; 718-596-2506; www.bwac.org)* located on the waterfront in a pre-Civil War warehouse next to the Fairway Market. The warehouse offers two large floors of exhibition space. Check the schedule for the upcoming shows as they occasionally host live performances. When I was there they were showing a production of Shakespeare's *Much Ado about Nothing*. There is also a small area where you can pick up a coffee or pastry. In the warmer months, vendors line the walkway by the waterfront selling their wares—everything from pottery to pocketbooks.

Recently galleries have been popping up in other areas of Brooklyn, although they aren't as densely populated with galleries as Williamsburg and Dumbo. One such addition to the scene is **Bond Street Gallery** *(297 Bond Street; 718-858-2297; www.bondstreetgallery.com)*; this gallery in Carroll Gardens displays photographs, just two blocks from the neighborhood's Restaurant Row on Smith Street. Also, if you're in the 'hood, visit the **Micro Museum** *(123 Smith Street; 718-797-3116; www.micromuseum.com)*, a gallery that is much more of a gallery space than a museum. The exhibits change frequently and are always worth a weekend visit.

Local Art Events and Studio Tours

APRIL
Tribeca Open Studio Artist Tour
212-479-7317
www.toastartwalk.com

MAY
Long Island City Artists Open Studio Tour
917-843-3836
www.licartists.org

JUNE
Red Hook Open Studio Tour
718-596-2506
www.bwac.org

Red Hook Waterfront Arts Festival
718-643-6790
www.redhookfest.org

Bushwick Open Studio Tour and Arts Festival
www.artsinbushwick.org

Bronx Council of the Arts Mott Haven Open Studio Tour
718-931-9500
www.bronxarts.org

SEPTEMBER
Dumbo Art Under the
Bridge Festival
718-694-0831
www.dumboartscenter.org

Greenwich Village Art Fair
www.rockfordartmuseum.org/
gvaf.html

OCTOBER
Harlem Open Artist
Studio Tour
www.hoast.org

NOVEMBER
Artist Alliance on the Lower
East Side Open Studio Tour
212-420-9202
www.aai-nyc.org

ONGOING
Lower Manhattan
Cultural Council Public Art
Walking Tours
Download a self-guided audio
tour from their Web site.
212-219-9401
www.lmcc.net

Chapter Four

Sports in the City:

Go Out and Get Active

From retro roller-skating to cycling, enjoy getting active in the five boroughs. If you don't have the energy to indulge in a sports-filled escape, you can plan a weekend of watching sporting events, drinking at sports bars, or touring the Sports Museum of America. Go grab your sneakers, skates, skateboard, golf clubs, saddle, or simply wear some sweats, and explore what this city has to offer on your athletic weekend getaway.

You can spend a weekend going to baseball or basketball games and cheering for your favorite New York teams, but wouldn't it be fun to actually participate in some sports? You don't have to join a league or team; just enjoy your commitment-free weekend of athletic activities.

What's the best way to beat the summer heat? Head to an ice rink for an open skating session, where you can cool off and get down to the tunes blasting from the speaker system at the rink. Don't forget to pack a sweatshirt for the excursion or you'll freeze, as I did when I wore a T-shirt. If you want to stay in Manhattan, take the A train to 23rd Street and walk toward the water to the **Chelsea Piers** *(23rd Street at the Hudson River; 212-336-6100; www.chelseapiers.com)*, where they house a skating rink with skate rental. You can spend an entire day enjoying all that the Chelsea Piers has to offer; the complex has a 23-foot-high indoor climbing wall as well as driving range, bowling alley, and batting-cage rentals. Many of the activities like the batting cages need to be booked at least the day before, so call ahead to confirm availability for your desired activity.

If you are a golf pro or just enjoy an hour at the driving range like me, make your way over to 3rd Avenue and catch the shuttle from either 72nd, 77th, 86th, or 96th Street or drive to the **Randall's Island Golf Center** *(1 Randall's Island; 212-427-5689; www.randallsislandgolfcenter.com)*, where you can enjoy the outdoor driving range, improve your golf game at the short game area, or have some beers and then head into the batting cages. A note to those with cars: You don't have to pay a toll while leaving Randall's Island, but you do have to pay one upon entering. If you're better suited for miniature golf, there are two miniature golf courses that are absent of cheesy fixtures like windmills and statues. You can have lunch at their beer garden or surf the Web from your laptop at their outdoor Wi-Fi lounge while relaxing on their comfortable cushioned chairs.

Across from the golf center is **Sportime Tennis** *(212-427-6150; www.sportimeTFM.com)*, which just underwent enormous renovations. The 20,000 square-foot tennis center re-opened in January 2009 with twenty courts featuring ten Deco-Turf hard tennis courts and clay tennis courts. The remaining fifteen courts are housed in an air structure, where they can be played on outdoors in the warmer months and indoors in the cold. They also have a nice café and bar, as well as a pro-shop.

If you brought the car and the driving range inspires you to golf on a course, head over the Triborough Bridge to the Bronx. There are many golf courses in the Bronx; play a game at the **Pelham/ Split Rock Golf Course** *(870 Shore Road; 718-885-1258; www.pelhamsplitrock.americangolf.com)* just east of Co-op City. This is the city's only thirty-six hole course. The course offers a sign-up sheet for golf lessons and there are discounts available to NYC residents.

For a list of all the golf courses in NYC, check out the Web site www.golfinnyc.com, which lists the courses and prices for all available golfing within the city. You can also visit **Golf NYC**'s Web site, www.golfnyc.com, as they run five New York City golf courses.

Rather pick up a racket than a club? There are tons of places to play tennis in NYC. You can even play on the same courts as the stars that compete in the U.S. Open. Those courts are open to the public year-round except in August and September through the **USTA Billie Jean King National Tennis Center** *(Flushing Meadows-Corona Park; 718-760-6200; www.usta.com)*. For a list of other tennis courts, please see the Web site, *www.tennisnyc.com*, as it lists all of the courts in the city. There are also many free courts available through the city's parks department; see their Web site, *www.nycgovparks.org*, for more information.

Maybe you aren't into court tennis, but would like to indulge in a game of table tennis. If so, take the 1 train to the Upper West Side for an evening at the **Manhattan Table Tennis Club** *(250 West 100th Street; 212-864-7253)* to play at one of their seven tables. You can reserve an hour to try your hand at table tennis at this popular Upper West Side spot for an offbeat afternoon or evening activity.

Have an old bow and arrow lying around? If not, don't worry, because in

Queens you can rent them and spend your afternoon practicing archery at **Queens Archery** *(170-20 39th Avenue; 718-461-1756; www.archery-nyc.com)*. To get there, take the 7 train to the last stop and hop on the Q28 to 171st Street. This outfit offers you a chance to throw arrows on weekends from 10 a.m. to 5 p.m. Also, it's good to note that on Sundays from 10 a.m. to 1:30 p.m. they host tournaments, so it's better to come by after that time to use the range.

If finding a place to practice archery in New York City encourages you to explore other sports you wouldn't expect to find in the area, then make your way to the **Trapeze School New York** *(212-242-TSNY; www.trapezeschool.com)*. The school offers two locations in Manhattan; one is opened seasonally on the West Side Highway at Pier 40 in Hudson River Park from May through September and the other is located inside an indoor tent on West 30th Street between 10th and 11th Avenues. Make an appointment at least two weeks in advance as this art form is extremely popular and the school is often booked up. Wear yoga-style pants and T-shirt for this two-hour class, which might leave you a bit sore.

If you're a fan of heights and want to try something other than hanging from a trapeze, make an appointment to traverse the climbing walls in the city. On Sundays you can climb the wall at the **North Meadow Recreation Center** *(Central Park at 97th Street; 212-348-4867)*, where you can boulder climb on their twenty-foot indoor wall for $7. You can also head out to Brooklyn's amazing sports complex, **Aviator Sports** *(Floyd Bennett Field; 718-758-7500; www.aviatorsports.com)*, to climb the wall, which is available on both Saturday and Sunday. For $10 you get two climbs on a thirty-five-foot-high indoor wall.

Aviator Sports also provides one-stop shopping for your sports getaway and is located in restored airplane hangars at the now-defunct Floyd Bennett Field Airport. The complex has tons of weekend pick-up games—from basketball to soccer. When I went, there were even folks dressed in white to play a game of cricket on the lawn outside. Aviator has an indoor ice skating rink that has open skating sessions seven days a week throughout the day. Aviator is also home to the new Brooklyn Aces of the Eastern Pro Hockey League *(www.ephl)*, so make sure to check out a game. Aviator Sports has two skating rinks, so hockey games won't interfere with the open skating sessions. Open skating sessions last for three and a half hours and cost eight dollars. You can rent skates for four dollars.

At Aviator there is also a gym for kids, with drop-in gymnastics classes available. If you'd like to spend the day taking fitness classes and working out in their spacious gym, you can purchase a day pass to the facility. Aviator has a cafeteria-style dining area where you can score pizza and burgers to chow down after the big day of activities. There's also a fun sports bar on the second floor so that you won't have to miss any televised games while you spend your day enjoying the immaculate facilities.

An added plus to spending the day at Aviator is that you can explore the park surrounding the complex, including the Ryan Visitor Center where you can ask a ranger for a tour of the airport's old control tower. On Saturdays, you can head over to the old hangar to see planes from World War II and sit in a grounded helicopter (you don't get a ride though). Aviator is a great day excursion for those who want to enjoy the sports complex and also see some unique NYC history.

And if you appreciate history, then you might like a retro weekend reveling in the old roller disco days of New York City. Whether you are a child of the seventies who is nostalgic for the rink or not, grab your skates or rent them on-site at the last two places open for skating in the city. In Manhattan, you can skate the afternoon away at the roller-skating rink at seasonal **Riverbank State Park** (679 Riverside Drive at 145th Street; 212-694-3600) or really indulge your skates in Tottenville, Staten Island, at the indoor rink **Roller Jam USA** (236 Richmond Valley Road; 718-605-6600; www.rollerjamusa.com), which is open year-round.

Maybe you like the roll of only two wheels beneath you, and if so NYC is a biker's paradise with public bike lanes and parks offering great riding. Rent a bike at the **Boathouse in Central Park** (72 Central Park West; 212-517-2233; www.thecentralparkboathouse.com) and cycle through the park on the bike lanes.

Personally, I love cycling along the water. There are some great riding opportunities with scenic water views if you head over to the bike path that runs along the West Side Highway. Rent a bike at the **Bike and Roll Guided Tour and Bike Rentals** (Pier 84, Hudson River Park, 557 12th Avenue; 212-260-0400; www.bikeandroll.com) from March to November on the West Side Highway at 44th Street. The shop is open from 8 a.m. to 8 p.m. and bike rentals average about $10 an hour with a two-hour minimum. You can have the bike for as long as you'd like and some people even keep it overnight.

You can also cycle across the Brooklyn Bridge to Brooklyn, where you can cycle around the brownstone neighborhoods near the bridge. **Bike New York** (891 Amsterdam Avenue; 212-932-BIKE; www.bikenewyork.org) is an organization that promotes safe biking and information on cycling in the city. They also host the popular five-borough bike tour.

Apartment dwellers may not have a backyard with a pool, but that doesn't mean they shouldn't enjoy a refreshing swim. The city has both indoor and outdoor public pools that you can swim in year-round. A cool new addition to the city pools is the Floating Pool, which is a seven-lane pool complete with a pool house on a barge that, each summer, docks in one chosen borough. So far it has docked in Brooklyn and the Bronx, but check the city parks Web site for more information on the pool.

You can swim in the heart of the winter at the **Asser Levy Recreation Center** *(Asser Levy Place; 212-447-2020)*. Just off 23rd Street on the east side of Manhattan, this gorgeous building with the words "Bath House" engraved above the entrance is a step back into New York City's architectural past. You can swim in the outdoor pool in the summer for free, but you must purchase a $75 membership in order to use the indoor pool and recreation center throughout the year.

Many hotel pools are also open to the public, but they ask a hefty fee of $30–$50 for use of the pool. Lavish hotel pools to splurge on are **Le Parker Meridien** *(118 West 57th Street; 212-245-5000; www.parkermeridien.com)*, where you can use their pool and fitness facilities for $100, or the **Hotel Gansevoort** *(18 9th Avenue, 212-206-6700; www.hotelgansevoort.com)*, where for $250 you can pretend you are a celebrity, with a spa treatment, a day pass to their rooftop pool, a free drink, and a sun care pack.

Don't want to get wet? Go for a run. Of course, anybody can put on a pair of running shoes and take a jog around their block, but if you're new to running and want to race or find a running partner, consider joining the **New York Road Runners Club** *(9 East 89th Street, 212-423-2236; www.nyrr.org)*. This organization hosts running classes and races. If you join the club, you can utilize their Upper East Side facility to change, get water, use the bathroom, or get discounts on race entry fees.

Maybe you don't like to engage in sports, but you're a huge sports fan? You must visit the **Sports Museum of America** *(26 Broadway; 212-747-0900; www.sportsmuseum.com)*, a downtown museum that displays cool sports paraphernalia like the original Heisman Trophy and Derek Jeter's Little League jersey.

There are tons of interactive exhibits. You can cast your own vote for the Heisman Trophy winner or wear an interactive hockey mask in "A Goalie's Eye View" exhibit where you can see a video of what a Ranger goalie sees from the ice and feel pucks coming at you. For those who want to try their hand at being a sports announcer, there's a booth where you can record yourself reading a play-by-play of a game. The museum really touches upon all sports and their impact on America, using exhibits dedicated to everything from pro-bowling to more political installations like cultural barriers in sports.

This museum is a must-see for sports fans. They have tons of old footage of monumental sports moments, including a short film on sports in America. Don't forget to stop by the gift shop to pick up sports merchandise from your favorite teams.

You don't have to be a sports fan to enjoy a day at **ESPN Zone** *(1472 Broadway; 212-921-3776; www.espnzone.com)*. This restaurant, bar, and game room are exciting enough to satisfy anyone in need of a good meal and some video games or sporting events displayed on large-screen TVs. If you just want to stop in for a beer, head upstairs to the sports bar bustling with fans getting the latest scores and watching everything from football to basketball. Personally I love to head up to the game room for some foosball or to bowl a game at the two ESPN bowling lanes. Although the flat-screen TVs surrounding the game room can lead to a bit of an information overload, it is all in fun and unlike a typical sports bar, it's a great place to bring the family.

For a club feel in a sports bar setting, head to the Chelsea sports bar and lounge owned by acclaimed rapper Jay-Z. **The 40 / 40 Club** *(6 West 25th Street; 212-832-4040; www.the4040club.com)* is a 12,000-square-foot space that offers party rooms, although for smaller groups you can make table reservations. Folks can spend Saturday and Sunday afternoons and evenings here watching games and browsing the collection of sports memorabilia on display. The bar and lounge is open from 12 noon until 4 a.m. throughout the week.

If you like to hang out in clubs that offer you the chance to bowl a game, order a drink and lace up your bowling shoes at **Bowlmor** *(110 University Place; 212-255-8188; www.bowlmor.com)*. This bowling alley is open until 3:30 a.m. on Fridays and Saturdays so you can keep on hitting strikes until way after midnight. Brooklynites should enjoy bowling at another bar and bowling alley in Williamsburg, where it's hip to bowl. **The Gutter** *(200 North 14th Street; 718-387-3585; www.thegutterbrooklyn.com)* offers folks on the Bedford Avenue L stop a late night of bowling and brews.

Okay, admit it, you're a football fan, and we're not talking about the Jets or Giants. I've noticed an increasing number of European football fans in the city. The streets of my Brooklyn neighborhood were empty on the final day of the World Cup, and maybe that's why **Floyd NY** *(131 Atlantic Avenue; 718-858-5810; www.floydny.com)* in Brooklyn Heights offers large-screen viewing of European football games. Folks crowd the bar on Saturday and Sunday afternoons to watch the games and chow down on an English breakfast from the **Atlantic Avenue ChipShop** *(129 Atlantic Avenue; 718-855-7775; www.chipshopnyc.com)* located next door to Floyd. If the excitement of the game is too much, you are welcome to distract yourself with a game of bocce ball on their indoor bocce court.

Some Fun Sporting Events in the City

MAY
Five Boro Bike Tour
212-932-BIKE (2453)
www.bikenewyork.org

SEPTEMBER
NYC Skate Marathon and New York 100K
www.skatemarathon.com

NYC Century Bike Tour
212-629-8080
www.nyccentury.org

NOVEMBER
New York City Marathon
212-423-2249
www.nycmarathon.org

Chapter Five

At Sea in the City:

Sail on and Get in NYC's Waterways

Although the city is surrounded by water, New Yorkers don't get to spend enough time in and around it. Enjoy a weekend exploring New York's waterways, from scuba diving to party cruises—there are a myriad of ways to take advantage of the city's rivers and oceans. Relax on a free ride to Governor's Island or hop aboard a water taxi that takes you to a man-made beach in Long Island City. If you don't want to get wet, you can even have a picnic at a pier. The great thing about the activities in this chapter is that many of them are free. There are endless year-round options for your weekend at sea, so go forth and set sail!

Start your weekend kayaking on the Hudson River by heading to one of the three locations of the **New York City Downtown Boathouse** *(www.downtownboathouse.org)* open mid-May until mid-October on weekends from 9 a.m. to 6 p.m. The boathouse has locations throughout the west side of Manhattan: Pier 40 at Houston Street on the Hudson River; Pier 96, Clinton Cove at 56th Street and the Hudson River; and 72nd Street on the Hudson. You can sign up to use one of the kayaks at any of these locations. There is no charge to borrow a kayak and they will instruct you on how to properly use one. They do ask that people taking the kayaks out know how to swim and wear a life jacket on board at all times.

After exploring the city by kayak you might develop a taste for the sea air. You can book a longer kayaking excursion through **Manhattan Kayak** *(Boathouse, Pier 66, 26th Street and 12th Avenue; 212-924-1788; www.manhattankayak.com)*, which offers kayaking instruction at any skill level as well as kayaking tours. Tours range from outings around Coney Island or through Red Hook to romantic kayaking jaunts at sunset, which is a nice way to end your day sailing around the city.

Those looking to purchase a kayak should head over to the **New York Kayak Company** *(Pier 40, West Houston and West Street; 212-924-1327; www.nykayak.com)*. Since 1994 the New York Kayak Company has hosted tours as well as run a popular kayaking club and shop, where you can purchase a kayak or other boating accessories.

Now that you've mastered kayaking, how about trying out a canoe? Even if the closest you've gotten to a canoe is the one on display at the American Museum of Natural History, the Urban Park Rangers run comprehensive canoeing classes in the city. Check out the weekend canoeing activities on the New York City Department of Parks and Recreation Web site *(www.nycgovparks.org)* or call 311 for more information.

For over seventy years, the **Sebago Canoe Club** *(1400 Paerdegat Avenue North; 718-241-3683; www.sebagocanoeclub.org)* has been canoeing and kayaking in the waters off Canarsie in Brooklyn. On Wednesday nights and Saturday mornings they offer guided kayaking to the general public on a first come, first served basis; they provide the kayaks but the program is limited to fifteen people, so get there early. If you want to be a part of this historic club, request membership through their Web site. Member activities include canoeing in their six-person water canoes on weekend excursions and having access to Lake Sebago in Harriman State Park, which is a cool place to kayak on a weekend getaway.

If you'd like to kayak or canoe around the city on your own, you must obtain a permit from the **New York City Department of Parks and Recreation** *(311; www.nycgovparks.org)*. Their Web site lists the locations where you can get your $15 permit as well as the rules and regulations for kayaking or canoeing in the city. Also on the site is a helpful interactive trail map that shows locations for launching your kayak or canoe. From March through October you can spend your afternoon rowing in Central Park. At the **Loeb Boathouse** *(Central Park, East 72nd Street; 212-517-2233; www.thecentral-par boathouse.com)* you can rent boats and row along the water for a classic NYC activity. This is one city experience that every New York native should experience. Personally I thought it would be a lot easier to row a boat, but I did have a great time taking in the scenery while getting some exercise.

For a unique boating experience in Central Park, journey to the east side of the park from 72nd to 75th street and spend some time at the **Conservatory Water**, also known as the **Model Boat Pond**. This famed pond is the spot where model boat aficionados gather to sail their radio controller model boats. If you don't have a model boat, you can rent one from the concession stand by **Kreb's Memorial Boathouse**. This is a great activity for folks with kids or for those who are young at heart. I love to sit on a picnic bench and watch the boats race around the pond. On Saturdays at 10 a.m. from April through November you can also watch model boat races run by the Central Park Model Yacht Club *(www.cpmyc.org)*.

If you're like me and you'd just like to sit on a boat and relax, you won't be disappointed with the options available in New York City. There are various boats setting sail, from thematic cruises around Manhattan to free ferry rides to neighboring boroughs. For those on a budget, enjoy a ride on the classic **Staten Island Ferry** (www.nyc.gov; or www.siferry.com). The ride is free and the views of downtown New York City are stellar. After your twenty-five minute ride, you might want to explore Staten Island or simply take the ferry back to Manhattan.

For a quick ferry ride that will leave you on a rarely visited New York island that was once home to the U.S. Coast Guard, on weekends from June through October you can take a free ride on the **Governor's Island Ferry** (Battery Maritime Building, Whitehall Street; www.govisland.com). The ride only lasts about fifteen minutes so make sure to stand out on the deck to catch a glimpse of the views before you dock. When you arrive at Governor's Island, you should stop by the visitor center to see if they have any scheduled activities.

There are bikes available for rent through **Bike and Roll Guided Tour and Bike Rentals** (see page 42) in case some brisk exercise in the outdoors is all you need. I was surprised at the quality and selection of bikes available, including options for cycling with kids such as tandem-style bikes, bike seats for tots, and an attachment for the back of your bike that allows you to ride with two kids at the back. My one word of advice is to get there early as the line of customers gets pretty long and the number of bikes is limited.

Ride the bike path around Governor's Island and enjoy the greenery of this peaceful place. Pack a picnic for lunch at one of the many picnic tables or stop at the café located right past the Bike and Roll. Governor's Island offers activities for visitors all summer long, from a popular Saturday concert series in July to artistic installations and other interesting cultural events. It's also a serene environment to simply walk around.

On almost every boat tour of New York Harbor you will pass the Statue of Liberty, so why not hop aboard a boat that will take you to see her up close? You can get tickets for tours of the Statue of Liberty and Ellis Island through **Statue Cruises** (Castle Clinton at Battery Park or Central New Jersey Railroad Museum at Liberty State Park, Jersey City; 877-LADY-TIX; www.statue-cruises.com). The tour is a popular tourist attraction and at both departure points, Battery Park City and Liberty State Park in New Jersey, the boats tend to get quite crowded, so try to go early in the day.

Most New Yorkers think party boats are touristy, and maybe they are, but that doesn't mean they aren't good fun. Toss your New York attitude aside and book a ticket with funky **Affairs Afloat** *(Pier 40, West Houston Street; 212-987-BOAT; www.affairsafloat.com).* Their Web site says they have "New York City's Largest Showboats," and with a whole variety of thematic cruises—from dance nights to Sunday afternoon family-friendly cruises— you are guaranteed a good time on their ships.

For a classic New York City sightseeing cruise or a thrilling ride on a super-fast speedboat, book a trip on the **Circle Line**. Their two locations, **Circle Line 42** *(Pier 83, West 42nd Street; 212-563-3200; www.circleline42.com)* and **Circle Line Downtown** *(Pier 16, South Street Seaport; 866-925-4631; www.circlelinedowntown.com),* both offer a wide variety of cruises from boat rides with live bands to thematic holiday sails like the 4th of July cruise where you get an incredible view of the fireworks. For one of the quickest rides around the city, head on either "The Shark" or "The Beast," Circle Line's intense thirty-minute speedboat ride, which is a thrilling way to see New York City's waters. "The Shark" leaves from the South Street Seaport and "The Beast" sets sail from their 42nd Street location.

If you'd like the chance to dine at sea, get a table for lunch or dinner at **Bateaux New York** *(866-817-3463; www.bateauxnewyork.com),* a ship that sails from Pier 62 at Chelsea Piers, and on which you can dine while passing such sights as the Brooklyn Bridge and Ellis Island. Take note that there is a dress code on this ship; they recommend that men wear jackets to their dinner cruises and jeans are prohibited on all of their cruises. **World Yacht** *(Pier 81, West 41st Street; 212-630-8100; www.worldyacht.com),* also offers fun dinner cruises.

Don't limit yourself to a formal dinner or a wild night on a party ship; enjoy a ride on some excellent vintage vessels like a tugboat or a schooner at the **South Street Seaport Museum** *(12 Fulton Street; 212-748-8600; www.south-streetseaportmuseum.org).* From June through October, bring a picnic lunch and some drinks and hop aboard the wooden tugboat *W.O. Decker* for a lovely afternoon or a romantic evening at sea. The afternoon rides are an hour long, evening rides last for two hours, and on Saturday afternoons they offer a four-hour ride. You can also purchase tickets at the museum to ride the *Prairie,* a schooner that runs two-hour rides in the afternoon and evenings. The tugboat and schooner sail around the picturesque New York harbor and return to the dock at the seaport.

While you're at the seaport, enjoy a day at the museum touring the historic ships docked in the harbor and checking out the museum's art galleries. The seaport also has quaint cobblestone streets and a mall filled with good eats—some restaurants offering amazing views of the water.

If you get seasick you can still enjoy a jaunt—on boats that don't move. Book your next party on the **Frying Pan** *(Pier 63, North River at West 23rd Street; 212-989-6363; www.fryingpan.com)*, a once-sunken ship that was under water for three years before she was restored. The *Frying Pan* is a lightship—a type of boat once used as a floating lighthouse—and is now on the list of historic places on both the New York State and federal registries. Stop by and have a drink aboard the ship near the Chelsea Piers, or book your own private party on this unique vessel.

After two years undergoing restoration, the **Intrepid Sea, Air & Space Museum** *(Pier 8 at West 46th; 212-245-0072; www.intrepidmuseum.org)* re-opened to the public in November of 2008. Now a national historic landmark, the aircraft carrier *USS Intrepid* first set sail in 1943 during WWII and then was used in Vietnam. With many interactive exhibits, today the ship is used as a museum to pay tribute to our military history, as well as to aviation and nautical history. You may think it's cool enough to tour an aircraft carrier, but you can also tour the cockpit of the Concorde, ride in an A-6 cockpit simulator, and check out the hanger deck aboard the *Intrepid*, which houses WWII airplanes. Check for a current schedule at their Web site, since the museum also hosts educational workshops and events, including an array of benefits and personal parties.

Your weekend at sea would not be complete without a visit to the **Waterfront Museum and Showboat Barge** *(Pier 44, 290 Conover Street, Red Hook, Brooklyn; 718-624-4719; www.waterfrontmuseum.org)*, which is truly one of the most unique attractions in the city. Only open to the public on Thursdays from 4 p.m. to 8 p.m. and Saturdays from 1 p.m. until 5 p.m., admission is free, but donations are suggested at this restored barge that houses changing exhibits. When I was there they had an interesting exhibit on the history of showboats. The barge, which was used to transport cargo, was built in 1914 and restored in 1985 after owner David Sharps bought the barge for a dollar.

David is extremely friendly and is always willing to tell you about the history of the barge. Kids will be fascinated by collection of bells and gongs that were once used as communication between traveling barges. Kids and adults alike will be fascinated by a piece of art they call the "ball machine," a large Willy Wonka–like sculpture created by artist George Rhoades and on display as a part of the barge's permanent collection. Don't forget to say hello to friendly "Duey the barge bunny," an actual bunny that hops around the museum space. David Sharps spent many years on the cruise circuit performing as a clown and now hosts CIRCUSundays every June, with various circus acts performing at the barge. During my visit David juggled for visitors.

The views from the barge that look out onto the Statue of Liberty and the waters that surround Red Hook are phenomenal. Next door to the museum is the **Pier 44 Garden** where you can picnic with sandwiches from **Fairway Market** (480-500 Van Brunt Street, Red Hook; 718-694-6868; www.fairwaymarket.com), located adjacent to the barge. (They share the same parking lot.) Just a few blocks down the road is another great waterfront picnic spot, **Valentino Pier** (Coffey Street Pier, Red Hook, Brooklyn; www.nycgovparks.org), which offers a nice grassy patch for picnic blankets and also has awesome views. Don't forget to walk across the street to a place where eating pie can result in being addicted to **Steve's Key Lime Pies** (Pier 41, 204 Van Dyke Street, Red Hook, Brooklyn; 888-450-5463; www.stevesauthentic.com). Get a pie or a Swingle, a chocolate-covered key lime pie on a stick, and wash it down with a glass of their key lime iced tea. Sit outside the shop, surrounded by plants on their tiled tables, and you'll feel as if you're eating pies in the peace and quiet of Key West.

Don't hail a taxi back to the city, just head down to the pier by IKEA or Fulton Ferry Landing to hop aboard the **Water Taxi** (212-742-1969; www.ny-watertaxi.com), which will drop you off at Pier 11 in downtown Manhattan. Note that you must purchase something at IKEA to catch a water taxi back to the city from their pier. The water taxi is a great way to see the city and you can simply purchase tickets from the ferry stop at Fulton Ferry Landing or any of the New York Water Taxi stops. Purchase a one- or two-day weekend pass from April to October and have unlimited access to the ferry, with stops all over the city from the South Street Seaport to the Chelsea Piers.

Looking for something new to do this weekend? Have a beer and play some volleyball at the New York Water Taxi's man-made beach in Long Island City, Queens (www.watertaxibeach.com). You can also grab a hot dog or a soy dog at this cool waterside beach that is accessible by water taxi, car, subway, and bike.

If you take the water taxi from Fulton Ferry Landing, you must get an ice cream cone at the **Brooklyn Ice Cream Factory** (1 Water Street; 718-246-3963). Folks line up for the homemade ice cream at this establishment in an old fireboat house, and it is truly worth the wait. You can indulge in your ice cream on the pier looking at the view of the lower Manhattan skyline.

Those who like classical music should get tickets for a concert on the barge located on Fulton Ferry Landing directly across from the taxi terminal. **Barge Music** (718-624-2083; www.bargemusic.org) is an incredible venue to hear classical and jazz music. This is one of these true NYC experiences, which has been operating for over thirty years and is a must-visit.

If you don't want to head back to the city by water taxi just yet, hang out on the waterfront at scenic **Brooklyn Bridge Park** *(www.brooklyn-bridgepark.org)*, located next to the Fulton Ferry Landing, and which hosts outdoor movies and other great events all summer long on Thursday evenings.

You can also look down at the water while walking across the Brooklyn Bridge, which is easily accessible from the Fulton Ferry Landing. Walking across the Brooklyn Bridge is one of my favorite activities to do in the city.

Stick around Brooklyn and head to Prospect Park where you tour the lake in the center of the park on the *Independence,* an electric boat located at the **Prospect Park Audubon Center** *(see page 57)*. The twenty-five minute tour of the park's lake takes you through many scenic areas and departs every half hour. If you want to burn off some energy after your electric boat ride, head to the **Wollman Rink** *(718-282-7789)* which is also located inside the park. From May through mid-October this popular ice skating spot is occupied by pedal boats that are rented at an hourly rate.

Now that you've sailed over the water and enjoyed fantastic views, let's take a look beneath the sea. If you have your scuba license and want to head out into the waters surrounding the New York City area, go to the East Village to book a local excursion with **Village Divers** *(125 East 4th Street; 212-780-0879; www.villagedivers.com)*. They also offer classes on scuba certification. On Sundays, head to two local dive sites with the crew of the *Jeanne II (Pier 5, Emmons Avenue, Sheepshead Bay; 718-332-9574; www.jeanne-ii.com)* for their Leisure Sundays, which include a BBQ lunch. Check their Web site for their schedule of other local dives. You can also night dive with **Captain Mike's Diving** on City Island *(see page 76)*.

Interested in catching your own fish? Take your pick of the charter boats that dock off of the piers at Emmons Avenue in Sheepshead Bay. Lots of these fishing outfits have both half-day and full-day excursions for fluke and flounder as well as longer trips for tuna and other fish. Some popular fishing boats include the *Sea Queen VII (917-642-0265; www.seaqueenvii.com)* and the *Brooklyn VI (718-743-8464; www.brooklynvifishing.com)*. If you need fishing gear, head to **Bernie's Tackle** *(3035 Emmons Avenue; 718-646-7600; www.berniesfishing.com)*, which has been supplying local fisherman with bait and other fishing necessities for over fifty years. After a day of fishing in Sheepshead Bay head to the last remaining clam bar on this stretch of Brooklyn waterfront at **Randazzo's** *(2017 Emmons Avenue; 718-615-0010; www.randazzosclambar.com)*. This eatery has a great selection of classic seafood dishes and Italian food. The service is great and the food rivals any

New England clam bar. Randazzo's is open year-round and in the summer months, they offer outdoor seating. It's nice to have dinner and then walk along the pier, checking out the nightlife on Emmons Avenue and watching all of the fishing boats return from their day at sea.

Waterfront Restaurants:

The Café at Fairway Market *(480-500 Van Brunt Street, Red Hook; 718-694-6868; www.fairwaymarket.com)* This café is one of the most economical places in the city to dine along the water, barring a picnic on the pier or on the Brooklyn Heights Promenade. In the warmer months, sit outside this popular Brooklyn market with a great view of the Statue of Liberty and dine on goodies from their café. It's amazing that you can get such good grub at incredible prices, with a priceless view to boot.

The River Café *(1 Water Street; 718-522-5200; www.rivercafe.com)* Since June of 1977, folks have been dining at this classic Brooklyn restaurant with views of the Manhattan skyline. Open for lunch, weekend brunch, and dinner, the restaurant never fails to satisfy with a menu of classic American cuisine that includes dishes like the Cape Cod monkfish and crisp duck breast.

The Water Club *(The East River and FDR Drive, via East 23rd Street; 212-683-3333; www.thewaterclub.com)* Every table has a view in this upscale east-side-of-Manhattan restaurant that's open for lunch, dinner, and weekend brunch. The Water Club has a classic American menu. In the summer they open the Crow's Nest for casual outdoor dining with a menu of fun pub grub like burgers, hot dogs, and oysters. This is a great place to have a cocktail.

Water's Edge *(4-01 44th Drive, Long Island City; 718-482-0033; www.watersedgenyc.com)* This Long Island City restaurant offers stunning views of the water and the Manhattan skyline as well as a complimentary water shuttle from 35th Street and the East River. Taking a boat to your dinner adds to the excitement and the beauty of an evening at the Water's Edge. Dinner is served from 5:30 p.m. to 11:30 p.m., Mondays through Saturdays. If you'd like to dine outdoors, from the spring until the fall the Water's Edge offers guests the opportunity to dine on the Promenade, an outdoor area where you can dine al fresco as you soak in the views.

A Fun Day at Coney Island

Coney Island *(www.coneyisland.com)*
Take the D, Q, N, or F train to the last stop at Stillwell Avenue and head to this public beach. Find a spot to sunbathe on the sand or spend the afternoon walking around the vibrant boardwalk. If you are feeling gutsy, there's always the classic wooden roller coaster, the Cyclone. In June, check out the **Mermaid Parade** on the boardwalk which adds to the flavor of this unique beach. You can also spend the day at the **New York Aquarium** *(Surf Avenue and West 8th Street; 718-265-FISH; www.nyaquarium.com)* or take in a **Cyclones game** *(KeySpan Park, 1904 Surf Avenue; 718-507-TIXX; www.brooklyncyclones.com)*. A trip to Coney Island wouldn't be complete without grabbing a hot dog at **Nathan's** *(1310 Surf Avenue; 718-946-2705; www.nathansfamous.com)*.

In addition to Coney Island, there are many gorgeous public beaches in the city. In Queens, you can spend the day at **Rockaway Beach** *(www.nycgovparks.org)*, immortalized in the famous Ramones song "Rockaway Beach." This quiet stretch of beach has a boardwalk and good surf. You can also hop aboard the ferry and head to Staten Island's famous **South Beach** *(www.statenislandusa.com)*, with great views of the Verrazano-Narrows Bridge, and where you can sun yourself on the sandy beach and stroll along the boardwalk.

Chapter Six

Peace and Nature in the City:

Relax, Hike, or Enjoy NYC's Wildlife

You don't have to leave the city to embrace nature. New York City is home to over three hundred and fifty species of birds, as well as nature trails, coastal horseback riding, a campground on the site of a defunct airport, and some of the most beautiful beaches in North America. If you feel yourself in need of a mental health day, there are many ways to spend a day of peace and relaxation in nature.

For those who want less nature and more peace, there are also plenty of ways to relax, whether you spend the day strolling through a Tibetan museum on Staten Island or decide to picnic in the New York Botanical Gardens. Recharge and escape the hustle and bustle of this energetic city.

Bird-watching:

There's no better balance of nature and serenity than bird watching in New York City. If you're a novice bird-watcher who can only identify pigeons, and you want to find the best places to see other kinds of birds, take the Q, S, or B trains to Prospect Park station where you might find some lessons in birding at Prospect Park. Exit onto Lincoln Road and follow it up to the park entrance on Ocean Avenue. Walk along the park's roadway and cross the East Lake Drive, and continue following the path downhill through the Cleft Ridge Span Bridge to the **Prospect Park Audubon Center** *(718-287-3400; www.prospectpark.org)*. Every Saturday throughout the year they host an introduction to bird-watching session from 12 noon to 1:30 p.m. Don't worry about bringing binoculars, as the organizers of the seminar will lend you a pair for your excursion in the park to discover the beautiful birds of Brooklyn. This bird-watching event is free and open to the public.

There are many ideal locations in the city for viewing birds, especially during the birds' migrations in the spring and fall. For group outings, check with **New York City Audubon** (71 West 23rd Street; 212-691-7483; www.nycaudubon.org), which has many weekend programs, from local bird-watching around the boroughs to economical weekend trips away from the city. For both of these kinds of trips, they provide the transportation from their Chelsea location. The groups tend to be limited in size, so sign up well in advance. New York City Audubon also offers an introductory bird-watching class.

If you'd like to go birding on your own, purchase the handy guide *The New York City Audubon Society Guide to Finding Birds in the Metropolitan Area* by Marcia T. Fowle and Paul Kerlinger. The book outlines specific areas in the city that attract birds, such as Jamaica Bay Wildlife Refuge in Queens, which draws ospreys, and Green-Wood Cemetery in Brooklyn, which is popular with monk parakeets.

How about combining bird-watching with a nautical theme? Sign up for a relaxing boat ride on **EcoCruises** (212-742-1969; www.nywatertaxi.com), sponsored by the New York City Audubon Society. These cruises run on Sunday evenings from June until mid-August. Tickets cost twenty-five dollars for adults and ten dollars for kids. Tours depart from Pier 17 at the South Street Seaport and last from 7 p.m. until 8:30 p.m. This is a great way to see the herons that nest on the small islands around the city.

Nature walks:

For those who like to spend the day hiking, there are many nature trails throughout the city, with terrains from marshlands to lush greenery. Enjoy the trails offered at fifteen Urban Park Ranger Centers in the New York City parks. Each nature center hosts weekend activities, most free of charge; listings of the activities are on the NYC Department of Parks and Recreation Web site (www.nycgovparks.org). A subscription to *Outdoors in New York City*, a newspaper that lists all the activities for outdoor adventure through the parks department, will provide you with all the details.

My favorite nature center is the **Henry Luce Nature Observatory** (Midpark, 79th Street; 212-772-0210; www.centralparknyc.org) in Belvedere Castle in Central Park. Enjoy the views from this gorgeous building and don't forget to look at the collection of papier-mâché reproductions of the types of birds that can be found in the park. You can even bird-watch from this historic site that also serves as a weather station for the U. S. Weather Bureau. Young bird-watchers and nature lovers can borrow binoculars from the center to explore the wildlife in the area. Outside the observatory is an area known as the ramble, which is a less developed part of the park and is a great spot for bird watching.

If you want to head out of Manhattan to see nature, go to Brooklyn and the **Salt Marsh Nature Center** (*3302 Avenue U; 718-421-2021; www.saltmarshalliance.org*). Take the Q train to Avenue U / East 16th Street, where you can walk around the trail behind the nature center. The gorgeous trail takes you around the marshland and within seconds, you will feel completely removed from the city. The walk isn't challenging, so all can enjoy it; the length of the trail can be covered in fifteen minutes to an hour, depending on your pace.

There are also bike trails available for use and a large park across the street, where folks often spend the weekends playing games of cricket, dressed in white. If you are hungry after your walk, head a few blocks down Avenue U and grab a tasty deli sandwich or knish at **Jay and Lloyd's Kosher Deli** (*2718 Avenue U; 718-891-5298*). The Salt Marsh Nature Center offers different events throughout the year from an outdoor film series to family-oriented nature activities.

To continue spending the weekend with the elements, you should certainly plan a trip to the **Jamaica Bay Wildlife Refuge** (*718-318-4340; www.nps.gov/gate or www.nyharborparks.org*). If you happen to drive to the refuge, you can visit both the Salt Marsh Nature Center and the Jamaica Bay Wildlife Refuge in the same day since they are both easily accessible from the Belt Parkway, and after a trip to these nature centers you can compare the different marshlands and the various forms of wildlife you will see on the trails. The Wildlife Refuge has a much larger trail than the Salt Marsh Nature Center, as the refuge is over 9,000 acres, but the main trail is just a loop a few miles in length around the water. There are also many benches where you can sit and watch the birds. The rocky path is extremely accessible, which is why the trail attracts families from all over the area. They also host many nature-related activities throughout the year.

Take a break from the marshland and head on the 7 train to Main Street. From here, take the Q12 bus to Northern Boulevard until you reach **Alley Pond Park** (*228-06 Northern Boulevard, Douglaston; 718-229-4000; www.alleypond.com*). This park is over 600 acres wide and has bike trails, nature trails, and a nature center that houses an extensive collection of animals as well as a driving range and miniature golf course across the street from the center. The nature center hosts many guided walks throughout the year. They also run a series of nature classes for kids of all ages.

Head to Staten Island and explore over thirty miles of trails in the lush **Staten Island Greenbelt** (*200 Nevada Avenue; 718-667-2165; www.sigreen-*

belt.org). The Greenbelt consists of 2,800 acres of forests, meadows, streams, ponds, hiking trails, parks, and recreational areas in Staten Island that are free and open to the public. The easiest way to access the trails is by visiting the Greenbelt Nature Center *(700 Rockland Avenue; 718-351-3450)*, which is located within easy access of most of the trails in the Greenbelt. Don't forget to pick up a trail map at the nature center or download one from their Web site, so that you can navigate your way around the Greenbelt. The center offers guided walks and workshops focusing on nature and the environment, as well as being host to various family friendly programs from pumpkin festivals to story hours. Dog lovers will be especially pleased with their dog-friendly guided hikes.

Camping:

If you have kids and want to introduce them to the world of camping, try Queens. During the summer, Alley Pond Park hosts an extremely popular **Family Camping Program** through the Urban Park Rangers, where they will provide you with the tent, flashlights, and all the gear needed to get through one night in the park. The evening begins with a collective BBQ where they offer a wide range of grilled treats, including veggie burgers. The night's festivities conclude with an extremely interesting and informative night hike, complete with stargazing and s'mores. The program is free and runs on Friday and Saturday nights throughout the summer. The experience starts at 5 p.m. and ends at 6:30 the next morning, when they help you break down your tent and revive you with juice and muffins. It's a gentle introduction to family camping and is a great way to see if your urban family is ready to take their camping skills on the road. My daughter Lucy, didn't want to leave and once we got home I bought a tent and started to plan a camping trip for the entire family.

If you're really adventurous and want to camp on your own, take the 2 train to Flatbush Avenue, then the Q35 bus to **Floyd Bennett Field** *(Flatbush Avenue; 718-338-3799)* and the only campground in New York City where you can camp without a ranger. For fifty dollars, you can get a permit to camp at one of the four public campsites for three days. Once an operational airport, Floyd Bennett Field is a great place to bike on the old runways. They have a BBQ pit and public bathrooms. Many people rent the space for large family get-togethers and don't actually stay the night. If you'd like to have an unusual night doing some coastal camping at an airport that once hosted historic flights like Amelia Earhart's and Charles Lindbergh's, this is the place.

Shopping:

Looking for camping equipment? The city has a few good places to pick up the gear for a rural weekend. For tent rental, you can try **EMS Sports** *(591 Broadway; 212-966-8730; www.ems.com)*, where for $30 to $40 a day, depending on the size of the tent, you can rent the right tent for your party. You can also buy tents, sleeping bags, and camping essentials at this popular SoHo shop. Check out the bulletin board at the entrance for postings for hiking clubs, camping trips, and other outdoors-related info.

Another shop for tent rentals and equipment is **Tent and Trails** *(21 Park Place; 212-227-1760; www.tenttrails.com)*. You can rent a tent with prices starting at $30 for three nights. The shop is filled with helpful staff who will teach you how to use the equipment. The shop hosts events and talks so check their Web site for a complete listing of events.

If you're looking for a good pair of hiking boots or other assorted gear, take a trip to 18th and Broadway to visit **Paragon Sports** *(867 Broadway; 800-961-3030; www.paragonsports.com)*. This shop carries everything you'll need for your outdoor adventure, including clothes.

To continue your shopping excursion, head to the **Evolution Store** *(120 Spring Street; 800-952-3195; www.evolutionnyc.com)*. This unique SoHo store sells all sorts of nature-related oddities from purses made of old toads (yes, they're real, I asked) and framed centipedes to glass-encased butterflies. If you're looking for a unique nature-themed curiosity or gift, you should head to this shop. It's also a great place to browse.

Museums:

Spend a weekend exploring the world of nature inside the fantastic New York City museums. From incredible exhibits and IMAX films focusing on everything from snakes to planets to a farm museum where you can take a hayride, you can experience all facets of nature in this urban oasis.

Start your weekend taking the C or B train to 81st Street on the Upper West Side and the classic New York City museum, the **American Museum of Natural History** *(Central Park West and 79th Street; 212-769-5100; www.amnh.org)*. Check out the dinosaurs and old-school exhibits filled with dioramas of stuffed animals in their native environments, but don't forget to visit the large blue whale hanging above the Milstein Hall of Ocean Life. A great tip to beat the crowds is to arrive early or on the off-hours during the workweek. After your morning at the museum you can explore Central Park, which is directly across the street.

Head back downtown to the Staten Island Ferry Terminal and feel the breeze as you ride the ferry across to Staten Island. Keep a look out for local birds and also the evocative downtown skyline. Once you have your feet planted on dry land in Staten Island take the S74 bus to Lighthouse Avenue where you will see the **Jacques Marchais Museum of Tibetan Art** *(338 Light-house Avenue; 718-987-3500; www.tibetanmuseum.org)*. This museum has a lot to offer by way of Tibetan art, including a walk through their meditative gardens. The Jacques Marchais Museum is truly a relaxing place in the city as the environment makes you feel far removed from the city's urban grind.

To indulge in newfound relaxation, every Saturday morning they offer meditation sessions from 11:30 a.m. until 12:30 p.m. and in the afternoons tai chi chuan, a Chinese martial art that features gentle movements based on images found in nature, from 4:30 p.m. until 5:30 p.m. They host the popular annual Tibetan Festival in September, which features Tibetan food and crafts as well as talks on Tibetan culture and demonstrations by Tibetan artists. Note that the museum is located on a hilly block, and it's a bit of a hike from the bus. The neighborhood that surrounds the museum is also home to a Frank Lloyd Wright house among other eclectic buildings, which makes for an interesting walk around the area.

Enjoy an afternoon feeding the goats or taking a hayride at the **Queens County Farm Museum** *(see page 30)*. The farm museum hosts year-round events—from popular seasonal fairs to a sheep-shearing festival. Go see how a farm really functions at this 47-acre farm museum in the middle of Queens.

To really feel removed from the urban bustle, take the 1 train to 242nd Street and hop on the free shuttle to **Wave Hill** *(West 249th Street; 718-549-3200; www.wavehill.org)*, a stunning 28-acre public garden in the Bronx. Every Saturday at 10 a.m. in the garden, beginners are welcome to partake in a tai chi chuan class. You can also tour the galleries on Saturdays at 2:15 p.m. or tour the lush gardens on Sundays at 2:15 p.m. Those in search of peace, art, and nature will find themselves sated at Wave Hill, which has a perfect balance of all things cultural and natural. Wave Hill is also a popular place to get married.

Horseback-riding:

Think horseback riding is something you can only do on a weekend in the country? You can horseback ride on trails throughout the city, so hit the saddle and explore Manhattan by horse. If you want to ride in Central Park, the **Riverdale Equestrian Center** *(West 254th Street; 718-548-4848; www.riverdaleriding.com)* offers guided tours of the park. The Equestrian Center has four outdoor riding areas available or they can also take you on trails in Van Cortlandt Park in the Bronx.

Those who want to ride in scenic Prospect Park in Brooklyn should head to historic **Kensington Stables** *(51 Caton Place; 718-972-4588; www.kensingtonstables.com)*. If you have kids in tow, you might want to sign up for a pony ride that, for three dollars, will delight your child in a gentle ride up and down the block. You can also horseback ride in Staten Island and Queens; there is a list of trails and locations of where you can rent a horse on the NYC Department of Parks and Recreation Web site *(www.nycgovparks.org)*.

For coastal riding, drive the Belt Parkway to the **Jamaica Bay Riding Academy** *(7000 Shore Parkway; 718-531-8949; www.horsebackride.com)*, which boasts trails that follow along the quiet shoreline. Rides are available privately or for groups throughout the year. Their trails are located on about a mile of beach and in the wooded areas of Jamaica Bay.

Botanical gardens:

Brooklyn Botanical Garden *(1000 Washington Avenue, Brooklyn; 718-623-7200; www.bbg.org)* The 52-acre Brooklyn Botanical garden boasts magnificent greenhouses, a stunning rose garden, and an interactive children's garden and other beautiful gardens. Relax as you spend the day walking through the immaculately landscaped grounds including my favorite, the Japanese Hill and Pond Garden, not to mention the wonderful Steinhardt Conservatory. Simply strolling through the garden or relaxing with an iced tea in the outdoor café is a great way to escape the stress of the city.

Conservatory Garden at Central Park *(Central Park, 105th Street; www.centralparknyc.org)* This 6-acre garden in Central Park offers Saturday morning tours at 11 a.m. from April through October. Access to the grounds is free, and it is a true pleasure to walk through the gardens and their blooming flowers.

Narrows Botanical Gardens *(Shore Road, Bay Ridge, Brooklyn; www.narrowsbg.org)* Stroll through this 4 ½-acre sanctuary that was created by volunteers who transformed this stretch of waterfront property into a gorgeous flowerbed boasting a lovely rose garden.

New York Botanical Garden *(Bronx River Parkway, Bronx; 718-817-8700; www.nybg.org)* This 250-acre Bronx garden will satisfy any nature lover. An added plus is that admission is free on Saturdays from 10 a.m. until 12 p.m. In addition to flowers, there are historic landmark buildings like the Enid A. Haupt Conservatory and the Snuff Mill. Spend the day perusing the gardens and enjoying this quiet stretch of the Bronx. You can also picnic in the Botanical Garden's designated picnic area, which is near the lovely Everett Children's Adventure Garden.

These gardens are a true paradise located less than a half hour from Manhattan. We love to visit in the winter when they host the popular annual Holiday Train Show, where you can see model trains ride around replicas of New York City landmarks.

Queens Botanical Garden *(43-50 Main Street, Flushing; 718-886-3800; www.queensbotanical.org)* The Queens Botanical Garden, always free and open year-round, is lovely place for a nice stroll. The garden offers many special programs including a series that is devoted to lessons in composting and promoting a green lifestyle. The garden has also reserved some garden space for senior citizens to enjoy the chance to garden and meet up on weekdays. Parents might enjoy signing their kids up—ages 5 and over—for their classes on how to plant and tend gardens in the city.

Staten Island Botanical Garden *(1000 Richmond Terrace; 718-448-2500; www.sibg.org)* Every New Yorker must take a ferry across the river to visit the New York Chinese Scholar's Garden—one of the city's treasures—where it's hard not to find both peace and tranquility as you sit on a bench in the Moon Viewing Pavilion. Children will enjoy a romp through the maze in the Secret Garden. There is a minimal charge to enter these two gardens, but the rest of the grounds are free of charge. They offer educational programs for both adults and kids and host events throughout the year.

You can easily spend the entire day at the Staten Island Botanical Garden and the neighboring museums. Enjoy a day at the gardens followed by an afternoon at the Children's Museum or the Snug Harbor Cultural Center. This is the perfect outing for families who want to enjoy activities for both adults and kids.

Chapter Seven

Let's Spend the Night:

Hotels You'd Splurge On Even If You Live in NYC

Even if you live in New York City, there is no reason you can't play tourist for a night. Plan a romantic weekend or a fun girlfriends' getaway in your own hometown. From a homey bed-and-breakfast off of Prospect Park to a hip hotel in the Meatpacking District, there are plenty of overnight escapes to be had in the city. A night at one of these hotels will enhance your New York experience and you'll realize that these digs have a lot to offer natives. Who doesn't like having their cocktails on amazing scenic rooftop lounges? There are two hotels featured here that limit the use of their rooftop bars to hotel guests. Isn't that alone reason enough to spend the night?

Of course, the possibilities of hotels to choose from are endless, but I tried to keep the list to ten—an incredibly hard task. The list covers the city from the east to the west, and from downtown to Brooklyn.

Bed and Breakfast on the Park *(113 Prospect Park West, Park Slope, Brooklyn; 718-499-6115; www.bbnyc.com)* This charming Brooklyn B and B has great personality. In fact you can't help but be impressed by the building's antique wood trim and by the paintings displayed on the walls. Located on Prospect Park West in the heart of Park Slope, the warm and attentive staff of this seven-room B and B will make your stay feel as if you're among old friends.

This historic brownstone-turned-bed-and-breakfast is a great place for a romantic weekend "away." Book one of the three rooms with working gas fireplaces, so you can snuggle up fireside in the privacy of your own room. Don't sleep in though, as you won't want to miss the hearty, delicious breakfast served in the dining room. Breakfast is served promptly at 9 a.m. when guests gather around a grand wooden table on the main level. If you wake up early and are in need of coffee to start your day, head to the garden-level community kitchen, open twenty-four hours per day, and is stocked with coffee and other beverages, including a fridge filled with snacks like yogurt and ice pops.

After your day in Brooklyn, you can relax in the parlor, perusing their large collection of New York City–centric books and snacking from baskets filled with chocolates placed strategically throughout the B and B. In the warmer months you can unwind in their peaceful backyard garden. If you would prefer some private outdoor space, be sure to ask for the Lady Liberty room that is complete with its own roof deck. A true paradise in the city, Bed and Breakfast on the Park is a wonderful place for a perfect New York getaway.

Casablanca Hotel *(147 West 43rd Street; 212-869-1212; www.casablancahotel.com)* Despite its location, just a block away from Times Square, the Casablanca will transport you to a faraway land. With a mural of a Northern African town along the walls of the lobby and the large statue of a leopard outside the hotel's café, the atmosphere evokes images from the acclaimed film *Casablanca*. Fans of the film will enjoy dining on the complimentary breakfast and all-day snack service provided by the appropriately named Rick's Café. You may not find Humphrey Bogart here, but you will be delighted to discover the café's nightly wine and cheese fête, which lasts from 5 p.m. until 8 p.m. If you'd like to invite a date for the night, you're in luck as hotel guests are allowed to bring friends to join them.

If you haven't seen *Casablanca*, there is no better place to watch it than in your Moroccan-inspired hotel room, which has with great touches like ceiling fans and wooden blinds. They have copies of the film on DVD for watching in the comfort of your room as well as a large collection of films set in New York City and Broadway shows that were turned into movies. If watching the film inspires you to write your own screenplay, there's a computer and printer available for guests in the café as well as outdoor seating for sipping cappuccinos while you contemplate how to start the opening scene.

New Yorkers who have always wanted to watch the ball drop on New Year's Eve but have never wanted to stand out in the cold for twelve hours waiting in a large crowd, should book a room at the Casablanca for a fun New Year's stay. The hotel is the closest hotel to the ball drop, and offers free passes to the restricted Times Square celebration area, which most people only get to see on television. In addition to getting up close and personal to the monumental ball drop, this hotel package includes a dinner for two at Tony's DiNapoli restaurant, a classic family-style Italian restaurant that has been open since the 1950s, located off the hotel lobby and complete with Broadway-style entertainment and an open bar. You can also have a private celebration of your own with the complimentary bottle of bubbly they provide in your room.

Gramercy Park Hotel *(2 Lexington Avenue; 212-920-3300; www.gramer-cyparkhotel.com)* New Yorkers who have always dreamt of having both the key to the Gramercy Park garden and access to the private rooftop club should book a weekend getaway to this striking hotel across from Gramercy Park. Upon entering the hotel, you will be captivated by the scent of their signature candle that burns all day in the lobby. This aroma, combined with the stately fireplace and décor handpicked by artist Julian Schnabel are just some of the reasons why the charm of this hotel is plentiful. Run by the father of boutique hotels, Ian Schrager, the Gramercy Park Hotel will satisfy even the most discerning New Yorkers.

Start your evening with a drink at either the Rose Bar or the Jade Bar, atmospheric lounges with walls adorned by artwork from legendary artists like Damien Hurst and Andy Warhol. These two spots are quite popular with the locals and they tend to get crowded. Make sure you reserve a space after 10 p.m. or consider booking a table at Wakiya, the swank hotel restaurant.

The rooms in the hotel are equally as impressive. Thoughtfully decorated by artist Julian Schnabel, each space is filled with yards of red velvet and a mini bar with real-sized liquor bottles, so you can enjoy a getaway without ever leaving your room. Every room is designed a bit differently, although all have a picture of Andy Warhol up on the wall. The bath products were handpicked by the editors of *Allure* magazine and include fine products like Mario Badescu Vitamin E Body Lotion with Wheat Germ and Hamadi Ginger Soymilk Hair Wash. Book a room overlooking the scenic park or just close the blinds and enjoy the well-curated décor of your room.

Be sure to grab a table at the rooftop club, open only to hotel guests and club members. The views are awesome and the roof is retractable, so that you may drink beneath the stars—and quite possibly with the stars, as the rooftop club is a favorite celebrity haunt. The club is cleverly designed to feel like an intimate European café, with half-finished backgammon games left atop the coffee tables that sit alongside the plentiful and cozy couches. The complimentary continental breakfast is served up on the rooftop bar. What could be a better way to start your New York City morning? With amazing rooms, the hippest bars, and a private rooftop club, you can't help but feel like a VIP during your stay at this ultra-posh hotel.

Hotel Gansevoort *(18 9th Avenue; 212-206-6700; www.hotelganse-voort.com)* For a hip weekend in New York City's funky Meatpacking District, book a room at the Hotel Gansevoort, where you don't even have to leave the hotel to be a part of a great party. Reserve a treatment at the hotel's G spa, which also doubles as a nightclub as the G Lounge—massage rooms double as private cabanas for the nightclub. Dine at the hotel's incredible restaurant, Ono, or sip cocktails at the bar in their gorgeous outdoor garden.

Twenty-one of the luxurious 187 rooms are suites, and they do not disappoint. Splurge on a room with a view of the Hudson or a suite with its own small balcony. All rooms have the quintessential amenities for a proper New York City getaway, like free Wi-Fi. iPod docking stations, a 27-inch flat-screen TV, a safe big enough to store your laptop, and a complimentary bottle of EBOOST energy drink to keep you up all night or help you make it to breakfast on time. Rooms are decorated with artistic photos of the neighborhood and include complimentary turndown service.

If you are awestruck by staggering city views, head for a swim in their private rooftop pool, open until 11 p.m. Located next to the pool is Plunge, the hotel's extremely popular rooftop bar that is open year-round. After your swim, toast your friends as you literally sit atop the world, overlooking the inspiring view of Manhattan. Although you can't swim in the pool unless you're a hotel guest (see page 43), the rooftop bar is open to the public.

Hudson Hotel (356 West 58th Street; 212-554-6000; www.hudsonhotel.com) There aren't any names or hotel brands flanking the outside of this chic hotel. While taking the unmarked elevator up to the hotel lobby you'll feel as though you're about to enter a nightclub. No matter what time of day, the escalator that leads you to the second floor lobby is lit by yellow, almost chartreuse light. The lobby has a glass ceiling covered in ivy with a single large, stunning chandelier hanging over the reception desk. With tables that are wrapped in tree bark and chairs that are upholstered in sleek leopard print, the décor is an eclectic balance of modern design with hip safari overtones. Modeled after a college dormitory, the hotel, which was once a former YMCA, has many aspects that incorporate the feeling of collegiate life. The restaurant, aptly named the Hudson Cafeteria, was inspired by college dining halls, complete with long wooden tables where patrons dine together on comfort food—try the mac 'n' cheese, you won't regret it!

If you've come for nightlife like most folks who visit the Hudson, you will not be disappointed. The hotel offers four exclusive bars for hotel guests, although two of them are only open seasonally. The Library is decked out with a large college-lounge-style pool table. The walls are lined in books that guests may borrow as they retire to their rooms. The Private Park is a gorgeous outdoor space with large trees and ivy-covered garden walls, where folks can relax during the day and socialize in the evenings. Those who enjoy the New York City party scene have probably already enjoyed a cocktail or two at the famed Hudson Bar in the hotel, which is modeled to look like the world has been flipped upside down—the floor composed of ceiling tiles and the ceiling deceivingly similar to a floor. All of these bars are worth a visit, even if you don't decide to spend the weekend. However, only hotel guests have access to the unbelievable Sky Terrace. In lounge chairs, atop this fifteenth floor terrace, you can soak in the rays while relaxing in one of the most tranquil places I've ever been in the city. Guests spend their downtime lounging, reading, or socializing with the other hotel guests as they drink from the bar menu. Honestly, just a day and night on this terrace is worth the price of the room: it's the perfect escape for harried New Yorkers.

The rooms tend to be on the small side, but what they lack in size they make up for in amenities. They are well designed with trendy wood-paneled walls, Philippe Starck lighting, and a wonderful selection of bath products by Agua. The 805 rooms range in size from a standard Queen, which is ideal for two, to a Double Double, which is the best bet for a fun girlfriends' getaway, to elegant and spacious Deluxe Studios. Although you don't have to the leave the hotel to have a fun night, you might be a bit tempted, since it's near Columbus Circle, Lincoln Square, and just blocks from Hell's Kitchen nightlife.

Mandarin Oriental *(80 Columbus Circle; 212-805-8800; www.mandarinoriental.com)* The unassuming entrance is deceiving as you enter the elevator to the lobby located on the 35th floor of this Columbus Square building. The views of Central Park alone are worth a visit to the Mandarin Oriental, from thirty-five floors above the city, overlooking the park and Columbus Circle, you will feel as if you are on top of the world. Afternoon tea or cocktails in the lobby lounge are delightful alongside the large windows that line the walls of this luxurious hotel. In addition to being one of the best places to take a gander at the beauty of Central Park, this five-star hotel offers guests gorgeous Asian-inspired décor outfitted with tons of amenities, from free books and high end bath products to a flat-screen TV in each bathroom so you can soak while watching your favorite shows.

Book a treatment at their spa with six massage rooms that have private baths. If you're planning a romantic weekend, get a couple's massage at the VIP Spa Suite with private steam and sauna facilities, and order off the spa menu or enjoy a cup of tea with a private meal. Those in search of some quality workout time can take the private elevator straight to the fitness center and pool to enjoy an invigorating swim. If you forgot your iPod, the Mandarin Oriental offers preloaded iPods at the gym, so you can work out to some of the latest tunes.

After a day of relaxation at the spa, slip out of the complimentary plush bathrobe that was hanging in your room, and get dressed up for a dinner at Asiate. Fans of good vino will appreciate the vintage wine bottles that line the walls, some dating back to the 1800s. Their delectable prix fixe dinner is $85 and consists of Asian-inspired cuisine. Asiate also offers a wonderful brunch on both Saturday and Sunday. Like most of the Mandarin Oriental, the views from Asiate are stunning, so request a table by the window.

New Yorkers who've always wanted to watch the Macy's Thanksgiving Parade but who never dared to brave the chilly autumn air should book a stay at the Mandarin for Turkey Day. The hotel opens the ballroom to hotel guests, who receive a complimentary breakfast complete with an amazing view of the parade from the large windows overlooking Columbus Circle. The Thanksgiving parade is broadcast on big screens within the hotel, so you won't miss out on any of the action. This is a fun and lavish way to spend a weekend with the kids.

NU Hotel *(85 Smith Street; 718-852-8585; www.nuhotelbrooklyn.com)* First came the five-star restaurants, then the swank bars, and now there's even a boutique hotel in Brooklyn. Housed on Smith Street, one of Brooklyn's famed restaurant rows, the hotel pays tribute to old Brooklyn with cool relics of Brooklyn history located throughout this eco-chic hotel. The lobby has a large sign that reads "YES," the letters of which were taken from a 1930s sign for Bayside Oil and Fuel, a Brooklyn-based company. Next to the elevator is a size-twelve clothing model from the 1950s, taken from a garment warehouse in Brooklyn.

Quotes from famous Brooklynites are written on the walls of each floor, which adds to the unique Brooklyn flavor of this boutique hotel. The rooms are mindfully designed with green materials that include white cork floors and furniture made from recycled materials, and the rooms include wicker baskets filled with treats instead of mini fridges. This hotel has all the amenities of the upscale lodges across the river, like iPod docking stations, flat-screen TVs, and blackout curtains so you can sleep in. Book one of the three suites, so you can relax in your own personal hammock that hangs within each of the three deluxe rooms. If you have kids in tow or if you'd like to cram a few friends in, book the NU room, which offers rooms with bunk beds. This fun hotel is economical, offering folks a great escape from the city and leaving them with more cash to spend at the many diversions in the neighborhood.

If you are in search of a Brooklyn souvenir, stop across the street at **Brooklyn Industries** (100 Smith Street; 718-596-3986; www.brooklynindustries.com), where you can score some of the coolest Brooklyn tees around. Although the hotel doesn't offer a spa, **Providence Day Spa** (329 Atlantic Avenue; 718-596-6774; www.providencedayspa.com) is a personal favorite of mine and is located just down the block from the hotel.

After checking into your room, have a cocktail at the NU Bar in the hotel's lobby, or step out the door and experience the culinary delights of Brooklyn.

SoHo Grand (310 West Broadway; 212-965-3000; www.sohogrand.com) Stay among galleries, great shops, and funky nightlife at this uber-hip SoHo hotel that is also known as a celebrity magnet. Don't forget to bring your pet to this extremely animal-friendly hotel that offers a room-service menu for both you and your pet's every need, including food bowls, plush pet beds, and dog-walking services. If you are without your furry friend, this hotel treats guests to a complimentary pet goldfish, which you have the option of bringing home at the end of your stay. The SoHo Grand is also very kid-friendly and has Maclaren strollers on hand to lend guests. If you wish to see the city by bike, the hotel offers free bikes to its guests, including a selection of kid bikes if you have younger ones in tow.

The rooms are outfitted in amenities like bath products by Malin+Goetz, flat-screen TVs, and a mini bar with New York–centric goodies like snacks from Citarella. With art from the Howard Greenberg gallery on the walls and large windows with views of SoHo, the vibe is both arty and cool. Grab a drink at the Grand Bar in the lobby or hang outside during warmer months at the Yard where you can have dinner and drinks in the SoHo Grand's urban oasis restaurant and bar. The Yard is open to only guests from 11 a.m. to 4 p.m; from that time on it is open to the public for dinner and drinks. This restaurant is a must-visit even if you don't stay at the hotel. It is divine to relax in private and soak in some rays while you dine on lunch.

The SoHo Grand offers a ton of packages, from the staycation package for New Yorkers who want to spend a weekend in their own city to a great girlfriends' getaway package. For those who love the world of film, check out the SoHo Grand's other hotel, the **Tribeca Grand** (2 Avenue of the Americas;

212-519-6600; www.tribecagrand.com), located just two blocks from the SoHo Grand in Tribeca. The Tribeca Grand is all about the movies, with classic films inspiring the overall design of the hotel and its rooms. The Tribeca Grand also provides pet goldfish to their guests, although the ones in Tribeca are black while the fish at the SoHo location are gold. Even if you aren't a hotel guest, don't miss their outrageous Sunday brunch buffet at the Church at the Tribeca Grand. Bring the kids because during brunch they show free children's films in the hotel's posh screening room.

Library Hotel (299 Madison Avenue; 212-983-4500; www.libraryhotel.com) Get inspired to write the great American novel in this funky hotel where the rooms are arranged by the Dewey decimal system. Choose to stay on the Social Sciences floor where you can spend the night in the Political Science room. Looking for a romantic weekend amidst a literary enclave? Book the Erotic Literature room. If you do book the Erotica Literature room, they have a popular erotica package that includes such well-thought-out goodies like a Kama Sutra pocket guide and strawberries with whipped cream in your room

Although the exterior of the hotel blends into the midtown landscape, as soon as you enter the lobby you'll be transported far away from the office. Like a library, the hotel is peaceful. Aside from being saturated with books, this hotel has tons of clever finishing touches from the room design to the door signs that read SHHH…PLEASE LET ME READ, or PLEASE DUST OFF MY BOOKS.

Dine on complimentary pastries and coffee all day in their Reading Room. The room is lined with bookshelves and books to borrow, but unlike a library, you can eat and talk as you relax inside. If sitting in a room where the walls are lined with classics inspires you to write one, take a seat at the computer down the hall from the Reading Room, which is complete with a printer. There is a good space to set up your laptop in each room, so you can burn the midnight oil at the Library while donning a plush robe and comfy slippers. If you need further inspiration, ask for a room with a view of the main branch of the New York Public Library.

Of course all good writers are in search of some libations. After the complimentary wine and cheese pairing that occurs nightly from 5 p.m. until 8 p.m., head upstairs to the rooftop bar where you can order drinks like the Jackie Collins and the Pearl S. Buck. Even if you aren't staying in the hotel, it is definitely worth a visit to this cool bar, which offers views of midtown and a bit of peace in the city.

The Plaza *(5th Avenue at Central Park South; 212-759-3000; www.fair-mont.com/theplaza)* Be a part of New York City history during your stay at this classic New York institution, which reopened in 2008 after extensive renovations that cut the hotel's size from well over 800 rooms to a more manageable 282 rooms. Half of the hotel was turned into private condos, but they are kept quite separate from the hotel and don't detract from the beauty and elegance of this grand landmark. The hotel is still as stunning as you will have remembered from the classic children's book *Eloise*, the story of the quintessential city kid living with a nanny, a pet turtle, and a dog in the famed hotel. A painting by *Eloise* illustrator Hilary Knight hangs in the lobby.

The hotel rooms are quite spacious. The standard room is the size of most hotel suites at 475 square feet. You'll feel like Eloise or a Plaza VIP with the twenty-four-hour butler service and a very impressive touch screen on the wall that does everything from control the temperature in the room to booking reservations at restaurants around the city. The décor of the rooms, which have 24-karat gold-plated fixtures and white marble vanities, is inspired by the French Louis XV style. With flat-screen TVs and modern amenities like free Wi-Fi, the hotel does a fantastic job of combining the old and the new.

Have breakfast, afternoon tea, or dinner in the historic Palm Court, where kids can order from menus with pictures of Eloise. The Palm Court, like the rest of the hotel, was carefully restored to its original condition. For the first time in sixty years, the Palm Court's gorgeous lay-light ceilings have been fully restored. Feel like a starlet from the 1920s as you dine in this piece of old New York.

Don't forgo a cocktail in the intimate and wood-paneled Rose Club, which is now located in the space that was formerly occupied by the Persian Room. The famed Oak Room reopened in the fall of 2008 after extensive renovations that returned it to its former grandeur. In a city that changes daily, this hotel pays tribute to New York's glorious history. The hotel, which graced a myriad of movies, served as home to renowned architect Frank Lloyd Wright and attracted famous guests from the Beatles to Marilyn Monroe. The Plaza is a great place to stay and feel a part of the living history of this amazing, energetic city.

Chapter Eight

Are We in New England?:

A Weekend on City Island at a Classic Bed-and-Breakfast

Driving directions: I-95 North to Exit 8B.

Public transportation: Take the 6 train North to Pelham Bay Park, which is the last stop. Transfer to the BX29 bus to City Island.

Surrounded by the Long Island Sound, this part of the Bronx offers folks a New England escape within an hour of midtown Manhattan. When you're sitting by the water having a drink and eating fried clams, you'll forget you are actually within city limits. Filled with a plethora of choice seafood restaurants, you can eat at literally a different fish establishment every night of the week. With its priceless views, City Island is the perfect place to recharge, year-round. You can eat at a waterside restaurant, hop aboard a fishing boat or rent your own small motorboat, or just sit in the park while you chow down on ice cream. There are many ways to spend time on City Island or you can simply spend a weekend doing nothing at all.

Places to see:

As you drive toward the bridge to City Island you'll notice stables for the Bronx Equestrian Center on your left, right before City Island Bridge. At the **Bronx Equestrian Center** *(9 Shore Road; 718-885-0551; www.bronxequestriancenter.com)* you can go on a trail ride for $35, no appointment needed. Guided rides usually last between one and two hours, and the Equestrian Center also offers lessons and pony rides.

After the stables, you'll pass **Turtle Cove Golf Center** *(1 City Island Road; 718-885-2646)*, where you might want to spend sometime improving your golfing stance at the driving range. Turtle Cove is open year-round, weather permitting. The outdoor driving range is heated, so you can practice your swing in the heart of winter. Open Mondays through Saturdays from 8 a.m.

until 8 p.m. and on Sundays from 8 a.m. until 7 p.m., this is a great place to stop even if you have kids in tow, and to suit a range of interests, they also offer miniature golf and batting cages.

Crossing over the City Island Bridge, you will enter City Island's main street, City Island Avenue, filled with notable restaurants and shops where you can easily fill an afternoon just browsing and stopping for lunch. A walk around the stately neighborhood that is comprised of many different styles of buildings, many of which date back to the 1800s, is an enjoyable way to entertain yourself.

On the first Friday of the month, the City Island Chamber of Commerce offers visitors a chance to ride the **City Island's Seaside Trolley** *(718-885-9100; www.cityislandchamber.org)*. The trolley begins its route through town at the Pelham Bay Station and stops at the **Bartow-Pell Mansion** *(see page 24)*, followed by a stop on City Island Avenue. The trolley runs from 5:30 p.m. through 9:30 p.m., every hour on the half hour. The ride is free and you can hop on and off as you wish. Many shops and restaurants offer specials and discounts on the nights the trolley is in operation, so check the City Island's chamber of commerce Web site for participating vendors.

Since you're on an island, you might want to skirt along its edges. If so, you can rent a four-person fiberglass boat from **Jack's Bait and Tackle** *(551 City Island Avenue; 718-885-2042; www.jacksbaitandtackle.com)*. The boats are available all week from 5 a.m. until 5 p.m. on a first come, first served basis, so be sure to get there early. Along with the rental of the boat, you will be outfitted with a rod and reel and a brief lesson on how to operate the craft. Bring your driver's license and credit card since you need them to rent the boat. There is also fishing gear available for purchase at the shop.

If you want to get into the water, contact **Captain Mike's Diving** *(530 City Island Avenue; 718-885-1588; www.captainmikesdiving.com)* for scuba instruction and scuba outings. They host night dives and organize local diving trips for all levels of divers. If you'd rather catch fish than swim with them, get aboard one of the party boats that dock in City Island's many harbors. The **Riptide 3** *(701 Minnieford Avenue; 718-885-0236; www.riptide3.com)* leaves daily at 8 a.m. for an eight-hour fishing excursion. They also offer popular four-hour sunset cruises on Wednesdays and Sundays at 6:30 p.m. with spectacular views of the Hudson.

At some point during your stay in City Island, you may be tempted to search for some good ice cream. If you're looking for a small-town ice cream parlor, reminiscent of the New England variety, one which offers a good selection of flavors as well as frozen yogurt *and* outdoor seating, head to **Lickety Split Ice**

Cream *(295 City Island Avenue; 718-885-9195)*. Next to Lickety Split is a park where kids can crawl on the statues of maritime life—as you top off your City Island escape by relaxing and looking out onto the island's lively main street.

Places to eat:

The Black Whale *(279 City Island Avenue; 718-885-3657; www.dineatblackwhale.com)* This restaurant was recommended to me by a City Island native, who quickly regretted sharing her favorite restaurant for fear that it would get too busy and become difficult for her to get a table. Lucky for you, the secret is out. The Black Whale is a refreshing find in an island filled with big seafood joints. The menu, a combination of sophisticated entrees from both land and sea, has an epicurean touch in its salmon with pesto and meatloaf with a red wine mushroom sauce. Save room for dessert, since they offer such goodies as hot fudge fondue for two. If it's warm outside, be sure to get a table in their garden. The Black Whale also has a fantastic Sunday brunch buffet.

Lobster Box *(34 City Island Avenue; 718-885-1952; www.lobsterboxrestaurant.com)* This classic City Island seafood restaurant has great views of the water from inside their homey establishment. The menu includes seafood as well as a nice selection of pastas and some Italian specialties like chicken or veal parmigiana and penne alla vodka. They have lobster, of course, so be prepared to wear a bib to devour a tasty crustacean. And if you are looking for a night out, the Lobster Box also has an extensive bar menu.

JP's *(703 Minneford Avenue; 718-885-3364)* Ask for a seat outside at JP's, where you can dine at their waterside tables and watch the fishing boats pass. JP's is not the kind of restaurant that kids around with their portions. Dine upon extremely generous portions of yummy seafood classics like lobster or baked clams. If you aren't a fan of fish, they have a large selection of Italian specialties to sate you, and they offer a children's menu, if you've brought your kids along.

Johnny's Famous Reef Restaurant *(2 City Island Avenue; 718-885-2086)* Located at the end of City Island Avenue on the water, this restaurant seems a throwback to a bygone era. Food is served fast-food style, where you order fried lobster tails or frogs' legs at the counter and then dine on large picnic tables on the deck by the water. The view is great and there is something timeless about this experience. It's definitely a great way to end a fun day on the island.

Sammy's Fish Box *(41 City Island Avenue; 718-885-0920; www.sammysfish-box.com)* The menu here is filled with tons of great seafood to share, like Sammy's feasts for two, which include an array of cold seafood such as legs of fresh snow crabs, and Sammy's ultimate seafood feast, featuring lobster, jumbo shrimp, and much more. With a jovial atmosphere and a good drinks menu, locals love this place, so it's no wonder why it's always filled.

Tony's Pier Restaurant *(1 City Island Avenue; 718-885-1424)* This seafood mecca is located directly across the street from Johnny's Famous Reef Restaurant, and I can only assume that there must be some fierce competition going on between the restaurants, which keeps the quality of food at both at high standards. The day I went they were packed equally full with diners. Tony's serves its delicious seafood cafeteria-style and has amazing views from its outdoor dining area.

Places to stay:

Le Refuge Inn *(586 City Island Avenue; 718-885-2478; www.lerefugeinn.com)* Who knew that a B and B could exist in the Bronx? New Yorkers in the know head to this gorgeous six-room French inn housed in a beautiful historic home in the heart of City Island. Le Refuge Inn is owned by Pierre Saint-Denis of the classic Upper East Side restaurant Le Refuge—one of Jackie O's favorite spots. The inn's history and décor are intoxicatingly beautiful and the staff is extremely friendly. The inn is located in the historic Samuel Pell house, which dates back to 1876.

The ambiance and the cuisine make Le Refuge Inn a special escape for New Yorkers, just as its name implies. It's the perfect spot to celebrate an anniversary or to simply get away; the peaceful atmosphere of the Inn will certainly help you recharge, and it's suitable for any season—sit by their fireplace in the parlor during winter months or walk to the water in the summer.

The Inn's prices are consistent throughout the year: a single bedroom is $125, and a double is $145, which includes a continental breakfast of fresh coffee and pastries. If you'd like to book a dinner reservation, they will reserve a table during your stay. They offer an incredible prix fixe dinner for $50, and a lunch option for $45, both of which include French culinary delights that will impress any foodie.

part two

weekends
away

Chapter Nine

A New England Escape:

Mystic, Connecticut, and Westerly, Rhode Island

Travel time from NYC: 2 1/2 hours

Driving directions: I-95 North to Exit 90

Public transportation: Amtrak (800-USA-RAIL; www.amtrak.com) to Mystic.

Spend your morning climbing aboard a historic wooden whaling ship from the 1800s, your afternoon walking into the first nuclear-powered submarine, and your evening strolling through the charming town of Mystic. In the summer, you will have your pick of area beaches and great hiking. In the fall, visit a working cider mill and picnic on the lush grounds of a local vineyard. Mystic is an ideal escape for all New Yorkers—from couples in need of a weekend at a bed and breakfast to families off to the aquarium, there are many ways to plan a Mystic weekend. You can take a short ride over to the Rhode Island shore and spend the day at the beach in Watch Hill or you can go antiquing in Connecticut's picturesque Stonington Borough. Try your luck at the local casinos or indulge in a weekend at the spa: Mystic has it all.

Places to see:

If you want to take in all the sites of Mystic, you should think about purchasing the **Mystic Pass Card** (www.mystic.org), which includes both admission and free fountain drinks at the aquarium and the seaport, as well as major discounts at popular area hotels and restaurants.

    If you start your day at the **Mystic Aquarium and Institute for Exploration** (55 Coogan Boulevard; 860-572-5955; www.ife.org), don't feel rushed to get through the aquarium since you can have your ticket validated when you leave and use it for two more days. If you don't have time to go back, you should try to schedule your day around the sea lion show at the Marine Theater. A large portion of the aquarium is set indoors, so it's a great option for a year-round visit. Kids will love the Touch Pools, where they can get up-close-and-personal with starfish, crabs, and stingrays. If you want to get even closer to marine life, sign up for the Encounter Program, where you can have a one-on-one encounter with a beluga whale or a penguin. If petting a beluga whale doesn't satisfy your appetite for adventure, in the summer they also offer an outdoor climbing wall, which appeals to both older kids and smaller adults (there is a 150-pound weight limit).

Maybe watching all of the fish makes you long for the sea—if so head over to **Mystic Seaport: The Museum of America and the Sea** *(75 Greenmanville Avenue; 860-572-5315; www.mysticseaport.org)*, just a short drive or walk from the aquarium. At the seaport you can explore a re-creation of a 19th-century village, where you can visit everything from a one-room schoolhouse to a general store. As a fan of *Moby Dick*, I enjoyed exploring a wooden whaling ship called the *Charles W. Morgan*. (This ship will undergo restoration in the fall of 2008, so call the museum before you visit to find out if it's available for touring).

You can also get out to sea on a boat ride along the port, which is included in the seaport admission. Honestly, the ten-minute ride just takes you from one side of the port to the other. If the short boat trip whets your appetite for a longer excursion, you can purchase tickets for a trip on the steamboat *Sabino*, which also leaves from the port. Or if you'd like to sail your own boat, you can rent a sailing boat from the boathouse. You can also combine the visit to the port with a trip into the town of Mystic. The seaport's water taxi will take you into downtown Mystic.

If you have kids with you, head over to the Children's Museum at the seaport. This museum has many activities set up where kids can play on wooden ships and pretend they are cooking for a crew in the play kitchen. This is a place that can keep younger ones occupied for hours and is a good place to escape the heat. I was able to just relax as my kids played; a much-needed break for me. They also have a nautical-themed playground and a building called the Art Spot, where kids can sketch water views and create other educational art projects.

For those who want to have a more casual day, you can spend the day soaking in the scenes of the seaport or having a meal at one of Mystic's restaurants. Explore the interesting sights at the port, like the Henry B. du Pont Preservation Shipyard, where you can see wooden boats being built and restored.

When I was at the seaport, they had a wooden submarine called the *Turtle* on display. The *Turtle* was the first combat submarine, built in the 1770s. Viewing it inspired me to visit a nuclear-powered submarine from the 20th century, docked a few miles from Mystic in Groton at the **U.S. Navy Submarine Force Museum** *(860-694-3174; www.ussnautilus.org)*. Touring the submarine made me realize that you cannot complain about the close quarters in your apartment until you've spent some time touring the bedroom space on a submarine. The museum features the history of submarines, which is quite fascinating. Both the museum and submarine are free to the public.

Take a break from museum hopping and head to the charming town of Mystic. The town has many interesting shops and restaurants like the renowned **Mystic Pizza** *(56 West Main Street; 860-536-3700)*, which made Mystic famous when Julia Roberts starred in the aptly named 1988 film, *Mystic Pizza*, about the pizza parlor. Personally I love taking a stroll through the town, checking out the various stores, and then getting Oreo ice cream by the drawbridge at the appropriately named **Mystic Drawbridge Ice Cream** *(2 West Main Street; 860-572-7978)* and admiring the view of the water. Afterward I usually look through the books at **Bank Square Books** *(53 West Main Street; 860-536-3795; www.banksquarebooks.com)*, which is a great independent bookstore. For some reason, my extremely urban husband always finds himself drawn to Mystic's **Army Navy Store** *(37-39 West Main Street; 888-536-1877; www.mysticarmy-navy.com)*, down the block from the bookstore. This large shop is jammed packed with everything from tents to fatigues and isn't the type of shop you'd find in the city.

Another fun place to shop is **Olde Mistick Village** *(Coogan Boulevard; 860-536-4941; www.oldemystickvillage.com)*, located across from the aquarium. This outdoor shopping area, designed like an 18th-century village, is a nice place to find unique gifts and trinkets at shops like **Mystic Magic**, a magic shop, or nice children's clothes at **Teddy Bearskins**. They also have restaurants in the village, like **Ten Clams**, where everything on the menu is $10 or less.

For those who like antiquing or who enjoy a visit to a quaint town, just a short drive from Mystic is the picturesque town of Stonington Borough. Browse through the local antique stores, enjoy some seafood at **Noah's** *(113 Water Street; 860-535-3925; www.noahsfinefood.com)*, or dine from the eclectic menu at the **Water Street Café** *(143 Water Street; 860-535-2122)*. Before you head back to Mystic, you must take a walk over to the dock and pick up a dozen frozen scallops at **Stonington Seafood Harvesters** *(4 High Street; 860-535-8342)*. Here, you can help yourself to scallops from a large freezer and just leave the money on the counter. I believe it might one of the few places in America where they still operate on the honor system.

If you want to spend a day at the beach, a short drive from Mystic is **Ocean Beach Park** *(98 Neptune Avenue; 860-447-3031; www.ocean-beach-park.com)* in New London. This beach offers changing facilities, a snack bar, a retro game room with personal favorites like skee ball and old school arcade games like Pacman, an immaculate pool with a water play area, miniature golf, as well as a playground. It's a great beach to bring kids along to since it's not too large and there are a ton of kid-friendly amenities. You can park in the lot and cram your car full of people since parking is a flat-rate fee, which also includes admission to the beach. If you take a bus over, they have a pedestrian entrance as well.

Beach lovers can also spend the day in neighboring Rhode Island, where they can relax in classic New England style in the affluent **Watch Hill** *(www.visitwatchhill.com)* neighborhood, just a short ride from Mystic. If you plan on going to the beach at Watch Hill, make sure to get there early since parking is hard to find in the summer months. There is a small charge for entrance to the beach and umbrellas and chairs are available for rental. Right by the beach is the historic **Flying Horse Carousel**. After a ride on the carousel, grab a scoop of unbelievably tasty homemade ice cream at the **St. Clair Annex** *(141 Bay Street; 401-348-8407)*. If you need a refresher at the beach, head to Bay Street and grab a Del's frozen lemonade, which once rivaled coffee milk for Rhode Island's state drink.

Looking for real food? Grab lunch or dinner at the funky **Olympia Tea Room** *(74 Bay Street; 401-348-8211; www.olympiatearoom.com)*—a Watch Hill institution. If you'd like to spend the night, you can book a room with a beautiful view of the water at the **Watch Hill Inn** *(44 Bay Street; 401-348-6300; www.watchhillinn.com)*.

Sunbathing on the beach isn't the only way to enjoy the outdoors. Hikers will love exploring the trails around Mystic. However, a word of caution, there are many cases of Lyme disease in this area, so please take precautions. Wear long pants and tuck your them into your socks when you hike. Use bug spray and check for ticks after your hike.

One popular place to hike is **Napatree Point Conservation Area** *(Westerly, RI; 800-732-7636)*. It has a mile-long walk along the shore and is a great place for bird watching. Or spend the day on the Long Island Sound at **Bluff Point State Park** *(Groton, CT; 860-441-6600)*, where you can hike and bike on the trails. You can also observe wildlife in their natural habitat at this spot. If you really want to see the wildlife, head over to **Barn Island Wildlife Management Area** in Stonington, Connecticut. This coastal area covers over 1,013 acres and offers hikers many trails as well as a boat launch.

There is deer hunting on the premises, so be alert when hiking during hunting season.

If you come in the fall, make sure to take a trip to the **B.F. Clyde's Cider Mill** *(129 North Stonington Road, North Stonington, CT; 860-536-3354; www.bfclydescidermill.com)*, an operational steam-powered cider mill, where you can grab a cup of cider and an apple doughnut. Kids will get a kick out of seeing apples being pressed into cider. It's the perfect way to spend a fall day in New England. The cider mill is open seasonally. Call or visit the Web site for a schedule.

A great place to picnic is the **Jonathan Edwards Winery** *(74 Chester Maine Road, North Stonington, CT; 860-535-0202; www.jedwardswinery.com)*, located right near the Foxwoods Resort Casino. The winery has a deck that overlooks the gorgeous grounds. Share a bottle of wine and enjoy the view.

Places to eat:

Azu *(32 West Main Street; 860-536-6336; www.bravobravoct.com)* If you want the big city dining experience in a small New England town, this is place to dine in Mystic. Azu has a large selection of grilled pizza pies. My husband ordered the "pizza salad" pie and there was an actual salad atop his pizza. It was quite tasty. They also have a good selection of traditional salads, exceptional tapas—I recommend the fish tacos—and scrumptious entrees like the fish stew. Azu is quite small, so you should make reservations. I was there on a Thursday night and by 7 p.m. the place was filled. Azu's festive atmosphere can get quite loud and despite the volume it doesn't appear to be kid-friendly. New Yorkers may not feel the sticker shock, but Azu is a bit on the pricey side for the area. The owner of Azu also owns the popular Bravo Bravo in the Whaler's Inn, which isn't vegetarian-friendly, but gets rave reviews from the locals.

Kitchen Little (*135 Greenmanville Avenue; 860-536-2122)* Located on the tourist strip, right near the Mystic Seaport, this gem is a local favorite. If you think New York City is the only place to get a good brunch then you are mistaken. This little restaurant has some of the best breakfast food around. Word of advice—it's also quite small so you must get there early to avoid lines. If there is a line, you should wait; lunch offers the most amazing clam chowder.

Mystic Pizza *(56 West Main Street; 860-536-3700; www.mysticpizza.com)*

Okay, I'll admit that I always grab a meal here when I'm in town or even when I'm en route to other places on I-95—maybe it's my teenage memories of watching a young Julia Roberts busing tables in the movie *Mystic Pizza*. I live in Brooklyn, so by default I'm a pizza expert, and I find their pizza to be quite tasty. Enjoy a pie or some pasta while reading the story on their menu about making the movie. There are also pictures from the film on their walls. Aside from the kitsch factor, the food is genuinely good and the atmosphere is fun.

Sea Swirl (*30 Williams Avenue; 860-536-3452; www.seaswirlofmystic.com*) I was happy to see Rachael Ray eating at Sea Swirl on the Food Network, so this roadside seafood restaurant will finally get the attention it deserves. Sea Swirl serves up all of your New England favorites like baked clams and fish and chips. Sit and watch the trains pass outside on one of their many picnic benches. If you're on a diet, put it on hold for this experience; I promise that you won't regret it.

Tim Horton's (*24 East Main Street; 860-536-6633*) I was both shocked and thrilled to find my favorite Canadian doughnut chain open in Mystic and immediately went in to purchase some doughnuts and "timbits," Tim Horton's version of munchkins. These doughnuts are soft and not too heavy, which makes me yearn for the day when they come to NYC. The coffee is also excellent.

Places to stay:

If you get the Mystic Pass, you'll get discounts at area hotels. There are a bunch of chain hotels within a few miles, which are similar but vary in amenities. When I book a room at a chain hotel, I always like to find out if they have an indoor pool since the pool is one aspect of city life that I don't get to indulge in very often. On my two visits in the area, I stayed at the **Gold Star Inn** (*156 Kings Highway*) in Groton and at **The Inn at Norwich** (*607 West Thames Street; 800-ASK-4-SPA; www.thespaatnorwichinn.com*). Here are some of the popular inns and bed and breakfasts in the area:

Another Second Penny Inn (*870 Pequot Trail; 860-535-1710; www.second-penny.com*) This historic B and B located in Stonington offers two rooms and a suite. Friends have mentioned that they serve up an exceptional breakfast. From November through April they offer hearth-cooking classes, where you can cook old-fashioned recipes over an open hearth. Call ahead for a list of weekends when the classes are offered.

Mermaid Inn *(2 Broadway Avenue; 877-myB-andB; www.mermaidinnofmystic.com)* People rave about this inn located in the heart of Mystic. The beautifully decorated rooms in this 19th-century Victorian home have private baths. In the mornings, you are treated to a wonderful breakfast and afternoon refreshments. They offer special packages, so check their Web site for more information.

Whaler's Inn *(20 East Main Street; 800-243-2588; www.whalersinnmystic.com)* If you want a little more luxury than a chain motel but have the kids in tow, this is the place to stay. Located in the heart of the downtown district and very close to the Mystic Depot train station, the Whaler's Inn offers rooms and suites with private baths. The Whaler's Inn offers discounts to those who purchased the Mystic pass.

Side trips:

A weekend at The Spa at Norwich Inn

Travel time from NYC: 2 1/2 hours
Driving directions: I-95 North to Exit 79A and follow onto CT-2A East. Take Exit 2 and follow signs to the Spa at Norwich.

Spend a weekend relaxing at this forty-nine-room charming inn where you can easily spend the entire weekend in a robe, decompressing from your hectic urban experience. Since the inn is from the 1920s, all the rooms differ in size and have an old-world charm. For instance, our standard room had eight windows and although it overlooked the restaurant's balcony, it was very quiet. I highly recommend booking this room (number 25) for the view alone. They also offer various suites ranging from apartment-style suites with kitchens and living rooms to options with terraces.

Upon entering your room at the inn, you should slip into a robe and head over to the spa for treatments. Make sure to book these before you arrive because they tend to fill up fast. Each morning while I was there they offered blackboard specials. The specials included deep discounts on treatments that were still available, which you could then add on to your list of services. By missing my chance to add a facial on to my treatment, I found out that these discounts go quickly. The spa menu is enormous—offering everything from traditional deep tissue massages to body wraps. My phytotherapy massage was wonderful and they used an oil to help clear up my chronically stuffed NYC sinuses.

The spa is immaculate and I liked that they had individual changing rooms in the locker room in addition to the changing area attached to the private showers. They also offer a robe and slippers. The spa is filled with high-quality products so you don't have to bring anything but yourself and your bathing suit. The spa amenities include an indoor pool, Jacuzzi, steam room, and sauna. Don't worry about carrying a wet bathing suit back with you, because they have a nifty little dryer for bathing suits in the locker rooms.

If you have a spouse that likes to golf, book a tee time with the front desk as the inn owns a golf course just a few minutes away. The spa also offers racket rentals if you would like to use their tennis courts. However, I opted to sit and read on the lounge chairs on the lawn by the reflecting pool and to dine on the outdoor deck of Kensington's, their popular restaurant. I learned a lot about food and its fat content as I perused their menu, which posts the fat and calorie content of each dish on the menu. This practice really helps you make wise choices, but even if you order a light entree, as I did, you won't be disappointed—the chef doesn't sacrifice taste for calories. The friendly executive chef Daniel Chong-Jimenez at Kensington's is happy to work with you if you have special dietary needs or want to keep kosher, but be sure to give advance notice.

The reason I enjoyed my stay so much is because unlike other spas, the rooms aren't based on double occupancy and you can pick and choose what you want to do. However, the only thing included in your rate is your room. You must pay for all meals, treatments, fitness classes, and guided hikes. A visit to this spa is for pure relaxation. If you want to indulge in nightlife other than the live music at Ascot's—the pub at the inn— they offer free shuttles to Foxwoods Resort Casino or you can drive five minutes down the road to the Mohegan Sun Casino.

All types of people co-exist at the spa at Norwich: Older couples, young couples, girlfriends on a getaway (who were quite loud at breakfast), as well as mothers and their daughters, who were all there to enjoy the weekend. The spa even offers elopement packages for those who want to run away and tie the knot. My weekend ended on a funny note when an older woman who was getting ready to leave the spa came out of the dressing room in her regular outfit, looked at me and said sadly, "Oy. I haven't worn clothes all weekend."

You're in the Money:
Weekends at the MGM Grand at Foxwoods and Mohegan Sun

The MGM Grand at Foxwoods

Travel time from NYC: 2 1/2 hours

Driving directions: I-95 North to Exit 92. Turn left onto Route 2 West. Foxwoods is eight miles west on Route 2.

You don't have to go to Vegas to enjoy a luxury boutique hotel casino anymore. The MGM Grand, which opened in May 2008, offers high-end restaurants, nightclubs, and an outpost of the popular G spa and casino. Get ready to have a soundtrack to your weekend getaway since everywhere you go you will hear music—even under the water in their outdoor pool. The energy at the Grand is intoxicating and although it's located in the middle of Connecticut, it has a very chic appeal.

When you make your reservation, make sure ask for an even number room so you can have one of the most stunning hotel views I've ever seen, overlooking the lush Cedar Swamp. To me, the cozy standard rooms have a very masculine appeal with green painted walls and a rain forest showerhead in the shower (note that they don't have bathtubs). They have all the amenities of a Manhattan boutique hotel like iPod docking stations and flat screen TVs. Although you won't get a complimentary breakfast, New Yorkers will feel at home chowing down at their enormous and clean Junior's Restaurant—straight out of Brooklyn! They have a nice outdoor deck where you can feast on their famous cheesecakes.

If you want to feel like a celebrity, you can book your own private table at their popular nightclub, Shrine. Even if you are a guest at the MGM Grand, you must pay a cover charge for the club. It is located across from the casino floor. The MGM Grand also houses many excellent restaurants like Alta Strada where you can have your pick of delicious antipastas while you sip some wine or you can enjoy some steak at chef Tom Colicchio's Craft Steak. Or, if you're in the mood for dessert, go to the Gelato Café and choose from twenty-four flavors of gelato.

The air in the casino is scented and they have a great air filtration system. I didn't feel like I needed to go outside for air from all the smoke, which often happens when I'm in a casino. If you want to play at a poker table, you'll have to walk over to the Foxwoods Resort Casino (there is an indoor bridge connecting all the casinos at Foxwoods as well as a shuttle) since there isn't a poker table at the MGM Grand. The MGM Grand does offer flat-screen TVs at some tables, so you can watch sports while you play blackjack and other table games.

After winning big, indulge yourself at the G Spa at the hotel. The spa houses an indoor pool and Jacuzzi where you won't get splashed by kids since the indoor pool is for folks ages twenty-one and up. There is an enormous outdoor pool that is kid-friendly, although the MGM isn't the best place to bring the family. It's really geared toward the twenty- and thirty-something crowd and with a MacAppeal store selling a variety of Apple products adjacent to the casino floor, they know their audience well.

The MGM is perfect for a bachelor or bachelor-ette party with the indulgent spa and the lively nightlife. Golfers will also like the fact that there are two golf courses available for guests. Music lovers and fans of comedians should check out the schedule of concerts and shows at their arena; they attract a ton of great acts and major headliners.

If you want to add an educational component to your weekend aside from counting your money, you should spend some time at the **Mashantucket Pequot Museum at Foxwoods** *(110 Peqout Trail; 800-411-9671; www.pequotmuseum.org)*. There is a shuttle bus from the casino that will drop you in front of the museum. The museum offers a glimpse into the lives of the Native American tribes of the region—with exhibits on the environment and a replica of a 16th-century Pequot village.

Mohegan Sun
Travel time from NYC: 2 1/2 hours
Driving directions: I-95 North to Exit 79A and follow onto CT-2A East. Take Exit 2 and follow signs to Mohegan Sun.

Spend a weekend high-rolling at this Native American–themed casino. When I arrived they gave me a booklet called *The Secret Guide* to finding Native American symbols throughout the casinos, but it's hard not to miss the artwork and the tribute to the culture.

There are three casinos at Mohegan Sun. When I was there they were in the process of finishing up the new Casino of the Wind, which is set to house Jimmy Buffet's Margaritaville and a forty-two-table poker room. The casinos that I enjoyed were filled with slots, tables, and great venues to see shows. You should really see a show at their 10,000-seat arena if you can—there isn't a bad seat in the house. The arena often hosts famous bands and this is a good place to see them since you'll get a great view of the stage. For an even more intimate experience with table seating, you can see visit the 350-seat cabaret theater to see live music or comedians. I also enjoyed a free show at the Wolf's Den, which has performances from groups like Soul Asylum and Jack Wagner.

The standard rooms at Mohegan Sun are spacious and when booking yours, ask for one with a view of the Thames River. I love the fact that when you check into your room you don't have to walk on a casino floor since the entrance to the hotel is separate from the entrance to the casino. You also can reach the Elemis Spa and the hotel's indoor pool without entering the casino, so those who stay to see a show won't feel overwhelmed by the casino's atmosphere.

The Casino of the Sky is set under a planetarium and features a bar where you can sit and stargaze as you watch the constellations pass overhead. I was also quite taken by the original of the three casinos, the Casino of the Earth. In the native language of the tribe, Mohegan means wolf, so this casino is fittingly decorated with animated wolves that howl when you win a progressive five-cent slot. I blew twenty dollars in hopes of winning the nickel slot jackpot and seeing the wolves perform. After the money ran out and I didn't win the jackpot, I quickly gave up.

If you want authentic Asian food, you must grab a meal at the Sunrise Square food court in the Casino of the Earth. In this area of the casino, they feature Asian-style games like baccarat in front of the Sunrise Square.

Mohegan Sun offers tons of shopping including a Tiffany's as well as many places to eat such as Todd English's Tuscany or Michael Jordan's Steak House. They also have a stunning seven-story waterfall, which peacefully washes out the casino noise while you are shopping.

Fun Stops along I-95

Whether you're stuck in traffic or looking for a good day trip, there are tons of exciting sights that are only minutes off the I-95. With good eats easily accessible off of the highway, you don't have to pull into a rest stop filled with fast food while you're on the road.

Exit 14:
South Norwalk

South Norwalk, which has come to be known as SoNo, is a funky town filled with boutiques and good restaurants. Besides stopping to take a break for some libations or funky threads, you can see the river otters at the **Maritime Aquarium** *(10 North Water Street, Norwalk, CT; 203-852-0700; www.maritimeaquarium.org).*

Exit 26:
Captain's Cove Seaport
(1 Bostwick Avenue, Bridgeport, CT;
203-335-1433; www.captainscoveseaport.com)
Stroll along the boardwalk or grab some yummy fish and chips at this seaport. If you want to shop, they have a stretch of stores housed in small Victorian and colonial-style buildings. The seaport hosts various events and live music. Stop by for a meal or to get one last glimpse of harbor life before you head to the Big Apple.

Exit 47:
New Haven
You can take a break and museum-hop around New Haven. Yale University has two museums open to the public; they are located across the street from each another and are free to the public. **Yale University Art Gallery** *(1111 Chapel Street; 203-432-0600; www.artgallery.yale.edu)* has an impressive art collection, including works by Picasso and Van Gogh. **Yale Center for British Art** *(1080 Chapel Street; 203-432-2800; www.ycba.yale.edu)* houses the largest collection of British art outside of the United Kingdom. The building itself is a work of art designed by architect Louis Kahn.

You can also visit the **Peabody Museum of Natural History at Yale University** *(170 Whitney Avenue; 203-432-5050; www.peabody.yale.edu)* to see exhibits on Native American and Pacific cultures, mammal evolution, dinosaurs, and more. This is a great stop if you have kids in tow. For those who want to grab a bite some other place than an I-95 rest stop, New Haven's Wooster Street is home to two great pizza places: **Pepe's** *(157 Wooster Street; 203-865-5762; www.pepespizzeria.com)* and **Sally's Apizza** *(237 Wooster Street; 203-624-5271; www.sallysapizza.net).*

Exit 56:
Thimble Island Boat Tours
Want a change of scenery? Sick of sitting in a car? How about hopping aboard a narrated tour of the Thimble Islands? Although you won't be

able to get out and explore these privately-owned, scenic islands, you do get to spend forty-five minutes on the water surrounding them. Your guide will tell you great stories about residents like Gary Trudeau and how at one time Captain Kidd lived on one of the islands and buried his treasure there. You can hop aboard one of the boat tours, which run throughout the weekend from spring through the fall, on either the **Sea Mist** *(203-488-8905; www.thimbleislandcruise.com)* or the **Volsunga IV** *(203-481-3345; www.thimbleislands.com)*.

Exits 62 and 64:
Lenny and Joe's Fish Tale
If you are even remotely close to these exits and like seafood, you must make a stop. I will admit that **Lenny and Joe's Fish Tale** *(Westbrook, CT; 860-669-0767 and Madison, CT; 203-245-7289; www.ljfishtale.com)* is my favorite seafood restaurant, so I had to include both locations. Their menu is filled with classics like fried clams and fish and chips, among other favorites. They do a great job with every fish on the menu—from broiled tilapia to salmon. Lenny and Joe's Fish Tale also sells their own durable T-shirts for only $6. The designs change yearly and come in a range of sizes, from toddler to adult. The two locations, a drive-in restaurant with a carousel in Madison and a family-style restaurant in Westbrook, are open year-round. Both are located along Route 1. It's best to visit in the Madison location in the summer when you can take a ride on the historic carousel and indulge in ice cream from a stand. There is a ton of outdoor seating with options underneath a sun covering, so you don't have to bake while you eat.

Exit 69:
Essex County Steam Train and Riverboat
Take a tour through the stunning countryside and then hop a riverboat at **Essex County Steam Train and Riverboat** *(1 Railroad Avenue, Essex, CT; 860-767-0103; www.essexsteamtrain.com)*. They also host special events like a day with Thomas the Tank Engine or a nighttime journey on the North Pole Express. If you don't want to ride the riverboat, you also have the option of riding the train.

Exit 72:

The Book Barn

If you love books, then you must head to the **Book Barn** (*41 West Main Street, Niantic, CT; 860-739-5715; www.bookbarnniantic.com*), right off the interstate in Niantic. This used bookstore is housed in six separate buildings. The buildings have names like Ellis Island, for all the used books that have just come in, or the Haunted House, for its collection of mystery books. If you have books you'd like to sell, they buy them at the Immigration Table. This quirky bookstore, which has a chalk outline of a body in their True Crime area, cats sunning themselves around the shop's shelves, a petting zoo, and a play area for kids, is a great place to browse and pick up moderately priced books. The have a wonderful children's section and offer patrons free coffee, water, Oreos, and mini doughnuts. This gives Book Barn an extremely inviting atmosphere. If you can imagine Manhattan's Strand bookstore relocated to an old farm, you have the wonderful Book Barn.

Chapter Ten

A Night at the Rodeo:

Pilesgrove, New Jersey, and the Brandywine Valley, Pennsylvania and Delaware

Travel time from NYC: 2 hours

**Driving directions: I-95 South to the New Jersey Turnpike.
Take Exit 1 on the New Jersey Turnpike.
Rodeo is located on Route 40, eight miles east of the Delaware Memorial Bridge.
You can reach the Brandywine Valley from the Wilmington exits on I-95.**

Public transportation: Amtrak (800-USA-RAIL; www.amtrak.com) to Wilmington.

You don't have to hop on a plane to go out west to see an authentic rodeo. In fact New Jersey is home to America's longest continuously running rodeo. Every Saturday night from Memorial Day until the last week of September, you can see cowboys and cowgirls attempt to break bull-riding and barrel-racing records in Woodstown, New Jersey.

The rodeo is only minutes from Wilmington, Delaware, and the scenic Brandywine Valley. Year-round in the Brandywine Valley, you can explore gorgeous gardens, old mansions, and museums displaying a time when the du Ponts changed America's landscape with their successful and potent black gunpowder. Spend a weekend immersed in Americana, where you can travel from the Old West to the home of the Industrial Revolution in just a short drive.

Places to see:

Driving down Route 40 in New Jersey, I saw a large statue with a cowboy hat in the distance and within seconds I had been removed from New Jersey and transported to the Old West at the **Cowtown Rodeo** (780 Route 40; Pilesgrove, NJ; 856-769-3200; www.cowtownrodeo.com). We arrived at the rodeo early Saturday morning to check out the flea market advertised on their Web site. The flea market is open on Tuesdays and Saturdays and is quite separate from the rodeo with vendors selling soy candles, socks, DVDs, and Avon products. There is one Western booth, which had inexpensive cowboy hats (I bought one for the rodeo). The flea market has some food vendors and a truck that sells authentic Mexican food. The market is housed across the street from the rodeo grounds in and around an old barn.

If you're looking for rodeo tickets, note that they don't go on sale until 6 p.m. that day. So if you want to pass up the flea market, you can buy tickets at the rodeo right when the rodeo doors open. You can also purchase tickets across the street from the rodeo at **Cowtown Cowboy Outfitters** *(761 Route 40, Woodstown, NJ; 888-761-4246; www.cowtowncowboy.com)*, where you can also get all the gear necessary to become a proper cowboy. Selling everything from hats to cowboy boots, they have a great kids' section, with Western-themed lunch boxes and toys.

If you need to use the restroom, use the facilities of the Outfitters since there are only portable toilets available at the rodeo. If you'd like to meet the owner of the Cowtown Cowboy Outfitters, he also runs the roasted peanut stand at the rodeo, as advertised on the wall of his shop. I couldn't resist and ended up buying some peanuts. After the rodeo, if you're inspired to buy more rodeo-related merchandise, the shop stays open for a few hours after the rodeo. They also have an outpost of the shop at the rodeo—a small booth where they have a large collection of rodeo T-shirts and other goodies for sale.

If you want good seats, get to the rodeo right when the gates open at 6 p.m. Food is available at the rodeo, but there are long lines and mainly meat-only options. The lack of veggie options might pose a problem for vegetarians (although I'm not sure how many vegetarians go to the rodeo). You can bring a cooler into the rodeo as long as it is no bigger than a milk crate, but snacks also abound like peanuts, chips, ice cream, and funnel cakes.

You might want to bring a cushion for the seat as there are only bleacher seats available and the rodeo lasts until around 10:30 p.m. I was pained by the end of the rodeo from simply sitting on the seats, not riding a bull. They also allow lawn chairs, which you can bring from home and set up. However, the rule of the rodeo is that the higher the seats on the bleachers, the better the view, so if you bring lawn chairs you will be compromising your view as you have to set them up on the ground level.

Even though you are not even two hours from New York City, the hosts of the rodeo have a twang to their accents and the house band is a country-western band. The rodeo is taken very seriously here and you can see young cowboys try their hand at various skills like bareback riding and team roping. If you're an animal lover, you might be pained by the tie-down roping event, where the cowboys are timed lassoing a calf, getting it to lie down, and tying its feet. After each event, however, the cowboys seemed a lot more hurt by the activities than the animals, who appeared to be in extremely good shape. Later on in the schedule, the cowgirls raced horses around barrels as the crowd cheered them on.

As I sat on the bleachers in the warm night, I couldn't believe that earlier that day I had been on line at my neighborhood bagel shop, overhearing a couple talk about heading to the Mermaid Parade; here I was feeling a thousand miles from Brooklyn. Watching small children dance around in cowboy hats and boots, I could have sworn I was in Montana. Then when after the event I drove just a few minutes to the parkway and onto the Delaware Memorial Bridge, the landscape changed again—especially once I booked myself into the Hotel Du Pont, a Manhattan-quality high-end hotel in Wilmington, Delaware, where a valet took my car. When I entered the posh lobby I was the only person wearing a cowboy hat.

To occupy yourself during the day before the rodeo or off-season, spend the afternoon exploring **Fort Mott State Park** (454 Fort Mott Road; Pennsville, NJ; 856-935-3218; www.state.nj.us), a ten-minute drive from the rodeo. At Fort Mott State Park you can get a ferry to Fort Delaware State Park, an island in between New Jersey and Delaware that houses an old fort that was once used as a Confederate prison during the Civil War. When you get off the half-hour-long ferry ride, take a guided tour of the fort or bird-watch in the bird sanctuary on the island. We aren't bird watchers, but I couldn't stop photographing all of the colorful birds that migrate to this area, which is known for the herons and egrets that frequent the island.

The ferry leaves every two hours from Fort Mott, starting at 10:30 a.m. The last ferry from Fort Delaware is at 2:30 p.m., which places you back at Fort Mott at 4:30 p.m. Fort Delaware is also accessible from Delaware City and the ferries leave hourly from the park in Delaware City. The ferry costs $11 for adults and $6 for children. Access to the island is seasonal, with ferries running weekends from late April until late September.

For year-round fun, spend the day relaxing in the lush Brandywine Valley in Delaware and Pennsylvania. We stayed in Wilmington and were able to access all of the locations in the Brandywine Valley quite easily. Start your day with the du Ponts, learning about where Delaware's history began at the **Hagley Museum** (Route 141, Wilmington, DE; 302-658-2400; www.hagley.lib.de.us). The museum was once the du Pont estate and mill where they produced black gunpowder, and now you can learn about the history of the du Pont family and their influence on Delaware and the Industrial Revolution.

You should allot about three hours to tour this museum and the extensive grounds. The museum has exhibits on the current innovations of the DuPont company while the rest of the grounds focus on the family's past. There is a bus that shuttles you from the museum to the estate and various other stops around the grounds like a working gunpowder mill where you can see an interesting and extremely educational demonstration of how gunpowder was made and how rivers were used to operate mills. You can also see a demonstration on how a steam engine works. If you have kids, you must stop by the museum's discovery room, where they can learn all about science from hands-on exhibits. Fans of home décor will enjoy a tour through the du Pont estate to see the collections of china and fine furnishings. I was particularly impressed with the dining room wallpaper, a mural from France, which depicts the life of early American settlers. Apparently the wallpaper company still exists and I was tempted to order it for my Brooklyn dining room.

The garage on the estate houses an extensive collection of both antique cars and Conestoga wagons. The grounds are lovely with a large lawn and many ripening fruit trees. It's a peaceful place to visit and also quite informative; I was quite impressed with the knowledgeable staff who ran all of the demonstrations and worked in the museum. I felt as if I learned an entire semester of American history in one three-hour visit.

After the museum, we relaxed as we strolled in **Longwood Gardens** *(1001 Longwood Road, Kennett Square, PA; 610-388-1000; www.longwoodgardens.org)* a thousand-acre garden in neighboring Pennsylvania. Longwood Gardens is so enormous, it makes the Brooklyn Botanical Garden seem like someone's backyard. Upon entering the visitor center you are greeted by an enormous garden shop with gardening tools, books, and trinkets that even an urban gardener would enjoy. Plan at least two or three hours to see the gardens although you can allot an entire day to view them properly. They host many events throughout the year including concerts, and they even offer a concert series for children. You can picnic at the gardens or you can grab a lunch at the café or the more formal Terrace Restaurant.

The gardens are simply beautiful and can be visited throughout the year since they have twenty indoor gardens in four acres of greenhouses. The gardens are filled with fountains, beautiful blooming flowers, and walks, making the Longwood Gardens a must-see on your trip through the valley. If you have the kids with you, don't miss their spectacular indoor children's garden.

Afterward we dined in the lovely historic town of **Kennett Square** *(www.historickennettsquare.com)*, located minutes from the gardens. Kennett Square is called "the mushroom capital of the world" since over fifty percent of the country's mushrooms come from this region and they host a popular mushroom festival every September. The town has many cute shops including a couple of bookshops, a great place to purchase wool called the **Wool Gathering** *(131 East State Street; 610-444-8236; www.woolgathering.com)* and my personal favorite, **The Mushroom Cap** *(114 West State Street; 610-444-8484; www.themushroomcap.com)*, which sells fresh mushrooms and many other gift items.

Take note that Kennett Square is very sleepy on Sundays, when most of the stores are either closed or are open until just 3 p.m. There are only a few restaurants open on Sundays. If you are looking on the weekend for organically prepared foods for a picnic at Longwood Gardens, stop by **Tulula's Table** *(102 West State Street; 610-444-8255; www.talulastable.com)*. Open seven days a week, Tulula's Table has all that one needs for a proper picnic. You can also dine on the large table that sits in the middle of the gourmet shop and restaurant.

Another Brandywine Valley favorite is the **Winterthur Museum, Gardens, and Library** *(Route 52, Wilmington, DE; 800-448-3883; www.winterthur.org)*. Once the country estate of Henry Francis du Pont, this is a beautiful place to tour and to check out their collection of Americana. Kids will love their Touch-It Room where they can learn about handicrafts. Kids will also love the Enchanted Woods, a children's garden on the grounds.

Another du Pont mansion that is not to be missed is the **Nemours Mansion and Gardens** *(Route 52, Wilmington, DE; 302-651-6912; www.nemours.org)*, which recently re-opened after extensive renovations. This grand mansion and its gardens are a great place to spend an afternoon.

Wine lovers will enjoy a trip tasting the wines of the region on the **Brandywine Wine Trail** *(Southern Chester County, PA; 610-444-8842; www.bvwinetrail.com)*. With many vineyards throughout the region, check the map of the wine trail on the Web site to see which ones fit into your getaway itinerary.

For a change of pace, in nearby West Chester, Pennsylvania, you can tour the **QVC Studio Park** *(1200 Wilson Drive; 800-600-9900; www.qvc.com)*. Fans of the popular home shopping channel can tour the studio seven days a week from 10 a.m. to 4 p.m., where you can get a glimpse into the world of television retail and get to view the 20,000-square-foot broadcast area, where you might be able to see live TV productions in action. Although I missed the QVC tours due to time constraints, I'm currently planning a trip back to the area to see these studios, as they were quite fascinating.

Places to eat:

Green Room at the Hotel du Pont *(11th and Market Streets, Wilmington, DE; 302-594-3154; www.hoteldupont.com)* I was overwhelmed by the ornate ceilings and wood trim. Make sure you pack some fancy clothes if you want to dine at this swank hotel restaurant. Sunday brunch is much more casual with relaxed attire and piano music. The buffet brunch has tables of food for guests, offering everything from chicken to scrumptious waffles.

Half Moon Restaurant *(108 West State Street, Kennett Square, PA; 610-444-7232; www.halfmoonrestaurant.com)* If you are looking for a fun Saturday night dinner and some good pub food then stop by the Half Moon Restaurant in Kennett Square. They serve both buffalo and bison, so meat lovers will be pleased. They are also open for lunch. They have live music, so check the Web site for a schedule. Half Moon has twenty-seven beers on tap and a large selection of Belgian beer. The one caveat is that they aren't open on Sundays.

Olympia Dairy and Drive-In *(40 State Street, Carney's Point, NJ; 856-299-5255)* Down the road from the rodeo sits an old-school ice-cream stand and drive-in restaurant. The drive-in doesn't offer car hop service, but has a small indoor seating area and some tables outside where you can enjoy some yummy hamburgers, hot dogs, and grilled cheese sandwiches. Don't forget to order fries and onion rings on the side and save room for the custard. Olympia is open from April through September. It's the perfect spot for a pre-rodeo meal. Chances are you'll see all the folks from the rodeo eating at the Olympia (we did).

Newton's on State Street *(114 East State Street, Kennett Square, PA; 610-925-5055; www.newtonsonstatestreet.com)* You can dine on pub fare at this restaurant on Kennett Square's main street, which is also open on Sundays. Kids under four eat for free at their Sunday brunch. The dinner menu has pub favorites like wings and nachos. The entree menu is rather eclectic for a pub, serving up everything from to crab cakes to Reubens.

Toscana Kitchen and Bar *(1412 North Du Pont Street, Wilmington, DE; 302-654-8001; www.toscanakitchen.com)* This Italian restaurant located in hip Trolley Square *(www.visittrolleysquare.com)* offers some nightlife in the town of Wilmington with live music and good food. The menu consists of Italian food—mostly pastas and some meat dishes. They are also open for lunch.

Places to stay:

Comfort Inn and Suites *(634 Soders Road, Carneys Point, NJ; 856-299-8282; www.comfortinn.com)* This chain hotel is located close to the rodeo and nearby Fort Mott State Park. It's a clean and economical place to stay during your weekend getaway. They offer a complimentary deluxe continental breakfast.

Hampton Inn *(429 North Broadway, Pennsville, NJ; 856-351-1700; www.hamptoninnpennsville.com)* Conveniently located off the parkway and only minutes from the rodeo, this hotel chain offers immaculate rooms and amenities like a buffet breakfast and in-room coffee. If you are a fan of fast food, you can get your fill at several popular fast food chains that surround the hotel.

Hotel du Pont *(11th and Market Street, Wilmington, DE; 800-441-9019; www.hoteldupont.com)* Spend your weekend feeling like a celebrity in one of this hotel's many deluxe rooms, which make up about 80 percent of this luxury hotel. Built in 1913, the hotel has an intoxicating old-world charm, from its gorgeous lobby to the stately dining room. Adorned with ornate chandeliers and wood-trimmed walls, this classic hotel will make you feel like you've stepped back in time.

The hotel offers great weekend rates and packages for exploring the Brandywine Valley, which is mere minutes from the hotel. If you want to indulge in luxury and not break the bank, book a room here. My deluxe king room must have been at least six hundred square feet with a bathroom that was larger than my old studio apartment. Fans of long baths will enjoy ordering from the bath menu, which includes a romantic bath with rose petals to a relaxing bath that comes with a cup of chamomile tea. Don't worry about packing too much; they have amenities like plush bathrobes and slippers in the rooms. You might want to include some gym clothes for their twenty-four hour gym, where complimentary juice, water, and fruit are always plentiful.

Local Events

MAY

Wilmington Flower Market
Wilmington, DE
302-995-5699
www.wilmingtonflowermar-
ket.org

JUNE

Clifford Brown Jazz Festival
Wilmington, DE
302-576-3095
www.cliffordbrownjazzfest.com

St. Anthony's Festival
Wilmington, DE
302-421-2790
www.stanthonynet.org/Festival

AUGUST

Riverfront Blues Festival
Wilmington, DE
302-576-2136
www.riverfrontbluesfest.com

Salem County Fair
Woodstown, NJ
856-769-0414
www.salemcountyfair.com

SEPTEMBER

Mushroom Festival
Kennett Square, PA
888-440-9920
www.mushroomfestival.org

Chapter Eleven

Wine Country:

The North Fork of Long Island

Travel time from NYC: 2–2 1/2 hours

Driving directions: Long Island Expressway to Exit 73.

Public transportation: Long Island Railroad (718-217-5477; www.lirr.org) or the Hampton Jitney (212-362-8400; www.hamptonjitney.com) to Greenport.

The North Fork is a treasure. If you want to escape from the stress of the city and are looking for peace and quiet just a few hours from your daily commute, you are certain to find it on the North Fork. Unlike the South Fork, the northern fork of Long Island isn't saturated with celebrities and status-seekers. Even in the heart of the summer you won't feel overwhelmed by the congestion of the beachgoers; in other words, it's tranquil. Although the wineries do tend to get crowded on weekends and the main road can get a bit backed up, the views from your car or bus window will be well worth it. If you don't want the added hassle of traffic on your way to and from the area, you can always hop aboard the Long Island Railroad, which runs through the North Fork regularly.

The North Fork can be visited in all seasons and though some places do close in the winter, most are open from the spring until the late fall. In autumn, roads are lined with farm stands selling fresh corn and other vegetables. Throughout the year in the North Fork, folks line up outside Breiermere Farms in Riverhead to purchase homemade fruit pies and other baked goods. The North Fork ends in Orient Point at the northern tip of Long Island, where you can spend the day relaxing or kayaking at Orient Park. Another ideal city escape is Greenport, a quaint New England–style whaling town filled with amazing restaurants, shopping, convenient ferry access to Shelter Island, and roads lined with vineyards and tasting rooms.

Places to see:

Orient Point, Greenport, and Southhold

A great way to explore the North Fork is on bike—the terrain is fairly flat, so it's not very challenging. You can rent a bike in the town of Greenport at **Bike Stop Rentals** (200 Front Street, Greenport; 631-477-2432; www.bike-stop.com). Bike Stop also rents baby seats, kid bikes, tandems, and accessories like bike helmets. They deliver and pick up bikes around the local area. In the warmer months they tend to get busy, so get to the shop early or call ahead to order your bike.

If you just want to relax on the waterfront, you can sit and enjoy the view from **Mitchell Park** (115 Front Street, Greenport; 631-477-2200; www.greenportvillage.com), a four-acre park lining Greenport's waterfront, designed by an architectural team in the 1990s. In the winter, you can ice skate at Mitchell Park and in the summer months the ice-skating rink becomes a mist walk to help visitors cool off from the heat. If you have the kids in tow or if you're a kid at heart, you must ride the vintage 1920s-era carousel in the Jess Owen Carousel House—open weekends year-round and every day in the summer. One of my favorite things to do in Mitchell Park is to head into the camera obscura. Walking into this freestanding structure is like walking inside of a giant camera—you can see a live image of the harbor and the park from outside the camera obscura projected onto a table inside the building. Once a popular novelty, sadly there are very few camera obscuras left in existence, so don't miss out on this unique opportunity.

If staring at the sea by Mitchell Park is enticing you to go water bound, walk along the water to the terminal for the **North Ferry** (Shelter Island Heights; 631-749-0139; www.northferry.com), where for $2 you can take the ferry to Shelter Island. The ride takes about ten minutes and ferries run every fifteen minutes. For an additional charge you can bring your car or bike on the ferry, which will only makes it easier to explore Shelter Island. A good place to grab lunch or have dinner and drinks is at **Chequit Inn** (23 Grand Avenue, Shelter Island Heights; 631-749-0018; www.shelterislandinns.com) just a few minutes from the ferry dock. If you don't want to spend an evening here, keep in mind that the last ferry to Greenport is at midnight—although it's so lovely on Shelter Island that you may want to stay the night.

If you'd rather earn your dinner, next to the ferry at the railroad dock is the **Peconic Star II**, on which you could spend your day fishing for fluke, porgies, or black fish depending on the time of year. Fishing boats run from May through early December. They also offer cruises and charters (Railroad Dock, Greenport; 631-289-6899; www.peconicstar.com).

For people like me who like to enjoy themselves on boats and let the captain do all the work, set sail on the historic schooner named the **Mary E**, a 75-foot authentic clipper from 1906. As Greenport's official tall ship (101-A East Broadway, Port Jefferson; 631-332-0699; www.schoonermarye.com), the schooner Mary E offers sailing trips throughout the day in season starting in mid-May.

The eco-minded should hop aboard the **Glory** (Prestons Dock, Greenport; 631-477-2515; www.greenportlaunch.com), an electric powered "environmentally friendly" vessel that offers four different bay tours focusing on everything from nature to local history. They also offer a sunset cruise that includes wine tastings from local vineyards. The Glory sails on weekends from Memorial Day until July 4th and then every day from July 4th until Labor Day. Both boats depart from Preston Dock next to Claudio's Restaurant, just a couple of steps from Mitchell Park.

If you want to take a ferry ride to New London, Connecticut, where you can spend the afternoon gambling at Foxwoods or walking around Mystic (see page 81), then hop aboard the **Cross Sound Ferry** (Orient Point; 631-323-2525; www.longislandferry.com) at Orient Point. The ferry trip takes one hour and twenty minutes and it departs hourly in the summer months, although it does run all year-round. Cars can also be brought on this ferry.

Train fans will be fascinated by the **Railroad Museum of Long Island** (440 Fourth Street, Greenport; 631-727-7920; www.rmli.org) located across the street from the North Ferry Terminal. There is also another location in Riverhead adjacent to the Long Island Railroad tracks (416 Griffing Avenue, Riverhead; 631-727-7920). The Greenport museum has two old trains out front—an old caboose and a snow-plow car with painted teeth named "Jaws III." Inside the former Long Island Railroad freight house-turned-museum is an exhibit on the railroad's history and a gift shop filled with Thomas the Tank Engine merchandise as well as other assorted train paraphernalia. If you have a train-obsessed child, you should definitely take the five-minute drive to the **Frank Fields Peconic County Miniature Railroad** (Webb Street, Greenport; 631-477-2433). This miniature train offers little ones a fun ride and is open Sundays and holidays, from May through September from 1 p.m. to 4 p.m.

After a day at sea on the ferry, what's a better way to end an evening than stargazing? On Saturdays at dusk, you can watch the stars at **Custer Observatory** (1115 Main Bayview Road; 631-765-2626; www.custerobservatory.org) in neighboring Southhold.

Spend your Sunday at the beach just fifteen minutes past Greenport, located at the very end of Long Island. Here, you will find Orient Point. Pack the bathing suits and a kite and spend your day relaxing at **Orient Beach State Park** *(631-323-2440; www.nysparks.com)*. This state park has a beach with canoe and kayak rental, two large nautical-themed playgrounds for children—from toddlers up to age 12, old wooden swings for couples to share, hiking trails, bike paths, and a grassy ball field. You can spend an entire day here, but remember to pack your sunscreen. If you do happen to forget the cooler full of goodies, don't worry as they have a refreshment stand that sells everything from fresh eggs to hot dogs.

If canoeing or kayaking is your pleasure, stop by **Eagle's Neck** *(49295 Main Road; 631-765-3502; www.eaglesneck.com)* in Southold, where you can explore the creeks and marshes of the North Fork with an experienced guide. Eagle's Neck also offers a paddling school and sunset tours on Saturday evenings.

Fans of nature should stop by the North Fork Audubon Society's **Red House Nature Center** in Greenport *(65275 Route 48; www.northforkaudubon.org)* and take a walk on one of their trails that extends just under two miles over about fifty acres of preserved parkland. The scenic trails are open daily from dawn until dusk. They also host events and children's activities; just check their Web site for their current schedule.

If you just came to shop, you are in luck as Greenport has a large selection of shops for such a small quaint town. My first stop is always at **Metal Monk** *(110 Front Street; 631-477-2722; www.metalmonk.com)* to check out their unbelievable selection of funky jewelry. This shop has an urban edge and would fit nicely in a hip Brooklyn neighborhood. Another good shop for jewelry and home decor is **Verbena** *(123 Main Street; 631-477-4080; www.verbena.net)*. If you're in need of a beach read, you must visit **Burton's Books Store** *(43 Front Street; 631-477-1161)*, which has a quality selection of books, including literary fiction, best-sellers, a large collection of books on Long Island, as well as a healthy selection of kid's books. **Now and Zen Yarns** *(15 Front Street; 877-477-2585; www.nowandzenyarns.com)* has a gorgeous selection of yarns for those who would prefer to knit the day away. Also, don't forget to stop by the **Arcade Department Store** *(14 Front Street; 631-477-1440)*, a classic five-and-dime that sells everything you might have forgotten.

If you're on a family weekend, don't miss **Goldsmith Toys and Electronics** *(138 Main Street; 631-477-0466)*, which will be a lifesaver if toys are what is needed to occupy your kids while you relax with a book. Fans of dollhouses and miniatures will love **Freda's Fancy** *(213 East Front Street; 631-323-0055;*

www.fredas-fancy.com), which has a large selection of dollhouses and accessories.

North Fork Wine Trail:

You don't have to be a wine connoisseur to spend the afternoon at the North Fork wineries. Most wineries provide entertainment on weekend afternoons and have lush, scenic settings with picnic benches and patios where you can munch on cheese and crackers while your friends drink the wine. If you are a fan of wine like me, you'll enjoy sampling many varietals at various East End wineries. Almost all offer a nominal tasting fee—usually $5—to sample their wine. A few wineries in the area even offer complimentary scheduled tours. It's good to note that some wineries offer discounts or even refund your tasting fee if you purchase bottles.

In the last thirty-five years, the North Fork has undergone a transformation into wine country. The first commercial vineyard was planted in 1973 and in 1975 the first winery, Hargrave Vineyard, opened in Cutchogue, New York. There are now over thirty wineries open to the public on the North Fork. You can see the full list of wineries at the Long Island Wine Council Web site, www.liwines.com; local wineries also use this site to post their special events.

If you don't want to drive or you'd like to spend the day tasting and touring the vineyards with a local wine expert, you should book a wine tour. Popular tours are given by **Off the Vine Tours** *(Riverhead; 631-779-3278; www.offthevinetours.com)* and **Vintage Lovers** *(Peconic; 631-765-4689; www.vintagetour1.com)*. Tours include pick up and drop off in an air-conditioned van and provide a picnic or boxed lunch with a complimentary glass of wine. You can also book a private tour for large parties through either of these outfits.

If you want to take a tour on your own, here are some wineries to see while you're on the North Fork. All the wineries on the North Fork are worthy of a visit; I have only included those I visited in recent trips. I'd suggest limiting your wine tour to four vineyards to avoid feeling tipsy.

Bedell Cellars *(36225 Main Road, Cutchogue; 631-734-7537; www.bedellcellars.com)* White bed-board walls with dramatic black tile floors give this winery an upscale appeal—it seems more art gallery than farmhouse. Tastings and tours are available by appointment. The grounds are stunning, with a patio perfect for drinking a cool white in the summer sun. They also own Corey Creek vineyard in Southold.

Castello di Borghese Vineyard & Winery *(Route 48, Cutchogue; 631-734-5111; www.castellodiborghese.com)* This is the oldest vineyard on Long Island, originally called the Hargrave Vineyard. In addition to tastings, they also host Winemaker's Walk, which is a tour of the vineyard for $15 on Saturdays beginning at 1 p.m. In the summer they offer the walk on Sundays and Thursdays as well. Advance registration is suggested.

The Lenz Winery *(Route 25, Peconic; 631-734-6010; www.lenzwine.com)* I love this low-key winery because they don't offer live entertainment—they concentrate on the wine. In the summer they host a tasting in their courtyard along with two yearly wine events in the fall and the summer.

Martha Clara Vineyards *(6025 Sound Avenue, Riverhead; 631-298-0705; www.marthaclaravineyards.com)* This winery hosts many events throughout the year, from cooking demonstrations to book club gatherings. The vineyard and tasting room are roomy and the wine is tasty.

Osprey's Dominion Vineyards *(44075 Main Road, Peconic; 631-765-6188; www.ospreysdominion.com)* With scheduled entertainment and a spacious patio, the Osprey's Dominion Vineyard provides the perfect setting for enjoying their selection of wine. After a tasting, make sure to pick up a bottle and head to the picnic benches and snack as you listen to some live music.

Pellegrini Winery and Vineyards *(23005 Route 25, Cutchogue; 631-734-4111; www.pellegrinivineyards.com)* Besides their flavorful wine, another great reason to visit is the stunning grounds of this popular vineyard. This is a great place to spend an afternoon—or to get married.

Pindar Vineyards, Winery and Pavillion *(37645 Main Road, Peconic; 631-734-6200; www.pindar.net)* One of the oldest vineyards on the North Fork, they host live entertainment on weekends and offer free tours during the summer months. If you happen to pass vineyards that aren't open to the public, you might be able to sample their wine at the **Tasting Room** *(2885 Peconic Lane, Peconic; 631-765-6404; www.tastingroomli.com)* where they offer wine tastings and sell wine from private North Fork winemakers that don't have tasting rooms on their vineyards. The tasting menu changes weekly.

Riverhead:

As you head back to the city after a day on the North Fork, you'll pass through the town of Riverhead. Don't forget to head down to **Briermere Farms** (4414 Sound Avenue; 631-722-3931; www.briermere.com) to pick up the best pies in the North Fork—so good that you can't help but sample them on the ride home. If you have kids with you or if you head back early due to rain, watch a sea lion show at the popular Long Island aquarium, **Atlantis Marine World Aquarium** (431 East Main Street; 631-208-9200; www.atlantismarineworld.com. If you're a bargain hunter, don't get on the parkway without hitting the **Tanger Outlets** (1770 West Main Street; 631-369-2732; www.tangeroutlet.com/riverhead), filled with outlets for shops such as Pottery Barn, the Gap, Barneys, and many others.

Places to eat:

Claudio's Clam Bar (West Wharf, Greenport; 631-477-1889; www.claudios.com) This laid-back waterfront restaurant on the pier is only open from May until October. It's a great place to have a drink and indulge at the raw bar. If you're here off-season, try Claudio's Restaurant, which, according to them, is the oldest same-family-run restaurant in the United States.

Coronet Luncheonette (2 Front Street, Greenport; 631-477-9834) Inside this vintage restaurant in the town of Greenport, it looks as though you stepped back in time to the 1950s or onto the set of Happy Days. Very kid-friendly.

The Frisky Oyster (27 Front Street, Greenport; 631-477-4265; www.thefriskyoyster.com) For high-end cuisine that you'll rave about to friends, this is the place to grab your dinner and drinks.

Hellenic Snack Bar and Restaurant (5145 Main Road, East Marion; 631-477-0138; www.thehellenic.com) On your way out to Orient Point Park, you must stop here for a meal. When you do, make sure to order the lemonade even if you aren't a fan of the drink—believe me, you won't regret it. The food is phenomenal, probably because as the menu states, they make 90 percent of the food from scratch on the premises. If you aren't a fan of Greek food, they also have regular diner fare.

Seafood Barge (62980 Main Road, Southold; 631-765-3010; www.seafoodbarge.com) Don't let the name fool you, as this is not a casual seafood restaurant on a barge, but a rather upscale restaurant with high-quality food and a wine list filled with local wines.

The North Fork Table and Inn *(57225 Main Road, Southold; 631-765-0177; www.northforktableandinn.com)* Specializing in locally grown produce and freshly caught fish, this restaurant is a hit on the North Fork. I would suggest calling for a reservation in advance since it is popular and fills up quickly with urban weekenders in want of good libations. They also have a popular four-room inn available, if you are looking to spend the evening.

Love Lane Kitchen *(240 Love Lane, Mattituck; 631-298-8989; www.love-lanekitchen.com)* One of my favorite places to stop for brunch on the North Fork, tucked away on Love Lane in Mattituck, is Love Lane Kitchen. It's a great casual place to have brunch with freshly roasted coffee and a menu filled with comfort-food favorites like cheese blintzes and pancakes.

The Lobster Roll *(3225 Sound Avenue, Riverhead; 631-369-3039; www.lob-sterroll.com)* There are two locations of this traditional seafood restaurant where you can order such classics as the lobster roll. This location, unlike the one en route to Montauk on Montauk Highway (see page 195) which is just a casual roadside stop, is a large sit-down restaurant. It's very kid-friendly, but make sure to get there early because there is often a long wait. The location of the Lobster Roll always gives me the perfect excuse to peruse my favorite candle shop on their premises, **East End Candle Company**. There is also a teddy bear shop and a store where you can decorate your own cookies in the shopping area.

Sandpiper Ice Cream *(142 Main Street, Greenport; 631-477-1154)* This family-owned homemade ice cream parlor has been operating since 1979. It's open from May to October from 11 a.m. until 11 p.m.

Bruce's Cheese Emporium and Café *(208 Main Street, Greenport; 631-477-0023)* As a fan of cheese—this is a must visit. Stop by for a cup of coffee, grab some lunch or have some cheese at one of the tables in their market. You can also pick up some fresh bread and cheese for a picnic.

The Greenport Tea Company *(119A Main Street, Greenport; 631-477-8744; www.greenportteacompany.com)* Tea lovers will devour their selection of loose teas and tea accessories. With a menu full of healthy lunch options and the allure of high tea—this is a perfect place to have a meal or a spot of tea.

Places to stay:

Silver Sands Motel *(1400 Silvermere Road, Greenport; 631 477-0011; www.silversands-motel.com)* You'll have your choice of room or small cottage at this old-school motel with an extremely homey vibe. The grounds are beautiful and they have their own beach with an area sectioned off for swimming. This is an excellent place for families in a location that is saturated with bed-and-breakfasts and inns. This motel will remind you of the places that you may have vacationed at when you were a kid. With a fridge in every room, the motel provides food for you to prepare breakfast in your room, so you are encouraged sleep in.

The Bartlett House Inn B & B *(503 Front Street, Greenport; 631-477-0371; www.bartletthouseinn.com)* A ten-room inn, located in a stunning Colonial Revival building in Greenport Village, offers breakfast with a two-night minimum stay on weekends from May through October.

The Greenporter Hotel and Spa *(326 Front Street, Greenport; 631-477-0066; www.thegreenporter.com)* This fifties-style motor lodge was transformed into a chic boutique hotel. They are pet-friendly and offer dog walking services. They have a minimum two-night stay from May through October, and a three-night minimum stay on holiday weekends. Rates include continental breakfast.

Harbor Knoll *(424 Fourth Street; 631-477-2352; www.harborknoll.com)* This gorgeous four-room B and B is located on the Peconic Bay. Two of their rooms have water views and all rooms have private baths. Breakfast and afternoon snacks are included in the price of a room. They also rent out the "enchanted cottage"—a one-bedroom cottage that sleeps four. They have a two-night minimum stay on weekends. Harbor Knoll is located within a block of the railroad station, so it's a perfect escape for someone who is traveling by train.

The Inn at the Blue *(7850 Main Road, East Marion; 631-477-0907; www.stayattheblue.com)* Located on Main Road between Orient and Greenport, this inn has an array of rooms from standard motel-style rooms to cottages. They also have pet-friendly rooms and a dog run on the premises. The inn has a pool and a grill with a shaded picnic area.

Holiday Inn Express East End (*1707 Old Country Road, Riverhead; 631-548-1000; www.hiexpress.com*) This chain hotel offers reasonable rates and clean rooms. Rates include breakfast and access to a workout room. This is a good place to stay if you have your kids in tow.

Local events

JUNE
Mattituck Strawberry Festival
631-298-5757
www.northfork.org

SEPTEMBER
Greenport Maritime Festival
631-477-2100
www.eastendseaport.org

JULY
Tall Ships Weekend in Greenport
631-298-5757
www.northfork.org

Golfing

Island's End Golf and Country Club
Route 25, Greenport, NY
631-477-8190
www.islandsendgolf.com
Semi-private club open to the public. Tee times can be reserved a week in advance.

Indian Island Country Club
Riverside Drive, Riverhead, NY
631-727-7776
www.indianislandcountryclub.com
Public course run by Suffolk County.

The Links at Cherry Creek

900 Reeves Avenue, Riverhead, NY

631-369-6500

www.cherrycreeklinks.com

Public course with a driving range on premises. You can reserve a tee time online.

The Woods at Cherry Creek

967 Reeves Avenue, Riverhead, NY

631-506-0777; 888-455-0300

www.thewoodsatcherrycreek.com

Public course with renowned Stonewall's Restaurant on their premises.

Long Island National Golf Club

1793 Northville Turnpike, Riverhead, NY

631-727-4653

www.longislandnationalgc.com

Open March through December

Chapter Twelve

A Weekend of Peace in the Woods:

Woodstock, New York

Travel time from NYC: 2 hours

Driving directions: I-87 (New York State Thruway) North to Exit 19. Continue onto Route 28 West and make right onto Route 375. Make left onto Route 212, which becomes Woodstock's Main Street.

Public transportation: Adirondack Trailways bus (800-776-7548; www.trailwaysny.com) to Woodstock. The bus drops off and picks up in the center of town.

Did you know that the town of Woodstock wasn't home to the famed 1969 concert? The concert was actually held almost fifty miles away in Bethel. Although this charming town didn't host the monumental festival, Woodstock was home to artists and free spirits well before it became the household name synonymous with 1960s music. A visit to Woodstock will bring peace to any harried New Yorker since the town operates at a much slower pace: Shopkeepers indulge in conversation, people relax over long meals, and locals take long walks in the lush woods. From gorgeous hiking trails to the laid-back vibe of Woodstock's Tinker Street, there is much to enjoy about this small town in the Catskill woods. With skiing nearby during the winter, tubing available in a creek nearby during the summer and abundant autumn foliage, Woodstock is an ideal escape for all seasons.

If you are trying to spend a quiet weekend without the stress of traffic, it might be best to avoid Woodstock in the heart of the summer, when the streets tend to get a bit crowded and the main road gets backed up with weekend traffic.

Places to see:

City folks who overbook themselves with activities might have a hard time adjusting to Woodstock's pace. They might find themselves wondering what to do after a stroll down Tinker Street and a visit to a gallery, but the reason one goes to Woodstock is to relax, and there are a lot of ways to find relaxation in this part of the woods.

For those who want to catch a glimpse of Woodstock's historic arts community, the first stop should be a tour of **Byrdcliffe Arts and Crafts Colony** *(59 Tinker Street; 845-679-9967; www.woodstockguild.org)*, one of the nation's oldest operating artist colonies. Guided tours are available only during the summer months, but pamphlets are available for self-guided tours year-round.

Check out the current photography exhibit at the **Center for Photography at Woodstock** *(59 Tinker Street; 845-679-9957; www.cpw.org)*. There is no cost to tour the galleries and they are open Wednesdays until Sundays from 12 noon to 5 p.m. If you haven't yet had your fill of photography, see the latest show at **Galerie BMG Contemporary Photography** *(12 Tannery Brook Road; 845-679-0027; www.galeriebmg.com)*, which is open to the public Fridays through Mondays from 11 a.m. to 6 p.m.

You can easily spend an afternoon exploring Woodstock's charming town filled with galleries and unique shops. Book lovers will be impressed with the selection of literary and commercial books at the **Golden Notebook** *(29 Tinker Street; 845-679-8000; www.goldennotebook.com)*. This is a definite stop when I'm in Woodstock, especially because of their separate children's bookstore next door. I also enjoy browsing through the spiritual and yoga books at **Mirabai** *(23 Mill Hill Road; 845-679-2100; www.mirabai.com)*. Woodstock is known for its boutiques; one to check out for tasteful pottery and home decor is **Timbuktu** *(2 Tannery Brook Road; 845-679-1169; www.timbuktuwoodstock.com)*. If you're in the mood for retro candy and delicious fudge, stop by **Woodstock Candy & Fudge** *(60 Tinker Street; 877-383-4311; www.woodstockcandy.com)*, where you can get everything from pop rocks to funky lunchboxes. **Candle Stock** *(16 Mill Hill Road; 845-679-8711; www.candlestock.com)* is not your typical mall candle shop. It has a unique collection of candles and accessories as well as a large selection of Judaica.

Fans of flea markets should stop by **Mower's Saturday Market** *(Maple Lane; 845-679-6744; www.ulster.net/~fleamarket)*, located on Maple Lane behind the bakery **Bread Alone** *(22 Mill Hill Road; 845-679-2108; www.breadalone.com)*. This cool market has been in Woodstock for over thirty years and is a great place for bargain hunting. The market is open from mid-May until November. Although it's called a Saturday market, Mower's is open on Saturdays and Sundays.

For those who like to do something other than shop, there are many great hikes in Woodstock. A popular hike is climbing up **Overlook Mountain**

Fire Tower *(www.catskillcenter.org)*. This five-mile hike is located about two miles outside the town of Woodstock. The trail takes you up Overlook Mountain where you can see the ruins of the once-grand Overlook Mountain House, a fire tower, and stunning scenic views. The gravel road trail is a bit buggy, so pack some bug spray.

If you'd rather stay on level land, view a six-acre outdoor sculpture, which took the late Harvey Fite almost forty years to create, hence the "40" in **Opus 40** *(50 Fite Road; 845-246-3400; www.opus40.org)*. Head to Saugerties, New York, to see this amazing work of art built out of quarry tools. The site also houses the **Quarryman's Museum**, which displays tools that quarrymen have used over the years.

If you're an animal lover and don't mind getting your hands dirty, volunteer to spend the day helping out at the **Woodstock Farm Animal Sanctuary** *(Van Wagner Road; 845-679-5955; www.woodstockfas.org)*. If you don't want to volunteer, just stop by on weekends from 11 a.m. to 4 p.m. to visit the animals.

If you're a train buff or have kids in tow, you should head to the **Empire State Railway Museum** *(845-688-7501; www.esrm.com)* located on Route 28 about fifteen minutes from Woodstock, where kids or the young-at-heart can enjoy looking at the caboose and other trains that are currently being restored. The museum also offers tons of photos of the old railway line. The museum is open weekends and holidays from Memorial Day through Columbus Day from 11 a.m. until 4 p.m. While at the museum you can hop aboard the **Catskill Mountain Railroad** *(Station Road, Phoenicia; 845-688-7400; www.catskillmtrailroad.com)*, which runs from May through October. This scenic one-and-one-half-hour train ride along the Esopus Creek is a relaxing way to spend the afternoon. If sitting in a train and watching the Esopus whets your appetite for a day on the creek, rent an inner tube at Town Tinker Tubing.

Town Tinker Tubing *(10 Bridge Street, Phoenicia; 845-688-5553; www.towntinker.com)* in the heart of Phoenicia, is located about twenty minutes from Woodstock. Town Tinker is open Memorial Day through the end of September from 9 a.m. to 4 p.m., with the last rental at 4 p.m. At Town Tinker you can rent an inner tube to ride down the Esopus, but you have to be a good swimmer and at least twelve years old. You must wear sneakers or sandals since it's a rocky way down the creek—I can vouch for that! Before you hit the creek, fill up on pancakes at **Sweet Sue's** *(49 Main Street; 845-688-7852)*, the place to grab some grub in Phoenicia.

Too much snow on the ground for tubing or hiking? Head to the extremely laid-back **Belleayre Mountain** *(Route 28; 800-942-6904; www.belleayre.com)*, a state-owned ski resort. There are two lodges: one for beginning skiers at the base of the mountain and one for the more advanced skiers a bit farther up the slope. The lodge for the beginners houses a ski and snowboarding school as well as day care for kids. There are eight lifts and forty-seven trails. Cross-country skiing is also available at Belleayre. It's easy to park your car and since it's a small ski resort, you don't have to lug your equipment very far. There is no "scene" at Belleayre; it has the feel of a public park, and has picnic benches inside where you can chow down on food from their snack bar or you can bring your own lunch to eat. Families tend to visit the resort due to its small size and laid-back vibe. However, the intimate appeal of Belleayre might change in the future since there are plans to build a larger ski resort adjacent to it.

When the slopes close for the summer, Belleayre takes on another life and offers sky rides on their lifts, hiking, swimming at their beach, boating, fishing, camping, as well as hosting various festivals ranging from music to craft.

After a day of hiking, tubing, or skiing, you might want to soothe your aches with a day at the spa. **River Rock Health Spa** *(62 Ricks Road; 845-679-7800; www.riverrock.biz)* in Woodstock has a calming atmosphere that will rejuvenate you. Enjoy a massage or indulge in a spa package. Another spa option is only a few miles away at the **Emerson Resort Spa** *(5340 Route 28; 877-688-28282; www.emersonplace.com)* in Mount Tremper, where you can choose from an extensive spa menu of massages, facials, and other body treatments. They also have yoga and Pilates classes. The treatments book up fast, so call ahead to schedule an appointment.

Even if you opt out of a spa treatment, you must make a side trip to the Emerson Resort and Spa to peruse their **Emerson Country Store** filled with tasteful home goods. The country store also houses **Kaleidostore,** the home of the world's largest kaleidoscope. You get to enter the 65-foot tall kaleidoscope, housed in a restored dairy farm silo, and watch a trippy light and sound show. The best way to watch the show is lying on the carpeted floor of the scope (this was recommended to us by the woman who sells the tickets), although you can watch it standing up. The show, which has an American theme with pictures of the American flag and patriotic music, is not to be missed. Once you leave the kaleidoscope you have the chance to purchase a kaleidoscope of your own to take home. They have tons of kaleidoscopes in various price ranges.

For a spiritual experience, visit **Karma Triyana Dharmachakra** *(352 Meads Mountain Road; 845-679-5906; www.kagyu.org)* a Buddhist monastery, and take a free guided tour on Saturdays or Sundays at 1:30 p.m. They advise that you call before coming in case the tour has been cancelled. For those who want to partake in meditation on a Sunday, you should go to the Sunday program at **Zen Mountain Monastery** *(Mount Tremper; 845-688-2228; www.mro.org)* in Mount Tremper. The Sunday program introduces newcomers to Zen meditation. The program is offered year-round and runs from 9 a.m. to 1:30 p.m., during which you meditate, receive an introduction to the monastery, listen to Zen liturgy and dharma teachings, and have lunch there.

Instead of meditation, you might want to relieve some stress on the court. If you have brought along a racket, you can rent a court in nearby Saugerties at **Total Tennis** *(1811 Old Kings Highway; 845-247-9177; www.totaltennis.com)*. If you really want to improve your game, they offer classes and have a year-round tennis camp with overnight accommodations for all levels of players — even ones who never picked up a racket. For golfers, hit the nine-hole course just twenty minutes away at a public course called **Rip Van Winkle Country Club** *(Route 23A, Palenville; 518-678-9779; www.rvwcc.com)*.

For local nightlife, check the schedule for the **Bearsville Theater** *(291 Tinker Street and Route 212; 845-679-4406; www.bearsvilletheater.com)*, a mile down the road from Woodstock's main shopping district. The theater has an eclectic schedule, including everything from theater to amateur boxing. If you're in Woodstock during the summer months, check out the **Woodstock Playhouse** *(Routes 212 and Route 375; 845-679-4101; www.woodstockplayhouse.org)* a semi-enclosed theater that hosts various theatrical and artistic productions. The original playhouse burnt down in 1998 and over the past few years it has been in the process of being rebuilt.

For music lovers, the summer offers the experience of listening to chamber music in a peaceful wooded setting at the Maverick Concerts. This historic concert series has been in Woodstock since 1916 when volunteers built the gorgeous music hall that is now on the National Register of Historic Places. The acoustics are great here and if the concert series is in season, it really shouldn't be missed *(www.maverickconcerts.org)*.

Fans of folk music, should head to the **Midnight Ramble** *(160 Plochmann Lane; 845-679-2744; www.levonhelm.com)* at the studios of Levon Helm of The Band. Rated "the best Jam of 2008" by *Rolling Stone* magazine, tickets carry a hefty price tag of $150. Helm invites accomplished musicians to join his house band and past performers have included Elvis Costello, Joan Osbourne,

Nick Lowe, Donald Fagan, and many other notables. Despite the price, these concerts sell out fast so book it in advance.

Places to eat:

The Bear Cafe and the Little Bear *(295 Tinker Street; 845-679-5555; www.bearcafe.com)* This wood-paneled restaurant with a fireplace and large windows overlooking a meadow is a popular restaurant in neighboring Bearsville. The menu will satisfy both meat-lovers and vegetarians. Make reservations early as the Bear Cafe tends to get very busy. I was there in the winter and it was crowded. If you are dining in the warmer months, make sure to get a table outside by the gorgeous stream. Fans of Asian food might try eating at the more casual Little Bear, which serves up Asian-style food right next door. You can also grab a drink at the bar and have some appetizers while you wait for a table.

Bread Alone Café and Bakery *(22 Mill Hill Road; 845-679-2108; www.bread-alone.com)* If you're a fan of the Bread Alone Union Square Greenmarket booth, you must head to their Woodstock location. You're sure to be intoxicated by the fragrant smell of homemade bread and cookies upon entering this charming café. Savor the aroma as you sip some coffee and enjoy freshly baked goods.

Joshua's Café *(51 Tinker Street; 845-679-5533; www.joshuascafe.com)* Since 1972 Joshua's Café has been serving the Woodstock community. The menu has a Middle Eastern influence with dinner appetizers that include stuffed grape leaves and baba ghanoush. There are a plethora of vegetarian options at this moderately priced restaurant. You can also stop in for breakfast or lunch. Vegans will enjoy their yummy tofu scramble and meat lovers can chow down on a lamb shish kabab. Upstairs from the café is the **Java Lounge** where you can have coffee or a cocktail while playing a board game. They also host concerts, readings, and other arty events.

Garden Café on the Green *(6 Old Forge Road; 845-679-3600; www.wood-stockgardencafe.com)* Calling all vegetarians to this relatively new vegan restaurant! Although they have garden seating, the place isn't very large and I'd suggest calling ahead for reservations.

Landau Grill *(17 Mill Hill Road; 845-679-0481)* This is one of my favorite places to dine in Woodstock during the warmer months. Sit outside on their patio and relax while having a salad or oysters from their raw bar. They also serve alcoholic drinks for those who'd like to have a nightcap.

Places to stay:

Woodstock Inn on the Millstream *(48 Tannery Brook Road; 800-420-4707 / 845-679-8211; www.woodstock-inn-ny.com)* This moderately priced inn has eighteen rooms ranging in size. The inn's grounds overlook Tinker Creek, where you can just sit on the rocks by the stream and relax. They also have a large lawn with hammocks, tables, and chairs. The inn is family-friendly and family travelers might be interested in their two-bedroom unit. Breakfast includes locally baked pastries, bagels and lox, granola, and other yummy treats.

Emerson Resort and Spa *(5340 Route 28; Mount Tremper; 877-688-282-8845/845-688-2828; www.emersonplace.com)* This luxurious spa also houses an inn and lodge. The inn is for adults only, so if you're planning a family vacation, they'll give you a room at the lodge. The inn consists of twenty-five suites, all of which have views, decks, and gas fireplaces. The resort is stunning and you'll truly feel pampered.

Kate's Lazy Meadow Motel *(5191 Route 28, Mount Tremper; 845-688-7200; www.lazymeadow.com)* Fans of the B-52s should "hop in their Chrysler that's as big as a whale" and set sail to this kitschy eight-room motel owned by B-52s singer Kate Pierson. Located twelve miles from the town of Woodstock, this colorful motel's rooms are filled with mod furniture and a fifties-style kitchen stocked with all the tools needed for cooking and, more importantly, mixing drinks. For those who really indulge in ultimate kitsch, you also have the option of staying in "Bubbles" or "Tinkerbell," the two restored vintage Airstream trailers. For larger groups, you can rent out the Lazy Cabin, a three-bedroom cabin decorated by Kate, which is only five miles away from Woodstock's main drag.

Saugerties Lighthouse Bed and Breakfast *(168 Lighthouse Drive; 845-247-0656; www.saugertieslighthouse.com)* If you have ever dreamt of spending the night in an actual working lighthouse, this is your chance. There are only two rooms available at this lighthouse, so book well in advance, sometimes even up to a year. The two rooms share a bath and have double beds. The lighthouse is accessible by a half-mile trail.

The Villa at Saugerties *(159 Fawn Road, Saugerties; 845-246-0682; www.thevillaatsaugerties.com)* When I told a friend about this book, she kept telling me the Villa at Saugerties must be included. Maybe she fell in love with the place because of the Egyptian cotton sheets or the five tastefully decorated rooms on four lush acres or the 40-foot pool. Located a few miles from Woodstock, this bed-and-breakfast with five guest rooms with private baths is open from mid-May until November. Off-season *(from November to May)* you can rent the entire house with a one-week minimum stay.

Local events

JULY/AUGUST
Belleayre Music Festival
800-942-6904
www.belleayremusic.org

SEPTEMBER
Hudson Valley Garlic Festival
Saugerties, NY
845-246-3090
www.hvgf.org

OCTOBER
Belleayre Fall Festival
800-942-6904
www.belleayre.com

Woodstock Film Festival
845-679-4265
www.woodstockfilmfestival.com

Chapter Thirteen

It's Not the Sixth Borough:

Philadelphia, Pennsylvania

Travel time from NYC: 2 hours.

Driving directions: I-95 South to Exit 4 and merge onto Route 73 North toward Camden/Philadelphia. Exit onto Kaighn Avenue (Route 38 West) and continue on Admiral Wilson Boulevard (US-30 West). Exit onto I-676 West (US-30 West) and make a right at North 7th Street.

Public transportation: Amtrak (800-USA-Rail; www.amtrak.com) or Greyhound bus (www.greyhound.com; 800-231-2222)

When most people think of Philly, they imagine a day visiting the Liberty Bell, Independence Park, and Betsy Ross's house. Sure you can spend a fun day learning about our Founding Fathers, but Philadelphia is also home to a world-class art museum, the largest collection of Rodin sculptures outside of Paris, and a penitentiary tour that rivals Alcatraz's. Like many American cities, in recent years this city has seen a revitalization and development in many areas and is also home to numerous up-and-coming trendy neighborhoods like Northern Liberties and Fishtown—all filled with eclectic restaurants and funky nightlife. Of course you don't have to limit yourself to dining at hipster haunts, you can also chow down on Philly's famous cheese steak and pretzels.

Philadelphia holds its own as a city, despite being referred to as the "sixth borough" because of its proximity to New York City. A getaway to the city of brotherly love is a worthwhile urban escape that appeals to all. Even jaded New Yorkers will enjoy exploring Philly and appreciating how much this city has to offer, aside from retracing Rocky's steps by running up the steps of the Philadelphia Museum of Art.

Places to see:

Being a native New Yorker, one aspect that appealed to me about Philadelphia is that you can get around easily by foot since the center of the city isn't too large and sites aren't that far from each other. However if you're tired, you don't have to rely on your feet; you can also hop on a bus, train, or trolley through Philly's extensive and user-friendly SEPTA transit system. Like NYC, you can also buy an all-day travel pass. You can pick one of these passes up at over four hundred locations throughout the area just check their Web site (www.septa.org) for locations, schedules, and a map. If you want to forgo public transportation for your getaway, there are cabs available all over the city for your trips around town. If you book a hotel near the city's center, you will be able to reach all locations mentioned here quite easily.

Shopping, museum hopping, and eating might be on your agenda for your escape to Philly, but if you're fan of the eccentric, you must start your trip with a visit to the **Mütter Museum** (The College of Physicians of Philadelphia, 19 South 22nd Street; 215-563-3737; www.collphyphil.org), created in the 19th century to educate medical students about human anatomy and medical issues. Today, the Mütter Museum is an interesting and educational journey through the world of medical practices. The museum is filled with everything from fetuses of various ages in jars to a cancerous growth removed from John Wilkes Booth's thorax. The wooden display cases give the museum an almost timeless appeal and you might feel as if you're in a 19th-century apothecary or a mad scientist's lab. In fact you can take a step back in time and view an authentic doctor's office on display in the Mütter room, with the exact desk and equipment from a local doctor who practiced in Philly from 1911 to 1923.

You can spend hours examining the displays of human skulls or a collection of foreign objects removed from human bodies. Those with a strong stomach can view the preserved body of the "soap lady" who died in the 1800s. Due to a chemical reaction after her death, her body turned to a soap-like substance. Though some might find the museum creepy, with its corpses on display and grotesque models of various skin conditions, the museum does provide us with a look at how far the medical profession has come in the last few centuries. If you're a fan of kitsch, check out the gift shop, which sells coffin handbags, syringe pens, and other fun goodies.

If perusing exhibits on medical oddities doesn't satiate your desire for the eccentric, head over to Fairmount section of Philadelphia and take a tour of the **Eastern State Penitentiary** (22nd Street and Fairmount Avenue; 215-236-3300; www.easternstate.org) Eastern State opened in 1829 and was the first prison in America. The prison's architecture is stunning: It looks more like a castle than a prison. The narrated audio tour by native New Yorker and actor Steve Buscemi is a must while touring the prison. In addition to Buscemi, they have ex-inmates and guards talk about their time at Eastern State. The prison also offers, for no additional charge, guided tours on various topics that run throughout the day. When I was there, they had a tour on prison riots.

The doors of Eastern State closed in 1971 and were reopened for public tours in 1994, although you might be surprised to find that not much of the prison has been renovated as you walk through the eerie remnants of this once state-of-the-art 19th-century prison. The first inmates at Eastern State were forced to serve their time in silence and isolation. Separated from each other in small cells, inmates were punished if they were caught talking to each other. The forced silence received much criticism and when Charles Dickens came to America, one of the first places he wanted to visit was Eastern State since he was horrified by the idea of isolating humans, which he believed might drive people into insanity. As the prison grew, inmates had to share rooms and eventually Eastern State's rules changed. It even once housed famous inmates like Al Capone, who, oddly, had his tonsils removed at Eastern State. You can tour his cell amongst other interesting locales at this historic structure.

After your visit to the big house, you might want to revive yourself with some coffee. Across the street from the penitentiary is the cleverly named **Mug Shots Coffee** (2100 Fairmount Avenue; 267-514-7145; www.mugshotscoffeehouse.com). This coffee shop also serves wraps—check out the Capone and the Slammer—and has good selection of vegetarian options. It's a nice place for a breather after an afternoon of quirky adventures.

For those who are less about macabre and more about Monet, spend your morning strolling though the **Philadelphia Museum of Art** (26th Street and Benjamin Franklin Parkway, 215-763-8100; www.philamuseum.org). Sunday is pay-as-you-wish day at the museum, so folks on a budget might spend the last day of their getaway checking out the museum's collection of over two-hundred-thousand works of art, ranging from contemporary art to the collection of arms and armor. The museum is also famous because Rocky ran up the steps of the main building in the movie *Rocky* and there is even a Rocky statue at the foot of the museum steps at the east entrance.

The museum is housed in both the main building and the Perelman building. The Perelman building, a former office building, was transformed into gallery space in 2007 to give the museum more room to house its collections. It's conveniently located across the road from the main building. The Philadelphia Museum of Art hosts popular exhibits and if you're in town to see a special exhibit that requires tickets, you can purchase tickets in advance on their Web site. The museum also offers a good amount of family programming including family guides available in the entrance of the main building for those who've brought their little artists out to explore. You might also want to start your weekend at the museum since on Fridays the museum hosts Art After Five, a program featuring live music and cocktails from 5 p.m. to 8:45 p.m.

Food options are scarce in the area surrounding the museum, since there is a lot of ground to cover with both spaces, so you might plan on having lunch at the Museum's café, which is a moderately priced option and has everything from fresh paninis, a salad bar, as well as kid's meals. For a more upscale culinary experience, check out the museum restaurant, where you can devour scrumptious goodies during their Sunday champagne brunch buffet while listening to live music. You can also dine at the museum restaurant for lunch and dinner on Friday evenings.

Even if you feel you've had your fill of art, I recommend stopping by the **Rodin Museum** *(2600 Benjamin Franklin Parkway; 215-568-6026; www.rodinmuseum.org)* even if it's just to sit out in the front garden to stare at Rodin's famous sculpture *The Thinker*. The Rodin museum houses the largest collection of Rodin sculptures outside of Paris. The building itself is stunning and the light, airy space is perfect for viewing the collection of sculptures. Fans of Rodin will be pleased with their gift shop, which must sell every Rodin-related item in existence today, from Rodin T-shirts to replicas of *The Thinker*.

For the book lovers among us, head over to Rittenhouse Square to the **Rosenbach Museum and Library** *(2010 Delancey Place; 215-732-1600; www.rosenbach.org)*. Located off the square on Delancey Place, this 19th-century townhouse is filled with a collection of rare books and manuscripts. The admission fee includes exhibits on view and a tour of this grand house. The Rosenbach Museum and Library houses the original manuscript for James Joyce's *Ulysses*. Fans of the book should plan a visit to the Rosenbach on June 16th for Bloomsday, where they host readings of *Ulysses* and one can view their collection of Joyce material.

If you want to play the role of traditional tourist, your trip to Philly wouldn't be complete without a day visiting the **Liberty Bell** and **Independence Hall**. Your first stop should be the **Independence Visitor Center** *(6th and Market Street; 215-963-7676 / 800-537-7676; www.independencevisitorcenter.com)*, where you can buy everything, from tickets to Independence Hall to a SEPTA pass, and get information on bus tours throughout the city. If you are going to spend the weekend touring the sights, you might want to purchase the **Philadelphia Pass** *(www.philadelphiapass.com)*, which offers you discounted admission to various attractions. Once you get the pass, it alleviates the stress of purchasing tickets at each location since admission fees to all participating sites are included in the cost of the pass.

In addition to getting tourist info and tickets to all the local historical sites at the Independence Visitor Center you can also get tickets for the **Lights of Liberty Light Show**, an outdoor light and sound show about the Revolutionary War, which runs from April through October, or tickets for **Breakfast with Ben** in the ballroom on Saturday mornings, where you can eat breakfast with Ben Franklin. Obviously, this is a lunch with a Ben Franklin impersonator since Ben Franklin is buried across the street at Christ Church Burial Ground). At the breakfast, you can ask this Founding Father questions about United States history—and even take a family photo with this historical figure.

For interesting shopping and people watching, you should take a walk over to South Street, which was once the stomping ground of the early punk rockers like the Dead Milkmen. These days it's less edgy, as it has a Starbucks and a Dairy Queen, but there is still a vibrant nightlife and cool shops like **Atomic City Comics** *(642 South Street; 215-625-9613; www.atomiccity-comics.com)*, and also legendary **Jim's Steaks** *(400 South Street; 215-928-1911)*, which some claim is the best Philly cheese steak in town.

If you want to check out new neighborhoods that are still considered edgy, take a trip to **Northern Liberties** *(www.northernliberties.org)* and spend a night having a pint at one of the many cool bars to pop up in the past years like the **Standard Tap** *(2nd and Poplar Streets; 215-238-0630; www.standardtap.com)* or the **700 Club** *(700 North 2nd Street; 215-413-3181)*. Or hear jazz at **Ortlieb's Jazzhaus** *(847 North 3rd Street; 215-922-1035; www.ortliebsjazzhaus.com)*. You could also spend the evening bowling and drinking cocktails at the über-cool, retro-designed **North Bowl** *(909 North 2nd Street; 215-238-2695; www.north-bowlphilly.com)*. This is a fun trip for a night out, but unlike most of the other neighborhoods, it's not walking distance from the center of the city.

Searching for more cheese steaks? A nice side trip would be a walk down to south Philly's Italian market where two opposing cheese steak restaurants sit on opposite corners: **Geno's Cheesesteak** *(1219 South 9th Street; 215-389-0659; www.genosteaks.com)* and **Pat's King of Steaks** *(1237 Passyunk Avenue; 215-468-1546; www.patskingofsteaks.com)*. It's up to you to perform a taste test to figure out which one is the best. Being a vegetarian, this part of my Philly excursion was a bit limited. I spent the time walking around the vibrant Italian market—filled with store selling meats, cheeses, and pastas—while my husband and I made *Rocky* references.

Places to eat:

Since Philadelphia is a large city, there are endless dining options in addition to cheese steaks, including cleverly named cafés and museum restaurants. Here are a few restaurants that I happened upon during my Philly excursion.

Reading Terminal Market *(Between 12th and Arch Streets; 215-922-2317; www.readingterminalmarket.org)* This famous large indoor market is one of America's oldest markets and is a great place to pick up some casual fare. Filled with food vendors, stores for housewares, and restaurants, there is something in the market to satisfy any palate. Restaurants vary from ethnic to vegetarian. Don't forget to leave room for dessert at **Bassetts Ice Cream** *(1211 Chestnut Street; 215-864-2771; www.bassettsicecream.com)*, which dishes out tasty homemade ice cream—I swear by the dark chocolate chip—or enjoy chocolate-covered chocolate chip cookies at **Famous 4th Street Cookie Co**. *(215-625-9870; www.famouscookies.com)*. Be sure to stop by **Blue Mountain Vineyards and Cellars** *(610-298-3068; www.bluemountainwine.com)* to pick up a bottle of vino, since many restaurants in Philly are BYOB.

Alma De Cuba *(1623 Walnut Street; 215-988-1799; www.almadecubarestaurant.com)* Drink mojitos and enjoy excellent Cuban food in a lively atmosphere. This Philadelphia hot spot has a funky interior, tasty food, and the occasional celebrity sighting. Although the food isn't cheap, the experience is not to be missed. For those who enjoy a nice midday break, Alma De Cuba has recently added a lunch menu.

Bindi *(105 South 13th Street; 215-922-6061)* Fans of Tabla's Bread Bar will enjoy dining at this funky Indian restaurant, which has tasty food and tons of vegetarian options. Although the restaurant is casual, entrees average about $20 but the portions are quite hearty. You can leave the credit cards at home since it's cash only, but you have to bring your own alcohol.

City Tavern *(138 South 2nd Street, 215-413-1443, www.citytavern.com)* Step back in time at this historic tavern that serves up cuisine inspired by 18th-century America. The original City Tavern that served folks like George Washington burnt down in 1834; the current location is an accurate reconstruction that opened in 1976. To keep in the spirit of American history, this is a good place to stop when spending the day visiting the historic sites. The tavern is open for lunch and dinner.

The Franklin Fountain *(116 Market Street; 215-627-1899; www.franklinfountain.com)* This quirky old city ice-cream parlor serves homemade ice cream, fresh fudge, and phosphates *(a fun fizzy drink)* with cool names like the Japanese Thirst Killer Phosphate. The parlor looks like you stepped back in time, with servers dressed like traditional soda jerks from the early 20th century. There is seating both indoors and outside, but the place tends to get crowded.

Mercato *(1216 Spruce Street; 215-985-2562; www.mercatobyob.com)* Our inn had their menu on display in the elevator and I couldn't stop salivating as I rode down to the lobby. Bring your own wine to this intimate Italian restaurant that focuses on slow-food cooking, with a menu featuring such yummy entrees like spring vegetable risotto and Parmesan-crusted veal cutlets. This is a great place for a romantic meal, but don't forget your wallet as it's cash only.

Moshulu *(401 South Columbus Boulevard; 215-923-2500; www.moshulu.com)* If you want to eat on a boat but don't want to spend a day at sea, have a romantic dinner on a four-mast century-old sailing ship docked at Penn's Landing. You'll be intoxicated by the views while enjoying a diverse menu of this award-winning restaurant.

Sabrina's Café *(910 Christian Street; 215-572-1599)* If you're not heading to South Philly's Italian market to eat cheese steak, stop in for lunch or enjoy a dinner at this popular BYOB restaurant that will appeal to late risers, since their brunch is filled with goodies like challah French toast and is served all day. The dinner menu has everything from goat cheese ravioli to pork chops.

Susanna Foo *(1512 Walnut Street; 215-545-8800; www.susannafoo.com)* This was the Citysearch.com pick for Philly's best Chinese restaurant. Its gourmet food isn't your typical Chinese take-out and has a menu filled with everything from tea-soaked Peking duck breast to slow-roasted Scottish salmon with sake and miso marinade.

Places to stay:

The official visitor site for greater Philadelphia *(www.gophilla.com)* often runs a popular overnight package, which offers deep discounts at area hotels. The one caveat of the package is that you must stay two nights, but there are many benefits to this package such as free parking, a Philadelphia-themed gift, and discounts at various tourist attractions. Check out the site for a list of participating hotels.

Alexander Inn *(12th and Spruce Streets; 877-ALEX-INN / 215-923-3535; www.alexanderinn.com)* We stayed at this boutique hotel located in Center City on a scenic street in a neighborhood filled with antique stores, quality restaurants, and gay bars. The historic building, dating back from 1901, was originally an apartment building. The inn's rooms are cozy and immaculate and the vibe is very laid-back. This is great escape for a couple or singletons away for a weekend. A continental buffet breakfast is available until noon on weekends, so you can sleep in. There is a gym in the basement and free use of the Internet. Twenty-four hour parking is available at a lot down the street for a nominal $10 fee.

Doubletree *(237 South Broad Street; 215-893-1600; www.doubletree.com),* If you have the family in tow you might want to check this 432-room hotel that offers free chocolate chip cookies when you check in. This hotel also offers a nice rooftop atrium pool. You have the option of self-parking or valet at the garage across from the hotel. The Doubletree participates in the GoPhilla package, but often has moderate weekend rates as well.

Loews *(1200 Market Street; 215-627-1200; www.loewshotels.com)* If you want to bring your dog away for the weekend, Loews offers a pet-sitting and walking service. Housed in the renovated historic Philadelphia Saving Fund Society (PSFS) Building, this hotel offers great views. Located in Center City, the hotel offers use of the health club and pool, and has a full menu of spa treatments.

Ritz Carlton *(10 Avenue of the Arts; 215-523-8000; www.ritzcarlton.com)* If you have ever dreamt of spending the night in a bank, this is the place for you. Housed in a century-old bank, with a lobby that is worth a visit even if you aren't staying the night, this historic landmark building is a great place to escape for the weekend. Located across from City Hall, this luxurious hotel is a bit on the pricey side, but weekend deals can be found since it's a participating hotel in the GoPhilla package. Bring your fancy shoes, since they offer a complimentary shoeshine for guests.

Sofitel *(120 South 17th Street; 215-569-8300; www.sofitel.com)* This hotel was recommended to me by a Philly native and is housed in the former stock exchange building. Large rooms await you at this grand hotel with a fitness center and complimentary fresh fruit; Sofitel is quite a luxurious place to spend your Philadelphia weekend.

Bringing the Kids to Philly

Philadelphia is a great place to bring the kids. It's an educational city that brings American history to life. However, aside from learning about Ben Franklin and our Founding Fathers, there are tons of other cool kid-friendly activities.

Please Touch Museum *(210 North 21st Street; 215-963-0677; www.please-touchmuseum.org)* Recently, this museum opened moved into bigger digs, making even more room for this well recognized children's museum that allows children to learn through play. With exhibits based on popular children's books, including a make-believe local grocery store, it's sure to please your little ones—especially on a rainy day.

The Franklin Institute *(222 North 20th Street; 215-448-1200; www.fi.edu)* Introduce your kids to the world of science by spending an afternoon at the Franklin. Tour interactive exhibits on the human heart as well as a train factory. If it's nice out, check out the 25,000-foot outdoor park where kids can learn about science by doing fun stuff like playing miniature golf and looking through a mini-periscope. For those who still have the Founding Fathers on the brain, there is the Benjamin Franklin memorial in the museum's rotunda.

Adventure Aquarium *(1 Aquarium Drive, Camden, NJ; 856-365-3300; www.adventureaquarium.com)* Half the fun of getting to this aquarium is that you can take the RiverLink ferry to get there from Penn's Landing. Located across the water in Camden, New Jersey, this popular aquarium, which opened in 2005, allows your little one to touch a shark and in the West African River Experience, observe real hippos.

The Philadelphia Zoo *(34th Street and Girard Avenue; 215-243-1100; www.philadelphiazoo.org)* This 42-acre zoo opened in 1874, and is the nation's oldest zoo. Walk around their gorgeous grounds and see animals from all continents. In their children's zoo, kids can feed sheep and goats or hop aboard a tractor. In addition to viewing the animals, kids can also enjoy taking a ride on a swan boat, a train, or a hot air balloon to get an aerial view of the zoo and the Philadelphia skyline.

Ride the Ducks of Philadelphia *(Ticket kiosk at 6th and Chestnut; 877-88-QUACK; www.phillyducks.com)* This eighty-minute combined land and water tour of Philadelphia on an amphibious vehicle also takes its passengers on a ride down the Delaware River. This is fun way to tour Philly. There are no restrooms on the tour, which might pose a problem for younger kids.

Chapter Fourteen

Back to School in New York:

New Paltz, High Falls, Rhinebeck, Hyde Park, and Millbrook

Travel time from NYC: 2–2 1/2 hours

Driving directions: For New Paltz, take I-87 (New York State Thruway) North to Exit 18. For Hyde Park, take I-87 North to Exit 18; follow Route 299 East and make a right at US-9 West. Take Route 55 East (US-44) until a slight right takes you to US-9 South.

Public transportation: Metro-North Railroad (www.metronorthrailroad.org; 800-638-7646) to Poughkeepsie; take a cab from the train station to either New Paltz or Hyde Park. Adirondack Trailways bus (800-776-7548; www.trailwaysny.com) to Main Street in New Paltz.

Would you like to know how to speak a foreign language? Or do you want to learn how to cook from top-rated chefs? How about brushing up on your American history? Well you can do it in New Paltz and Hyde Park. If you have ever wanted to change your life in forty-eight hours, here is your chance. There's never a better time to book a getaway that is both fun and educational.

There are a bunch of activities you can do in the area in addition to spending your time in the classroom. Maybe you want to improve your golf game or are adventurous enough to pick up a new sport like skydiving? You can also work this into your educational getaway. So brush off your books and sharpen your pencils because after a weekend here, you can fill up a notebook with a ton of new experiences.

Places to see:

If you're craving an academic atmosphere, you'll find it in this charming college town filled with bookstores, cool restaurants, and of course, a university. Really get into the spirit of academic life and sign up for a weekend class at the **Language Immersion Institute** (*State University of New York at New Paltz, 1 Hawk Drive, New Paltz; 845-257-3500; www.newpaltz.edu/lii*). This intensive program teaches beginner- to advanced-level weekend workshops in twenty languages ranging from Spanish to Yiddish to American Sign Language. You can show up with no experience at all in the language and by the end of the weekend you should understand the basics of the language.

When I was at the Institute, I sat in on a beginner-level Spanish course on a Sunday morning and was shocked at how well the students were talking to the professor. The students claimed they hadn't known a word of Spanish when they came in for the workshop that Friday. The enthusiastic professor shunned the use of English in the class, and whenever a student started to speak in English, the class repeated in unison, "Adios, Inglés, hola, Español!" The energy in the class was contagious, and the small class size gave all the students the opportunity to speak.

The language classes at the immersion center focus on speaking rather than writing the language, so the classes are focused on trying to communicate instead of conjugating verbs like most of us did in high school language class. The summer workshops offer on-campus housing, but during the school year you will have to find your own accommodations.

If you can't sneak away for a weekend but have the urge to speak a new language, they also offer monthly weekend workshops in New York City at the Affinia Dumont Hotel on East 34th Street. However, then you'll miss the collegiate experience as the New Paltz classes are housed in classrooms on-campus. All classes in New Paltz or Manhattan are booked through the office at New Paltz. Both locations keep the same schedule, classes run Fridays through Sundays. Classes start on Fridays from 7 p.m. to 9:30 p.m., Saturdays from 9 a.m. to 5:30 p.m., and Sundays from 9 a.m. to 2:00 p.m. Meals are not provided, but the class does go out to lunch on Saturday, where you'll continue to increase your conversational skills in your new language. You will have to pay your way and I've also been told that lunchtime conversations usually revolve around food.

After class you can stroll down New Paltz's Main Street, to visit the shops. If you collect vinyl, you must stop by **Rhino Records** (*3 Church Street; 845-255-0230*). Located in the same building is **Barner Books** (*3 Church Street; 845-255-2635*), which is a great place for browsing. The village is quite charming and there are tons of interesting shops to occupy your time after class.

If you arrive by car, you can also explore the local vineyards and farms in the area or take a side trip to Rosendale, a funky small town that hosts an annual pickle festival. Explore Rosendale by bike on your personalized bike tour of the region through **Table Rock Tours and Bikes** (*386 Main Street,*

Rosendale; 845-658-7832; www.trtbicycles.com), where you can rent a bike and organize a tour for any size group or simply book an individual tour. The guided service only costs $40 an hour. You also can explore Rosendale's small Main Street.

Maybe you are an adventure seeker? If so, you should head to **Skydive The Ranch** (845-245-4033; www.skydivetheranch.com), just six miles from New Paltz in Gardiner. This reputable school has taken folks like Kristin Davis of *Sex and the City* fame into the skies. They have a program for first dives, and for an additional charge you can get a photo of your first jump. This isn't a quick endeavor, and the ranch asks you to plan on spending your entire day there.

Less than half an hour away, across the Hudson from New Paltz, is the Culinary Institute of America. Are you hopelessly addicted to reading cookbooks and are your drawers filled with so many kitchen supplies that you can't close them? If you answered yes to either of these questions, you should sign up for a **CIA Boot Camp** Saturday class through the Enthusiasts Program at the **Culinary Institute of America** (Continuing Education Office, 1946 Campus Drive, Hyde Park, NY; 800-888-7850; www.ciachef.edu). The program is offered only on Saturdays throughout the school year.

The CIA Boot Camp offers you the chance to learn how to cook in various styles and ethnicities from BBQ to Spanish tapas. The classes start at 7:45 a.m. and end at 4 p.m. You get to experience a day at at one of the country's top cooking schools, housed on a scenic campus. If you can't sneak away for a day at the Institute, they also offer cooking demonstrations and weekend classes at the Astor Center in Manhattan. All classes are booked through the CIA office in Hyde Park. The Web site has an extensive list of all the upcoming Boot Camp classes.

Spend your Saturday night dining at the student-staffed restaurants on the CIA campus. On Saturday nights you have the choice of two restaurants, **American Bounty Restaurant** (845-471-6608) specializing in regional cuisine or **Escoffier Restaurant** (845-471-6608), which is a French restaurant serving dishes from all the regions of France. There is a business/casual dress code for both restaurants and they book up quickly, so make dinner reservations in advance.

You could fill up your Sunday learning about American history in Hyde Park. Start your day strolling through the gorgeous grounds and rose garden at the **Franklin Delano Roosevelt Home and Museum** (4097 Albany Post Road, Hyde Park; 845-229-9115; www.nps.gov) located down the block from the CIA. The museum was once FDR's summer home and is a fascinating look at the life of the influential president and his wife. There is also a museum on the premises and a presidential library. After a few hours here, I realized how much history I had forgotten but by the time I stepped in the New Deal gift shop, I felt as if I had just finished a class on the FDR years.

You can get tickets for the **Val-Kill**, the **Eleanor Roosevelt National Historic Site** *(www.nps.gov)* at Roosevelt's home. After his death, this became Eleanor Roosevelt's home and office. You can take a guided tour of the cottage and also see a short film on Eleanor Roosevelt here. They host various events at Val-Kill during the year, so check the Web site for the schedule.

If you haven't gotten your fill of historic homes, spend the day in the Gilded Age at the **Vanderbilt Mansion** *(www.nps.gov)*. A visit to this gorgeous estate is a lesson in architecture and history.

For those who want to soak in the scenery on a gorgeous walk, you can walk from the FDR Museum to the Vanderbilt Museum through the **Hyde Park Trail** *(311; www.hydeparkny.us)*, which runs along the Hudson River. The dirt path trail is easy to walk. Or if you want to head on to the Hudson to rent a kayak, you might want to take a lesson through the **River Connection** *(9 West Market Street, Hyde Park; 845-229-0595 / 845-242-4731; www.the-river-connection.com)*, which offers guided kayak tours and kayak instruction.

If you are fan of model trains, check out the model trains at the **Hyde Park Station** *(34 River Road, Hyde Park; www.hydeparkstation.com)*, a restored 1914 station that has model trains running throughout the museum. This station is open in the warmer months, so check the Web site for the schedule.

If you feel stuffed from all the food you made at the CIA, spend the afternoon or evening roller-skating at **Hyde Park Roller Magic** *(4178 Albany Post Road, Hyde Park; 845-229-6666; www.hydeparkrollermagic.com)*. Here, you can rent old-school skates or roller blades.

If you really want to feel as if you stepped back in time, during the late spring until the fall you can take in a flick at the **Hyde Park Drive-In** *(4114 Albany Post Road, Hyde Park; 845-229-4738; www.hydeparkdrivein.com)* down the block from the Culinary Institute on Hyde Park's main strip. This family-run drive-in has been in operation since 1950 and features one screen and a building with a fully stocked concession stand and restrooms. There are discussions about closing the drive-in within the next few years, which would be a shame, since so many drive-ins have gone dark in recent years. The drive-in also houses a popular farmer's market from 10 a.m. to 2 p.m. in the warmer months. Show your support and visit.

No trip to the region of Dutchess County is complete without a visit to the charming town of Rhinebeck, only a fifteen minute drive from Hyde Park. Spend the day antiquing and browsing around the shops or keep up with your American history lessons by learning about early aviation at the **Old Rhinebeck Aerodrome** *(Stone Church Road, Rhinebeck; 845-752-3200; www.old-rhinebeck.org)*, located off Route 9, where a large collection of old planes is housed in hangars. From June until October you can take in an air show. If you're really looking for a thrill, you can take a ride on an old biplane, an experience I opted not to do, although it looks like fun. You can also ride in an antique automobile around the aerodrome.

Rhinebeck is also the home to the **Dutchess County Fairgrounds** *(Route 9, Rhinebeck; 845-876-4001; www.dutchessfair.com)*, where many events are hosted annually, from juried craft shows to the state fair.

Places to eat:

Bacchus *(4 South Chestnut Street, New Paltz; 845-255-8636; www.bacchus-newpaltz.com)* I've been going for years to this New Paltz staple for the amazing food and the great atmosphere. The dinner menu is a mix of Mexican food including personal favorites like the Cajun Ahi tuna and fresh avocado quesadilla. The lunch menu has a nice selection of wraps and sandwiches. They recently opened a billiard hall next to the restaurant.

Del's Dairy Creme *(6780 Route 9, Rhinebeck; 845-876-4111)* This seasonal ice cream stand also serves fresh food like salmon with yogurt sauce, hamburgers, and fries. The ice cream is quite yummy and you can sit outside on the picnic benches while you indulge.

Eveready Diner *(Route 9 North, Hyde Park; 845-229-8100; www.theeveready-diner.com)* This kitschy fifties-style diner decorated in neon and silver is known for its pancakes. If you're in the mood for diner fare, this is the place to go. Fresh food and kitschy atmosphere abound. Don't forget to pose for a picture with the impressive statue of a man carrying an oversized coffee cup on your way out.

Main Street Bistro *(59 Main Street, New Paltz; 845-255-7766; www.main-streetbistro.com)* This Main Street favorite serves up breakfast all day. It's a good place to grab a hearty breakfast before you head to your language class. They also serve dinner on weekends and host a pasta night every Friday with an assortment of sauces ranging from vegetarian to seafood.

The Rosendale Café *(434 Main Street, Rosendale; 845-658-9048; www.rosendalecafe.com)* Vegetarians will find themselves with tons of options at this veggie-friendly café. I was quite taken by the tempeh Reuben, which was an interesting spin on the usually meaty sandwich. The homemade soups are also fabulous. The vibe is extremely laid-back and you don't feel rushed, so you can just relax and sip some tea and munch on healthy food. They have a regular schedule of live music in the evenings, so check their Web site for the schedule.

Terrapin *(6426 Montgomery Street, Rhinebeck; 845-876-3330; www.terrapinrestaurant.com)* Housed in an old church, the Terrapin allows you to dine in a more causal bistro or opt for the fancier dining room. The bistro menu has sandwiches, and amazing comfort food like baked macaroni and cheese, while the dining room menu has pastas, meat, and seafood. Both menus include a selection of tapas, with items like yummy goat-cheese-filled wontons. Terrapin is a local favorite and is known for their high-quality food. A definite stop if you find yourself in Rhinebeck and want good food.

Twist *(4290 Route 9, Hyde Park; 845-229-7094; www.letstwist.com)* The woman who ran the Roosevelt Inn suggested Twist for dinner since a former graduate of the Culinary Institute runs it. Twist is open for dinner from Tuesdays through Sundays and serves American fare with such goodies as seared tuna and Thai fish soup. I was impressed with their kids' menu, which treats them like adults, offering salmon with pesto sauce instead of the perennial chicken nuggets.

The Village Tea Room *(10 Plattekill Avenue, New Paltz; 845-255-3434; www.thevillagetearoom.com)* Stop in for some afternoon tea or enjoy a breakfast on their patio. The quaint tearoom is open for all meals and has a menu with items that will appeal to all. The tearoom makes all their baked goods on the premises with antibiotic- and hormone-free eggs. The food is extremely fresh and you can't go wrong with any sweet on the menu. It's also a nice place to study your notes from language class.

Places to stay:

Beekman Arms *(6387 Mill Street, Rhinebeck; 845-876-7077; www.beekmandelamaterinn.com)* This is America's oldest continuously operated hotel. The Beekman Arms is located in the center of town, so you can walk to Terrapin and other restaurants. It is a charming inn—perfect for a romantic getaway. If you have the family with you, they have more family-friendly accommodations behind the inn at the guesthouse, which offers motel-style rooms. They also rent out Rhinebeck's original firehouse, as well as rooms in the historic Townsend House. Be specific about the room you want when booking since there are many options.

Clove Cottages *(200 Rock Hill Road, High Falls; 845-687-4170; www.clove-cottages.com)* A local suggested these High Falls cottages to me. You can rent one of their seven cottages ranging in size from studio to a two-bedroom. Each cottage is stocked with breakfast food. Relax in your own cottage in the middle of the scenic country with hiking trails close by. They are also pet-friendly.

Journey Inn *(1 Sherwood Place, Hyde Park; 845-229-8972; www.journey-inn.com)* This charming bed-and-breakfast is located across from the Vanderbilt mansion. The rooms range in style from Japanese to Italian design. There are two suites available. They offer special rates for students at the CIA Continuing Education programs.

Mohonk Mountain House *(1000 Mountain Rest Road, New Paltz; 800-772-6646; www.mohonk.com)* This 265-room resort is both a stunning site and great destination for a weekend getaway. A popular location for weddings and business retreats, Mohonk has gorgeous grounds. In fact, even if you aren't planning to stay here, you are welcome to hike the trails. There are great hikes on the premises, for every level of hiker. Rooms range in size from a standard room to a suite. Children are welcome and they host a Children Stay Free program for kids under twelve with various activities for families throughout the weekend.

Olde Rhinebeck Inn *(340 Wurtemburg Road, Rhinebeck; 845-871-1745; www.rhinebeckinn.com)* If you want to take a romantic weekend in a more secluded location of Rhinebeck, you should consider staying at this historic inn built in 1745 and owned by the folks who run the Bed and Breakfast on the Park (see page 65) in Park Slope. The inn has four rooms—all with a private bath, including one suite. They offer a "Tiny Wedding" package, where you can rent out the entire inn for two nights and they will host your small weekend wedding.

Roosevelt Inn *(4360 Albany Post Road, Hyde Park; 845-229-2443; www.roo-seveltinnofhydepark.com)* This immaculate fifties-style motor lodge on Route 9 is economical and close to the Culinary Institute of America and all Hyde Park activities. The owners are extremely helpful and friendly. They serve a continental breakfast in their café. The rooms are typical motel rooms with an old-school comfort. The inn is open from March through December.

Golfing in Hyde Park and New Paltz:

Apple Greens Golf Course
161 South Street
Highland Park, NY
845-883-5500
www.applegreens.com
Typically eighteen holes, except after 4 p.m. on weekends when you can only play nine holes. There is a driving range and they also offer golf lessons.

Green Acres Golf
End of Harwich Street
Kingston, NY
845-331-2283
Nine holes and a driving range.

Mohonk Mountain Golf Course
1000 Mountain Rest Road
New Paltz, NY
845-256-2143
www.mohonk.com
Nine holes, a driving range, and a putting green. Lessons are available.

New Paltz Golf Course
215 Huguenot Street
New Paltz, NY
www.newpaltzgolf.net
Nine holes, a driving range, and a putting green. Lessons are available.

Red Hook Golf
650 Route 199
Red Hook, NY
845-758-8652
www.redhookgolfclub.com
A semi-private club with eighteen holes. There are restrictions on tee times for nonmembers.

Side trips:

Millbrook, New York

Travel Time from NYC: 2 hours

Driving directions: Take Millbrook Exit East (US 44) on the Taconic Parkway and follow signs to town center.

Millbrook *(www.millbrooknyonline.com)* is a great stop on your way up the Taconic Parkway to Hyde Park. The charming town is the second home to many of New York's elite and has a high concentration of celebrity country homes. You can either look for celebrities or antiques on Franklin Avenue, their quaint main street.

The best time to visit Millbrook is in the summer, when you can spend an afternoon strolling or picnicking at **Innisfree Garden** *(362 Tyrrel Road; 845-677-8000; www.innisfreegarden.org)*, a 150-acre picturesque public garden influenced by Chinese landscape design, filled with a 40-acre lake and flowers and rocks, making this once private Asian-inspired garden a must visit.

You should also plan a visit to **Wing's Castle** *(Bangall Road; 845-677-9085; www.wingscastle.com)*. Talk about eco-friendly—the owners of this castle built it entirely from recycled materials. Tours of the property are available in the summer. Wing's Castle is adjacent to the **Millbrook Winery** *(26 Wing Road; 845-677-8383; www.millbrookwine.com)*, so you can do a tasting after touring the castle.

See the wildlife at the **Trevor Teaching Zoo** *(131 Millbrook School Road; 845-677-8261; www.trevorzoo.org)*, housed on a boarding school campus. The vibe is extremely laid-back at this zoo, and you can get up-close-and-personal with the animals. I love their nocturnal animal section, housed in a dark room behind a curtain.

If you're stopping in Millbrook for lunch you can eat at my personal favorite, the retro **Millbrook Diner** *(224 Franklin Avenue; 845-677-5319)*, which has old-school jukeboxes at each booth. The food is Greek-influenced and delicious. For a fancier dining experience you can have dinner or brunch at the local favorite, **Charlotte's** *(4258 Route 44, Millbrook; 845-677-5888; www.charlottesny.com)*, housed in a 19th-century church.

Local Events

JUNE
Crafts at Rhinebeck
Rhinebeck, NY
845-876-4001
www.craftsatrhinebeck.com
Also runs in October.

MAY
Woodstock/ New Paltz Arts
and Crafts Fair New Paltz, NY
845-679-8087
www.quailhollow.com
Also runs on Memorial Day
and Labor Day weekends.

JULY
4th of July Great American
Picnic
Rhinebeck, NY
845-876-4001
www.dutchessfair.com

Ulster County Fair
New Paltz, NY
845-255-1380
www.ulstercountyfair.com

AUGUST
Dutchess County Fair
Rhinebeck, NY
845-876-4001
www.dutchessfair.com

SEPTEMBER
Headless Horseman Hayrides
and Haunted House
Ulster Park, NY
845-339-BOOO
www.headlesshorseman.com

OCTOBER
New York State Sheep and
Wool Festival
Rhinebeck, NY
845-876-4001
www.sheepandwool.com

NOVEMBER
International Pickle Festival
Rosendale, NY
845-658-9649
www.picklefest.com

Taste of Hudson
Hyde Park, NY
845-431-8707
www.tastehv.org

Chapter Fifteen

Zen Weekend:

Ananda Ashram, Monroe, New York

Travel time from NYC: 1–1 1/2 hours

Driving directions: I-87 (New York State Thruway) to Exit 16 toward Harriman. Take Route 17 West to Exit 130 and then take Route 208 South toward Monroe. Follow signs to town center.

Public transportation: Short Line Bus (800-631-8405; www.coachusa.com) to Monroe.

Devoted yogis as well as novices are welcome at **Ananda Ashram** (*13 Sapphire Road, Monroe; 845-782-5575; www.anandaashram.org*), run by the Yoga Society of New York. The ashram's beautiful 85-acre lush grounds are the perfect setting for a weekend away. Ananda's weekend schedule involves yoga classes, meditation, and the best vegetarian meals I've ever eaten. The one aspect of Ananda that drew me there and made me love it was its flexibility (and the unbelievable food). You don't have to attend any of the scheduled activities, and instead can just spend the weekend taking hikes around the ashram, using the canoes at their lake, swimming in the pool (open Memorial Day to Labor Day), or just relaxing. When I went, there was a woman who spent the weekend knitting and reading. The only rule on the ashram is that you must be respectful of the meditation of others and pay attention to signs in the houses that indicate whether people are meditating, which means you should be silent. In fact, my friend and I were actually asked to be quiet once, because we didn't realize that a meditation and fire ceremony were in progress within the building.

If you choose to follow the schedule, you are welcome to participate in any of the activities, which are all included in the flat rate. Meals and all other amenities are also included, with the exception of massage and other treatments at their healing center, as well as certain lectures and cultural activities. The delectable vegetarian meals are served buffet-style in the dining hall. Keep in mind you must wash your own dishes! I was happy to see that they have coffee at breakfast as some ashrams forbid caffeine. Although you can only eat meals at scheduled times, the dining hall is open all day and has various breads and tea available in case you get hungry.

If you need Internet access, which I strongly advise against in order to truly realize the stress relieving potential of a weekend at an ashram, there is an office that is open twenty-four hours and offers free use of the computer and Internet. Above the office is a gift shop that sells art, clothing, writings by the founder Shri Brahmananda Sarasvati, music, and other yoga-related items. They also sell bottled water and soy ice-cream sandwiches, which make a great snack when relaxing by the pool or lake.

You don't have to pack much for the ashram. Staple items to bring are comfortable clothes for yoga, a flashlight because the grounds get dark at night, and an alarm clock. Be sure to wear shoes that can be removed easily since you aren't allowed to wear shoes in most of the buildings on the ashram. If you visit in the warmer months, pack bug spray, sunscreen, and a bathing suit. They provide linens and towels for bathing, but don't bring valuables since none of rooms on the ashram have locks or safe boxes.

The weekend program starts at 6 p.m. on Fridays, but you can check in at 3 p.m. to get settled. The first class offered at 6 p.m. is a yoga and sound meditation class, which is a Hatha-style yoga class led by instructor Dalien, a Grammy nominated musician who incorporates music into his yoga practice. The schedule continues with various yoga classes, guided meditations, and cultural activities. The hour-and-a-half yoga classes are offered for all levels. For early risers, they have a gentle yoga class at 7 a.m. on both Saturdays and Sundays. They also have an open yoga class as well as an intermediate/advanced class that can be taken by all levels since they don't pressure you to do all the poses. One of my friends that came with me was pregnant, and my friend was able to modify the poses for pregnancy. There is word that Ananda is actually looking into having a weekend where they offer prenatal yoga workshops and classes.

You don't have to stay an entire weekend and Ananda is also open during the week for those who don't have weekends off. If you opt for a one-night trip to the ashram, you must check in after 3 p.m. and check out by 2 p.m. the following day. All rooms are dormitory-style, which means you have to share a bathroom. If sharing a bathroom is a turn-off (I must admit I was a little suspect at first), don't be deterred; the bathrooms are immaculate and there is a certain amount of respect for one another's space that is customary at the ashram. The housing accommodations are exceptionally clean but they are very sparse, so don't come here expecting to spend a weekend at a spa. In fact when I stayed here, I slept on a bunk bed.

There are two types of rooms on the ashram. One is a same-sex dorm-style room filled with bunk beds for $80 per night on weekends and $70 on weekday nights during the peak season. The other is a private double room with two twin beds, which is slightly more expensive at $100 per night on weekends and $85 on weekday nights during peak season. This is a good option if you are traveling with a friend or partner. You can also pay for the other bed in the private double room and spend the night alone. Camping is the other option, which gets you 20 percent off the dorm rate, but you must bring your own tent and gear.

The ashram tends to get very busy in the summer months, so book ahead. In the winter months, although the grounds get icy and you don't have the amenities of the pool and lake, the ashram is much quieter and you can have more space. The rooms are well heated for the winter so going during all seasons is no problem. Ananda Ashram is not only a great place to visit alone since you can enjoy the serenity of the ashram, but you can also take a friend along like I did. Just keep in mind that if you bring more than one person, you can't get a private room.

Other yoga retreats:

Sivananda Ashram Yoga Ranch *(Woodbourne; 845-436-4692; www.sivananda.org/ranch)* This popular ashram has locations throughout the world. The New York yoga ranch is located in the Catskill region on a former weight-loss resort. Sivananda's schedule is for serious yoga students. Just to give you an example of a typical day at Sivananda; the entire ashram is awakened by a bell at 5:30 a.m. to begin a day of satsang, meditation, and yoga. You must also take part in some chores during your weekend stay. Those that need a caffeine fix will find themselves in a bind, as there is no caffeine served here. That said, people swear by this yoga ranch and come back several times a year for a spiritual retreat. The ashram offers various weekend programs from cooking to specialized yoga practices. Sivananda Ashram has a bus that departs from their Chelsea yoga studio on Fridays for the weekend retreats.

The Tibet House Weekend Programs at Menla Mountain Retreat *(212-807-0563; www.tibethouse.org or 375 Pantherkill Road; 845-688-6897; www.menla.org)* The Tibet House, a Tibetan cultural center, offers weekend workshops in yoga, hiking, and Buddhism at the Menla Mountain Resort in Phoenicia. This 320-acre retreat in upstate New York is the perfect setting for a spiritual getaway; the area around the retreat is an Audubon Society bird sanctuary.

Kripalu Center for Yoga and Health *(West Street, Stockbridge, MA; 413-448-2400 / 800-741-7335; www.kripalu.org)* This popular Berkshires yoga retreat offers various weekend workshops and a year-round retreat-and-renewal program that focuses on yoga and relaxation. You can also take walks and hikes on their gorgeous grounds. For more information, see page 184.

Chapter Sixteen

The Home of Fly-Fishing:

Livingston Manor, New York, and Roscoe, New York

Travel time from NYC: 2–2 1/2 hours

Driving directions: For Livingston Manor, take Route 17 North to Exit 96. For Roscoe, take Exit 94 off Route 17 North.

Public transportation: Short Line bus (800-631-8405; www.coachusa.com)

Welcome to Trout Town, U.S.A.! Livingston Manor and Roscoe are both well known for their amazing creeks for fly-fishing. If you have ever wanted to fly-fish, this is the place to start. Livingston Manor is home to the Catskill Fly-Fishing Center and Museum, located on a stream. In addition to being New York's home of fly-fishing, both towns offer a small-town charm.

Roscoe is all about fly-fishing—on a one-block main street, there are three shops for outdoor gear and fly-fishing. Livingston Manor is cute and funky, with galleries, a large independent bookstore, and a hip coffee shop offering free Wi-Fi. Some of Livingston Manor's Main Street seems better suited for Williams-burg, Brooklyn, than a town that offers fly-fishers some of the best fishing locations in the country. Every June, Livingston Manor hosts the Trout Parade, a kitschy parade that is reminiscent of the early days of the Coney Island Mermaid Parade, which mixes the old-world feel of the town and the new arty life that is popping up.

Places to see:

Fly-fishing season peaks from April through June, although folks still fish throughout the summer and fall. If you've never been fly-fishing, consider signing up for a day at the fishing school **Catskill Flies** *(Stewart Avenue, Roscoe; 607-498-6146; www.catskillflies.com)*, a fly-fishing shop in Roscoe that offers lessons for beginners. A lesson runs about eight hours, from around 8:30 a.m. to 4:30 p.m. The cost of the lesson, $200, includes the rental of all gear. The instructor takes you to the stream and teaches you the basics of fly-fishing. Don't be discouraged if you don't catch a trout on your first outing because it's actually quite a challenge. They also offer intermediate- and advanced-level classes.

If you want to try your hand at fishing, but don't want to commit to purchasing the gear or a lesson, for $40 you can rent all the equipment (rod, reel, boots and waders) from Catskill Flies. Before you start fishing, you must obtain a fishing license (New York State Department of Environmental Conservation; www.dec.state.ny.us), which can be purchased in Roscoe at Catskill Flies, Beaverkill Angler, and the Little Store. The license is $15 a day for New York residents or $19 for a year.

Now that you're a fly-fishing expert, you might find yourself drawn to the **Catskill Fly Fishing Center and Museum** (1031 Old Route 17, Livingston Manor; 845-439-4810; www.cffcm.net). Located on a stream in Livingston Manor, this museum pays tribute to the history of fly-fishing and also to the preservation of the environment. The shop at the museum has lists for local fly-fishing schools and fishing maps.

I asked the salesperson working at the shop, which is filled with every trout and fly-fishing-related book and gift item, if people fish with the intent to kill the trout or to throw them back. She said that unless people were camping and planned on eating the fish, most throw them back since there is a large and popular movement to preserve the waters of the region. Instructors even teach a "catch and release method" of fly-fishing. It was here that I realized that fly-fishing is more about sport than mounting a fish. There is a spiritual aspect to fly-fishing, especially for those who catch and release.

In fact, the organization **Casting for Recovery** (www.castingforrecovery.org) offers fly-fishing retreats to breast cancer survivors, based on the philosophy that "the dynamics of fly-fishing provide a healing connection to the natural world." Simply by watching the fishermen in the creek, you can see their connection to nature and how peaceful it is in this area.

If you want to shop for gear, you should head to the neighboring town of Roscoe, ironically filled with swarms of actual flies in addition to fly-fishing shops. (I've never seen so many flies in my life.) Their small main street, Stewart Avenue, has three outdoor-sporting shops that sell fly-fishing equipment. **Catskill Flies** is the ultimate fly-fishing store; it sells the gear you need to fly-fish, local maps on where to fish, and antique books on angling. On their Web site they link to Yahoo maps that give directions to their favorite local fishing spots.

Next door to Catskill Flies is the **Little Store** *(59 Stewart Avenue, Roscoe; 609-498-5553)*. This shop is both an outdoor-equipment shop and a general store selling everything from hunting gear to toys. I was fascinated by the large collection of toy guns, some of which even came in pink. The shop is filled to the brim with merchandise and you can spend a while just browsing through the eclectic merchandise, and end by walking out with a pair of shoes or a kid's tackle box.

Across the street is **Beaverkill Angler** *(Stewart Avenue, Roscoe; 607-498-5194)*. With a staff of extremely friendly expert fishermen, the shop is an authorized Orvis dealer and sells Orvis fly-fishing tackle. They also have lots of gear to keep a fisherman occupied as well as offering instruction and rental equipment.

The fish in the streams and creeks in this area are abundant. You can't drive down Old Route 17 without passing a creek with a pull-over for parking or seeing a fisherman wading in the water. A popular place to fish is from 26.7-mile long Willowemoc Creek. It runs alongside Livingston Manor to Roscoe and has many prime fishing locations.

For those who want to enjoy nature without wading in the water, Livingston Manor is home to covered bridges like the **Livingston Manor Bridge**, a wooden bridge built in 1860. Or you can spend the day relaxing at the **Livingston Manor Covered Bridge Park** *(39 Covered Bridge Road, Monticello; 845-794-3000)*, where you can view the bridge while you picnic or grill.

If you brought the clubs or a racket, you can golf and pick up a game of doubles at the **Tennanah Lake Golf and Tennis Club** *(100 Fairway View Drive, Roscoe; 888-561-3935; www.tennanah.com)*. Explore the region on bike, renting one from **Cinder Track Bicycles** *(36C Main Street, Livingston Manor; 845-439-4590; www.cindertrackbicycles.net)*. The shop also organizes bike tours. If you need some outdoors clothing or a good book on local hikes or bike rides, chances are you'll find it at **Morgan Outdoors** *(46 Main Street, Livingston Manor; 845-439-5507; www.morgan-outdoors.com)*, located near the Cinder Trail Bikes.

If you're more arty than outdoorsy, you should spend the afternoon browsing around Livingston Manor's Main Street, stopping in at the new home of the **Catskill Art Society** *(48 Main Street; 845-436-4227; www.catskillartsociety.org)*, which has a gallery and gift shop. You can then head to **Hamish and Henry Booksellers** *(34B Main Street; 845-439-8029; www.hamishandhenry.com)*, stopping to peruse the fine selection of literary fiction. The shop has couches and a very cute cat on the premises. Oh, and did I mention the cookies?

Aside from the **Trout Parade** *(www.troutparade.com)* that happens every June and attracts quite a crowd, filling up the streets of Livingston Manor with floats and face-painting booths, there are two summer music festivals nearby.

Every August there is the **Shandelee Music Festival** *(845-439-3277; www.shandelee.org)*, which has been held in Livingston Manor for the past fifteen years.

About thirty minutes out of town is the historic site where Woodstock was held in 1969. Now it's the home to a popular summer concert series at the Bethel Woods Center. There is also the Bethel Woods Museum on the site, which focuses on the history of the 1960s and Woodstock. **Bethel Woods Center for the Arts** *(866-781-2922; www.bethelwoodscenter.org)* hosts concerts ranging from popular music like the Jonas Brothers or Lynyrd Skynyrd to the New York Philharmonic.

Places to eat:

Buffalo Zach's Café *(Old Route 17; 607-498-4149; www.buffalozachs.com)* Decorated in Old Western-style décor, you'd expect this place to serve only BBQ, when, in fact, the menu is filled with healthy wraps and paninis. There are tons of vegetarian options on the menu too, although they do have the staples like hamburgers. Buffalo Zach's Café is open for all meals.

Madison's Stand *(46 Main Street; 845-439-4368)* This cute and casual restaurant situated in the middle of Livingston Manor's Main Street has all the treats you'd love to eat for lunch, including pizza, hot dogs, and chicken wings.

Munson Diner *(18 Lake Street, Liberty; 845-292-1144)* Just a few exits from Roscoe and Livingston Manor off Route 17, is the diner that was made famous by *Seinfeld*. This beloved establishment moved from Manhattan's Hell's Kitchen to Liberty, New York in 2005 and it re-opened in 2007 in its new home. The day I went by it just happened to be closed, so I recommend that you call before going. You can pretend you're George, Elaine, Jerry, or Kramer and yada, yada, yada as you eat the famous Munson burger at a booth by the window.

Peez Leweez *(Pearl Street, Livingston Manor; 845-439-3300; www.peezleweez.com)* The café is quite charming and seems as if you'd find it in the East Village or Brooklyn. Peez Leweez has a lunch menu of comfort food like mac 'n' cheese, quiche, and soup. They also serve beer and wine. Stop in for a coffee and surf the Web on their free Wi-Fi. They also host live music.

Roscoe Diner *(Old Route 17, Roscoe; 607-498-4405)* Also known as the "famous Roscoe diner" since it's a big stop for folks traveling up Route 17, this diner has good-quality diner food and a menu filled with all the diner classics.

Places to stay:

Creekside Cabins *(Roscoe, 607-498-5873; www.creeksidecabins.com)* Spend the night in one of the cabins right near the Willowemoc Creek where you can fish for trout. Cabins sleep two to four people, depending on whether you choose "standard" or "deluxe." They also have a lodge available for rent, which sleeps six.

Roscoe Motel *(2054 Old Route 17, Roscoe; 607-498-5220; www.roscoemotel.com)* This moderately priced motel is a favorite of fly-fisherman, so if you are heading to Roscoe during peak season, you must book ahead. The sixteen rooms all have private baths and refrigerators. They also offer a free continental breakfast. The riverside motel has nice grounds and is family- and pet-friendly.

The Magical Land of Oz Bed and Breakfast *(753 Shandelee Road, Livingston Manor; 845-439-3418; www.ozbandb.net)* This bed-and-breakfast, located in a hundred-year-old home, has seven rooms all decorated in a *Wizard of Oz* theme. Upon entering the B and B, you are greeted by a life-sized Tin Man. You can stay in rooms like the Ruby Slippers Room or the Good Witch Room. All rooms are located on the second floor and share two baths. The owner, Dean, is quite friendly and cooks a traditional country breakfast.

If you really want to get close to nature, you can spend your night in a tent at these campgrounds in Livingston Manor. You can also park pop-up campers or trailers at these sites.

Covered Bridge Campsite *(68 Conklin Hill Road; 845-439-5093; www.coveredbridgecampsite.com)*

Willowemoc Campgrounds *(30 Willowemoc Road; 845-439-4250; www.willowemoccampgrounds.com)*

Side trips:

New Age Heath Spa

Spend a weekend on the lush grounds of the **New Age Heath Spa** *(7491 State Route 55, Neversink; 800-682-4348; www.newagehealthspa.com)*, where you can take yoga classes, eat salads with herbs and vegetables grown at the New Age greenhouses, book some treatments, or relax on the lawn reading a book. There is a two-night minimum stay at this moderately priced spa, which includes all of your meals and activities (except treatments) with rates averaging from around $300 a night. Those traveling alone have the option of keeping costs down by being placed with a roommate in a shared double room.

The appealing part of this spa is that there are activities throughout the day, although nothing is mandatory. There are daily guided hikes around the gorgeous grounds, as well as an indoor and outdoor pool. If there is a breeze, you can't help but hear music from the many wind chimes that are throughout the grounds of the spa. The spa is smoke- and alcohol-free, so prepare to detox. If you want to sweat out your impurities, they offer access to a sweat lodge throughout the year. Ask if it's available when you book your stay. If you don't want to cleanse yourself of caffeine, you get your fix at breakfast only, where they recently began to serve coffee.

If you have ever wanted to try a juice fast, the spa hosts a popular juice fasting program. The tasty food at the spa is also healthy, so those who don't want to subsist purely on juice shouldn't feel guilty about indulging themselves. The menu outlines the calories for each meal to help you plan what to eat.

It's easily accessible by public transportation; you can take the Short Line Bus to Liberty and get a cab to the spa. The office also has information on car services that take guests straight from New York City to the spa.

Camping and RV Rental

Maybe a weekend escape for you consists of camping in the woods. Besides the few places where you can camp in the city *(see page 60)*, there are several places to camp less than an hour from New York City. For a list of area campsites and their amenities, go to the **Reserve America** Web site *(www.reserveamerica.com)* to find various campgrounds and book your camping escape.

If you don't want to bring a tent, many campsites offer accommodations like small cabins and cottages, which are fun and economical getaways. In the heart of the summer, there is a one-week minimum stay in most cabins and cottages. If you do want to bring a tent, but don't have any equipment see information on renting tents in the city *(see page 61)*.

Did you ever want to rent an RV? Despite gas prices, people still enjoy cruising around the country. Since you don't have to pay for a hotel, an RV rental is a unique way to escape for the weekend with your friends. **Cruise America** *(800-671-8042; www.cruiseamerica.com)* offers rentals that can be picked up at JFK airport.

Chapter Seventeen

Ski Weekend:

Windham Ski Resort and Hunter Mountain, New York

Travel time from NYC: 2 1/2 hours

Driving directions: Take I-87 (New York State Thruway) North. For Windham, take Exit 21 and drive West on Route 23 for about 20 miles to the town of Windham. For Hunter Mountain, take Exit 21 off I-87 to Route 32 towards Saugerties. Make left at Route 32 North and continue on Route 32A North to Route 23 West.

Public transportation: See Web sites for Hunter and Windham Mountain for a complete list of bus companies that travel to the ski resorts. There are various bus companies that pick up skiers from locations throughout the Metro area.

Windham and Hunter Mountain offer challenging terrain for all levels of skiers and you don't have to hop on a plane or drive hours to get there. Between the upstate New York weather and the use of man-made snow, there is often more snow coverage here than in New York City. Both mountains offer good skiing conditions. In fact the weekend we went there, we awoke to about three inches of fresh snow and it was the middle of March.

A good way to spend your weekend is to divide your time between the two resorts since they are within a fifteen-minute drive of one another. Your weekend wouldn't be complete without visiting the neighboring town of Tannersville, which complements the ski resorts by providing weekenders shopping at funky shops and post-ski feasting at noteworthy restaurants.

Places to see:

Windham Mountain (Route 23, Windham; 800-754-9463; www.windham-mountain.com). Windham Mountain is open for skiing from mid-November to mid-April and has a total of ten lifts and forty-six trails, including a beginner's area. Windham is the smaller of the two resorts, which seems to appeal to families since all of the trails end at the same place and there is little fear of the kids getting lost. Windham also offers child care for kids ages two and up.

The big appeal of Windham is their night skiing. They have seven trails open for night skiing from 4 p.m. to 10 p.m. on Thursday through Saturday nights, and during select holiday periods. There are also various Terrain Parks, open to both skiers and snowboarders. For adult newbies like myself and for kids over four years old, they have a ski school on the premises. Since Windham is smaller and has more trails for beginners, this is a good place to learn how to ski or snowboard. For those folks who don't own gear, it is available for rent minus the ski outfit. A day of skiing on the weekend, between 8 a.m. and 4 p.m., costs $61, if you just want to ski at night, it costs $31. Kid's lift tickets cost $48 for the day and $31 at night and kids ages six and under are admitted for $10 anytime.

It's good to note that day lockers are available. If you get to Windham before 10:30 a.m., take advantage of their free curbside snow caddy to help bring your equipment from the car to the base lodge. The base lodge offers food, a bar, and a Starbucks to give you that extra energy before you hit the slopes.

For tubing and ice-skating fans, you can to drive over to the **Mountain Top Adventure Park**, which is located right down the road from Windham Mountain—about a two-minute drive. The fun thing about Mountain Park is that they offer night tubing. The Adventure Park has a 650-foot slope with twelve lanes, three lifts for tubing, and a self-contained base lodge. When we went at the end of the season, there were only three lanes open and the slope didn't seem that steep, but it was still a lot of fun. Since the ice-skating rink is outdoors, it is only available in the heart of the winter. In March, it looked more like a pond than a rink. Tubing takes place on weekends: Fridays, 4–10 p.m.; Saturdays and holidays, 10 a.m.–10 p.m.; and Sundays 10 a.m.–4 p.m. Tubing tickets are $17 per person for a two-hour session; all day passes are also available. Kids will also be drawn to the bungee trampoline at the park, which I wanted to go on, but the line was a bit too long.

Hunter Mountain (*Route 23A, Hunter; 800-HunterMTN; www.huntermtn.com*) Hunter Mountain is open to skiers and snowboarders and has eleven lifts and fifty-five trails for skiing from 8:30 a.m. to 5 p.m. A day of skiing for an adult is $59, for young adults ages 13–22, it costs $53, and for kids ages 7–12, it costs $40. They offer ski lessons for all levels throughout the day. If you need a brush-up on your ski skills or want to go to the next level, head to their learning center at the left of the base lodge to attend a lesson. All equipment is available for rental, except you must bring your own ski outfit. Hunter offers child care for kids ages six months and up and ski school for ages four and up. Hunter also offers snowboarding lessons using Burton's Learn-to-Ride program.

Hunter Mountain is a larger than Windham and attracts more advanced skiers due to the harder trails. Token-operated day lockers are available in their base lodge. The base lodge has a bar and restaurant, where you can hang out and take a break from skiing. I was surprised how laid-back everyone was with their ski and snowboard equipment, leaving it outside the lodge unattended while they hung out inside. Hunter has a friendly vibe and the bar was hopping when we were there, although I should mention that it was St. Patrick's Day weekend.

Hunter has snow tubing on the premises, which we enjoyed. The snow tubing area has its own lodge with a snack bar and restrooms. The parking is a bit removed from the ski area. There are up to nine chutes, each nearly one thousand feet long. In March, there were only three in operation, and it was very relaxed. There are two tube tows that haul you back to the top. There is a minimum height requirement of 42 inches and it costs $18 for two hours.

The great thing about Hunter is that it remains open when ski season is over and offers rides on the lifts for hikers and for those who just want to sit back and enjoy the view. They also host popular events like the TAP New York Craft Beer Festival—a festival of microbrews from New York that takes place in April—and an Oktoberfest in October. All events attract large crowds and sell out quickly. If you do decide to stay in the region during the off-season, take advantage of the easy one-mile long hiking trail, just a few miles from Hunter Mountain, to see the beautiful two-tiered 260 foot waterfalls (the highest in NY State) at Kaaterskill Falls . The area has trails for all levels. This is a popular tourist attraction and the trail tends to get quite crowded on the weekends. Parking is located on Route 23A, there is a pull off and entry to the hike.

Just to note, the roads in this area get pretty dark at night, so be mindful of deer making their way across the narrow streets. I mention this because we hit a deer on Route 23A. Be especially alert at both dawn and dusk when deer tend to be most active. Also deer rarely travel alone, so if you see one deer in the road, chances are that others will follow.

After a hard day of skiing or snowboarding, you might want a massage. Book a treatment at the **Windham Spa** (5369 Main Street, Windham; 518-734-9617; www.thewindhamspa.com) if you are sore from skiing or you'd just like to be pampered while your partner hits the slopes. This spa is the local favorite, located in the heart of Windham.

For some time off the slopes, head to the village of Tannersville. This small village has cute homegoods shops and restaurants. It's definitely worth a stroll and is a great place to head for a meal after a day at either Hunter or Windham. All shops are located within a few block radius and there is ample parking.

Places to eat:

Black Diamonds Grill *(6550 Route 23-A, Tannersville; 518-589-5444)* This restaurant is the closest to Hunter Mountain and is a local favorite. If you like steaks and seafood, this is for you. It's a good place to refuel and have a drink before hitting the slopes the next day.

Catskill Mountain Country Store and Restaurant *(5510 Route 23, Windham; 518-734-3387; www.catskillmtcountrystore.com)* This quaint country store has table service for folks in need of delicious baked goods or exceptional pancakes, and it has a menu filled with everything from eggs to wrap sandwiches. I had a hard time trying to decide what to eat because everything looked so fresh and appealing. This is the ideal place to grab breakfast before you hit Windham's slopes since it's right down the block from the resort. The restaurant is open for breakfast and lunch from 8 a.m. to 4 p.m. on Saturdays and from 8 a.m. to 3 p.m. on Sundays. The shop also sells cute home goods and educational toys.

Last Chance Antiques and Cheese Café *(602 Main Street, Tannersville; 518-589-6424; www.lastchanceonline.com)* The owner of this funky shop and restaurant was born and raised in Brooklyn, and he offers some of the best comfort food I've ever tasted. Their menu is eclectic, but cheese is their main focus. These folks are so serious about cheese that you can even get a knish covered in cheese. Their cheese fondue for two was exceptional, but it's so much food it could serve four. If you're a fan of chocolate, you must save room for the s'mores, which you can make at your own table, or try their chocolate fondue. For your road trip home, check out the chocolate and assorted candies in the shop. They also have an extensive beer list. This isn't the best place for folks on a diet; bring the family and your appetite.

Pancho Villas *(3087 Main Street, Tannersville; 518-589-5134)* With typical Mexican fare from burritos to quesadillas, this restaurant has a fun vibe and also tons of vegetarian options, which will make any vegetarians you may be traveling with very happy.

Village Bistro *(6033 Main Street, Tannersville; 518-589-5855)* If you're in need of a good burger after a day in the snow, this place is a favorite of locals and skiers alike.

Places to stay:

Catskill Lodge *(350 Route 296, Windham; 518-261-7150; www.catskill-lodge.com)* Located a mile and half from Windham Mountain is a family-run seven-room Victorian bed-and-breakfast that has the vibe of a fun, laid-back, ski share house rather than a traditional B and B. It attracts a friendly twenty- and thirty-something crowd that they cater to by offering amenities like a hot tub and a PlayStation that can be played on a projection screen in the common living room. The dining room has bookshelves filled with cool reads, including my favorite kitsch classic by Linda Goodman, called *Love Signs*. Catskill Lodge also offers DVDs that you can watch on the large screen or in the privacy of your own room as all rooms have DVD players. Three of the rooms have private baths and the other four have shared baths, but the rooms and the shared bathroom are located right next to each other and can be sectioned off with a curtain and turned into two-bedroom suites. We stayed in the only room on the first floor, which was conveniently located next to the living room, and so can be a bit noisy. However, if you don't want to miss out on any fun, this is the room for you. Aside from their yummy breakfasts, another great thing about the lodge is that you don't have to look for any local nightlife since the lodge is filled with such friendly folks. Catskill Lodge offers ski packages at Windham Mountain.

The Winwood Mountain Inn *(5220 Route 23, Windham; 518-734-3000 / 800-754-9463)* If you have the kids in tow or if you're not a fan of dragging your gear across the Windham parking lot, you can stay at the lodge owned by Windham Mountain. All rooms at the lodge have private baths and there are also suites, which are ideal for families. There is no additional charge for kids under thirteen. If you need a larger space, there are condos and private homes available for rental through the lodge's concierge service. Kids will be happy to know they have a movie theater and a game room at the main lodge to enjoy after your day at the slopes. The appeal of this lodge is that they have a shuttle that takes you and your gear to Windham Mountain. The Winwood Mountain Inn houses a great restaurant, Trails End Tavern and Grill, which is a nice place to pick up some food or have a drink, even if you aren't staying at the lodge.

Albergo Allegria Bed and Breakfast *(43 Route 296, Windham; 518-734-5560; www.albergousa.com)* For a romantic weekend, this B and B offers romance packages and rooms and suites with private baths at reasonable rates. Families or larger groups might want to stay at their other properties in Windham, including a cottage and farmhouse.

Kaatskill Mountain Club *(Hunter Mountain; 800-HUNTERMTN; www.KaatskillMtnClub.com).* If you'd like to stay close to Hunter Mountain, book a room at the new and luxurious Kaatskill Mountain Club. The mountain club is a time-share resort, where you can rent out everything from a studio to a three-bedroom apartment. They have amenities like a gym and a unique outdoor pool that is so heated it can be used even on the coldest day. There is also a spa on the premises so you can get a facial after a day in the cold brisk air. The Kaatskill Mountain Club is also a popular place to get married. I was surprised to hear that in the summer, couples have their guests take the ski lift up the mountain to get off and see them get married at the top. If you want more privacy or a larger space, you can rent out a condo at Lifeside Condominium Village through the Kaatskill Mountain Club.

Chapter Eighteen

A Funky Small Town

Hudson, New York: Art, Antiques, and Fine Dining

Travel time from NYC: 2–2 1/2 hours

Location: I-87 (New York State Thruway) North to Exit 21 toward Route 23/Catskill. Make left at CR-23B and make another left to merge onto Route 23 East.

Public Transportation: Amtrak (800-USA-RAIL; www.amtrak.com) to Hudson.

This quirky little town is one of the easiest and most relaxing escapes for a city dweller. It's only two hours away on Amtrak, and the station is located right near the center of town. You can enjoy browsing at the local antique shops and step out into the arty nightlife, and you won't even need a car. Book a room at one of the local bed-and-breakfasts and you'll feel as if you're staying at a friend's country house for the weekend.

Once an old whaling village and prosperous city, Hudson later fell into decline during the late 19th century, becoming a hotbed of prostitution, gambling, and corruption, and was even the focus of a book, *Diamond Street: The Story of the Little Town With the Big Red Light District*, by Bruce Edward Hall. In the 1980s antique dealers and New York artists started to set up shop in Hudson, and once again it's seeing a renaissance. Hudson is home to many noted artistic residents. Hudson itself is stunning; the town lies along the water and the eclectic architecture is from the Federal, Victorian, and Greek Revival styles as well as many other early forms of American architecture. Many buildings have been or are in the process of being restored. Just a simple walk through the town and a look at all of the buildings will impress any visitor.

Places to see:

The best way to see Hudson is by foot. Hudson's main drag is Warren Street, which houses tons of galleries, antique shops, and restaurants. Pick up a book and a beer at the **Spotty Dog Books and Ale** *(440 Warren Street; 518-671-6006; www.thespottydog.com)* or stop by the **Hudson Opera Company** *(327 Warren Street; 518-822-1438; www.hudsonoperahouse.org)*. This cultural center is one of the oldest surviving theaters in America. The opera company hosts readings, concerts, and other cultural and artistic events and workshops. Check out their schedule before planning your trip to Hudson to see if they have afternoon or evening events.

After an afternoon of gallery-hopping, shopping, and sipping herbal tea from **Verdigris Tea** (*13 South 3rd Street; 518-828-3139; www.verdigristea.com*), I was honestly falling in love with Hudson. I even spent a few minutes gazing at old Victorian homes in the window of the local real estate office trying to talk my husband into relocating.

Take advantage of Hudson's scenic waterfront and hop aboard **Hudson Cruises** (*Water and Ferry Streets; 518-822-1014; www.hudsoncruises.com*) to take a sightseeing tour of Hudson's lush landscape that was inspiration for many artists. They also offer thematic cruises like murder mystery events and lighthouse tours, but some of these events sell out quickly, so you must book them in advance. This cruise is conveniently located at the Waterfront Park, a short walk from the center of town.

Hudson's infamous Diamond Street was renamed Columbia Street, and instead of houses of ill repute, the block is filled with edgy art venues and my personal favorite, **Vasilow's Confectionary** (*741 Columbia Street; 518-828-2717*), an award-winning chocolate shop. Vasilow's was originally started in Hudson in 1923 by two brothers, but it closed in 1969. A grandson of one of the original owners, Jim Vasilow, reopened the business using the original chocolate recipes, just a few blocks from the original location. It's well worth a visit. Despite opening as recently as 1999, the building and chocolate factory feels timeless and the chocolate is memorable. Farther along Columbia Street is **Time and Space Limited** (*434 Columbia Street; 518-822-8448; www.timeandspace.org*), a former bread factory converted into an arts and performance center. TSL houses a theater with vintage 1940s theater seats where they screen independent films, host literary readings, theatrical productions, and other art-related events, like their popular opera series which features the Metropolitan Opera performances on the big screen. Call or check out their Web site for a calendar of events to see what's happening while you are there.

If you want to take in some theater, **Hudson's Stageworks** (*41-A Cross Street; 518- 822-9667; www.stageworkshudson.org*), once a 40,000-square-foot factory which might have been used for candle-making, was transformed in 2004 into an equity theater offering the dramatic arts to the folks of Hudson.

The **Hudson Farmers Market** *(North 6th and Columbia Streets; www.hud-sonfarmersmarketny.com)* runs from May to mid-November on Saturdays from 9 a.m. to 1 p.m. and offers you the chance to head home with some of the region's freshest food without having to do any farming of your own.

A bit off the main road, there is the impressive **FASNY Fire Museum of Firefighting**, *(117 Harry Howard Avenue; 877-347-3687; www.fasnyfiremu-seum.com)*. The museum is free and is open 10 a.m. to 5 p.m., seven days a week, with the exception of Thanksgiving, Christmas, and Easter. This place is great if you have kids with you, since it houses a large collection of fire trucks, both antique and modern. They also have a children's section with exhibits on fire safety. And yet you don't have to be a kid to like fire trucks and be interested in seeing their enormous collection of firefighting memorabilia. I must admit that I went without my children. My husband and I had a great time hopping aboard various fire trucks and looking at the way the equipment progressed over the past three hundred years. They also have a tasteful 9/11 tribute and a nice gift shop where you can buy firefighting-related merchandise.

Drive or call a car service to **Olana** *(5720 Route 9G; 518-828-0135; www.olana.org)*, a Moorish house that was once home to 19th-century artist Frederic Edwin Church. This is a must-see in the area and the historic home will impress even those who aren't interested in painting and home décor. Church's paintings decorate the walls of this home, which in itself is a work of art. Located on a scenic hillside overlooking the Hudson River, Church designed the landscaping around the property, where his artistic influence is clearly present. He even carved out areas on the Olana's grounds where one can set up one's canvas and paint the landscape.

Don't miss the film about the history of Olana in the visitor center, explaining the details of the years of work Church put into working on this home and how obsessive and driven he was to realize his idea of a Persian-style home in the Hudson Valley. The grounds offer incredible views of the Hudson Valley but the house can only be viewed on a guided tour.

Places to eat:

There are many restaurants on Warren Street in Hudson, from classic diners to restaurants offering high-end cuisine, but here are a few that I was able to sample during my stay.

Ca' Mea Ristorante *(333 Warren Street; 581-822-0005; www.camearestaurant.com)* For delicious Italian food at a place that seriously impressed a food snob like me, head to Ca' Mea. With their fresh pastas and tons of Italian staple dishes, it's sure to please all.

Da Ba *(225 Warren Street; 518-249-4631; www.dabahudson.com)* Fans of high-quality food will enjoy dining in a restaurant that seems straight out of Manhattan. The menu has monkfish, risotto, and many eclectic meat dishes.

Mexican Radio *(527 Warren Street; 518-828-7770; www.mexrad.com)*. Check out the Hudson Valley outpost of this NYC Mexican restaurant that is extremely kid-friendly and has a jovial atmosphere.

Swoon Kitchenbar *(340 Warren Street; 518-822-8938; www.swoonkitchenbar.com)* Foodies will love dining at this restaurant that is run by a married couple who left Manhattan's culinary world to open this gem in the Hudson Valley. The menu features dishes made with fresh, regional ingredients.

Places to stay:

There aren't many hotels or motels near Hudson, so a bed-and-breakfast, guesthouse, or inn is your best option. You can also camp at nearby **Lake Taghkanic Park** *(1528 State Route 82; 518-851-3631; www.reserveamerica.com)*, located eleven miles from the city of Hudson. If you'd like to stay at a B and B or inn, there is an area Web site with photos and reviews at *(www.stayinhudson.com)*.

Country Squire *(251 Allen Street, Hudson; 518-822-9229; www.countrysquireny.com)* We stayed at this bed-and-breakfast run by Paul Barrett, a friendly and accommodating ex-Manhattanite whose five-room B and B has all of the amenities that a city weekender might need, like wireless Internet access, private baths with claw-foot tubs, as well as a hearty breakfast. The Country Squire is also child-friendly, which is nice perk for a B and B.

Side trips:

If you're looking for a day trip on the way to Hudson, stop at one of these two art centers in the Hudson Valley Region. Head into Beacon, New York, to visit this up-and-coming artist haven with a main street filled with coffee shops and art galleries. Take Exit 17 off I-87 and follow the signs to Beacon. Spend the day at **Dia:Beacon, Riggio Galleries** *(3 Beekman Street, Beacon; 845-440-0100; www.diabeacon.org)* and stroll the galleries of this large contemporary art museum in a historic 300,0000-square-foot space that was once a Nabisco factory.

After the museum, head across the bridge over the river to Orange County to explore the sculpture garden at **Storm King Art Center** *(Old Pleasant Hill Road, Mountainville; 845-534-3115; www.stormking.org)* and have a picnic lunch of the grounds of this lush park where nature and art meet. Storm King has sculptures from famous artists like Henry Moore and Alexander Calder. Having a picnic lunch here, surrounded by sculptures, it beats eating at the rest stops along I-87. To return, you can access I-87 just a few miles from Storm King and continue on your way to Hudson.

Local Events in Hudson

JUNE
Flag Day Parade
518-828-1030
www.cityofhudson.org

DECEMBER
WinterWalk
518-822-1438
www.hudsonoperahouse.org

OCTOBER
ArtWalk
518-671-6213
www.artscolumbia.org

Chapter Nineteen

It's All about the Resort and Driving the Track

The Poconos

Travel time from NYC: 1 1/2 hours

Driving directions: I-80 West to Exits 309–298.

Public transportation: Greyhound bus (www.greyhound.com; 800-231-2222)

If you thought the Pocono Mountains were only filled with resorts that sported heart-shaped tubs and larger-than-life champagne glasses where couples can bathe in the moonlight, think again. The Poconos, located an hour and half from New York City, has a homey spa, an indoor water theme park, a casino, waterfalls, a 30-acre flea market, a racetrack where you can actually get behind the wheel, and, of course, some heart-shaped tubs. It's a great all-season destination and is easily accessible from the city—making it a perfect combination for a quick weekend escape.

Places to stay:

Deerfield Spa *(650 Resica Falls Road; East Stroudsburg, PA; 800-852-4494; www.deerfieldspa.com)*

Driving directions: I-80 West to Exit 309.

Public transportation: Greyhound bus *(www.greyhound.com; 800-231-2222)* to Stroudsburg/Delaware Water Gap. Cabs from the bus stop are available through WGM Car Service *(570-223-9289)*.

This destination spa is open from April until late October and is an unbelievable find for New Yorkers looking for a weekend escape that will invigorate them without breaking the bank. A two-night minimum stay at Deerfield ranges from $360 to $520, depending on room size. The rate includes all meals, countless fitness classes, guided hikes, nightly entertainment that ranges from tarot card readings to bingo, full use of the facilities, and the best "mocktails" I've ever tasted.

The spa's laid-back appeal makes it feel like a summer camp for adults, and you will feel at home the minute you walk through the door. The owner is Joan Wolff, who inherited the spa from her mother. She spends weekends there and often gives guests the kind of personal attention that is sometimes missing from many luxury spas. The staff is extremely friendly and the fitness instructors were very helpful in addressing my various exercise-related questions. It is the attentiveness of the staff that explains why the spa has a loyal following of guests that return every summer—some for more than ten years and others since the spa's opening in 1981—to relax and meet up with old friends.

The twenty-two rooms in the spa hold just over thirty people, giving it a very intimate appeal. At meals, spa-goers sit together at tables chatting and by the end of my two-day stay at Deerfield, my friend and I had met a bunch of people. The weekend I was there, the other folks at the spa were mostly women ranging in age from thirty-five to sixty-five. However, the clientele varies to include girlfriends getting away, mothers and daughters, and city folks coming alone. There were two men there, but they were far outnumbered. The spa definitely has a feminine touch—from the white wicker furniture to the beds adorned with decorative pillows.

The spa is housed in an old inn and the two fitness studios are located in a converted barn, where guests can choose from a menu of fitness classes. The heated pool, hot tub, and sauna are available all day. Although Deerfield is a spa, the accommodations are more like those you'd find in a nice bed-and-breakfast rather than a luxury spa. The air-conditioned rooms range from twin beds in a double room with a private bath to single rooms with a shared bath in the hall. They also have a cottage annex next to the inn near the pool, where we stayed, that is a bit pricier. This particular option is great for friends who are sharing a room since the cottage, with its full and king size beds and private baths has a lot more space than the rooms in the inn.

My friend and I took advantage of the spa treatments during our stay. Although the massages, facials, and wraps are housed in basic treatment rooms, there isn't a designated treatment spa facility. My massage, facial, and seaweed wrap were excellent and by breaking up my Saturday with various treatments in between fitness classes, I felt both relaxed and energized. If you want to bring the spa lifestyle back home, you can always head to the spa's shop, Frieda's Frocks, open from 3 p.m. to 5 p.m., to pick up some reflexology sandals and scrubs.

There is no pressure to do anything at Deerfield. You can simply spend the weekend in one of the two hammocks reading a book or just relaxing in the pool. The spa does focus on encouraging proper eating and many come here for their excellent weight-loss program, in which you can tailor your meals by calorie content. You place an order for all your meals the night before, circling your choice of entrees with a mini pencil on a printed menu. The menu offers various entrees and daily specials, all with printed calorie counts, and offers everything from tasty vegetarian meals to delicious baked fish. If you aren't there to diet, you are encouraged to order side dishes or even double portions.

If you want to get moving and start losing weight, begin your day with a morning stretch, yoga, or a sunrise hike followed by a day immersed in physical activity. A typical day at Deerfield is filled with guided hikes, power walks, and fitness classes. They have a wide range of classes offered like Yo-Wei (a yoga class that incorporates weights into the practice), chair aerobics, and pool aerobics, which was much harder than I thought. There are usually two fitness classes to choose from at all times during the day. Due to space limitations you must sign up for some classes in advance, like the Pilates Reformer class. If you haven't stepped on a scale in a while, on Saturday mornings, they offer to take your blood pressure and weight, but this like everything at Deerfield, is optional. Deerfield also offers helpful fitness lectures that address topics like smart snacking.

On Saturday night before dinner, they had a Mocktail Hour, during which my friend and I sat on the porch overlooking the main road eating healthy appetizers and drinking virgin sangria. It was fun and as moms who never get a chance to hit the gym, we felt happy about getting back into circuit training and yoga—activities that busy New Yorkers often put aside. Relaxed from the spa treatments and enjoying the fresh country air, we talked about how we wished we'd discovered this spa sooner and planned the next time we could sneak away for a weekend at Deerfield.

Great Wolf Lodge *(1 Great Wolf Drive; 800-768-WOLF; www.greatwolf.com)*
Driving directions: I-80 West to Exit 298.

Public transportation: Greyhound bus *(www.greyhound.com; 800-231-2222)* to Mount Pocono. Cabs for the 4-mile distance from the bus stop to Great Wolf Lodge are available through Roadrunner Taxi *(570-839-1500)* or Ace Taxi *(570-894-1500)*.

You don't have to head to Florida to spend the winter in 84-degree weather watching your kids splash around on a waterslide. In the Great Wolf Lodge, kids and adults can enjoy the 78,000 square-foot indoor water park (open for guests of the lodge only), which is kept at a warm 84 degrees year-round. After you drive up the windy road to the lodge, which looks as though it was constructed from Lincoln logs, head into the main lobby, where you are greeted by the energy of families strolling about in swimsuits. Look up and you'll see the large animated clock tower that actually puts on a show three times a day. Within minutes of surveying the area, you will realize that you have just entered a kid's wonderland.

Any parent will be pleased with the thoughtful design of the lodge's schedule of activities; your kids can be happily occupied all day. Pick up a copy of *Lodge Life*, a daily paper that lists all the day's activities. From pajama dance parties to bedtime stories by the fireplace, there is something to entertain children of all ages. In the summer, the lodge has an outdoor pool and volleyball court complete with a sandy floor to simulate a visit to the beach. In the winter, they simulate a winter scene complete with a snowfall lasting a few minutes in the lobby. They also have a 7,000-square-foot arcade with classic video games and skee ball that opens at 7:30 a.m. for your early risers and stays open until 10 p.m. each night.

Both kids and adults will love the MagiQuest game located throughout the lodge. At the MagiQuest shop on the second floor, parents can purchase high-tech magic wands that the kids can decorate. Once the wands are decorated, it's time to activate their power: the kids or adults go to a booth for MagiQuest training school, where you learn how to use the wand and choose your quest from the Quest Master. Afterward, kids are invited to go around the resort trying to fulfill their quests. There is a TV station at the lodge that teaches kids tips for succeeding at the MagiQuest game. The wand and game together cost $25, which is not included in the price for the weekend.

There are 401 rooms at the lodge and there are ten different types of suites. The Web site lists floor plans and photos of each suite to help you plan for your stay. There is an Aveda spa and a large fitness center on the premises, so the needs of the parents who are also staying for the weekend are not forgotten. The Starbucks in the lobby is also a welcoming sign for exhausted city parents who need to revive themselves after countless hours at a water park.

You get free unlimited access to the water park with your stay at the Great Wolf Lodge. The food on the premises isn't very pricey for city folks but a helpful tip is to bring in some outside food since all rooms are equipped with a mini fridge and microwave. You can also head down the road to the many reasonable restaurants near the lodge. There are deals for the lodge offered throughout the year, so check their Web site to try and get a promotional deal, which can often get you deep discounts for a night's stay. Another option is to book a large suite and share it with another family. The one caveat is that the large suite only comes with six passes to the water park; however if you have little ones under two, they don't need a pass to join in the water fun.

This is truly a great weekend escape for city kids and their parents. I was also a fan of the idea of an indoor water park because you don't have to lather your kids with sunscreen and you can always return to your room for naps. The only issue I can take with this resort is that I wasn't able to enjoy it when I was a kid.

Mount Airy Casino *(44 Woodland Road; 877-MT-AIRY1; www.mountairycasino.com)*

Driving directions: I-80 West to Exit 298.

Public transportation: Greyhound bus *(www.greyhound.com; 800-231-2222)* to Mt. Pocono. Cabs to Mount Airy are available through Roadrunner Taxi *(570-839-1500)* or Ace Taxi *(570-894-1500)*.

If you're a child of the seventies and eighties and grew up in the New York metropolitan area, you will probably recall the commercial for the "beautiful Mount Airy lodge" where all you had to bring was "your love of everything." The commercial offered scenes of loving couples playing tennis, embracing on a ski lift, and enjoying meals in the lavish dining rooms. Sadly the beautiful Mount Airy lodge no longer exists, but the good news is that they built a resort on the lush grounds of the old lodge.

The new Mount Airy Casino is a state-of-the-art hotel that feels more like Foxwoods than a Poconos resort. Although state laws prohibit table games such as poker or blackjack, the resort's casino is filled with every variety of slot machine that I've ever seen, including those that allow you to play poker and other popular table games on their computer screens. However, if you love gambling and you're not a fan of slots, you might find yourself disappointed at this casino.

The legendary Mount Airy golf course was under renovation while I was at the casino, but is slated to re-open in the spring of 2009. The Mount Airy Casino opened fairly recently, so the places have a modern design and all of the 188 rooms are either deluxe or suites. If you don't want to spend the day in your room, you can head to the beautiful Spa at Mount Airy, which offers an extensive menu of spa treatments from reflexology to serenity oil wraps. For dining and nightlife, the casino offers four restaurants as well as a nightclub called Gypsies. They are also in the process of expanding the resort to include an Olympic-size swimming pool among other amenities.

Although I was disappointed that I never got to spend a romantic weekend at the original beautiful Mount Airy Lodge, I did enjoy visiting this hotel and casino. It's a modern hotel with amenities that appeal to city folk and it's close to many of the Pocono Mountains attractions. If you don't want to stay at the type of Poconos resort where they try to sell you timeshares, this is a great weekend escape for you. I'm sure if the gaming laws of Pennsylvania change, this place is going to be a popular destination for many more New Yorkers who don't want to travel as far as Atlantic City or Connecticut to enjoy a casino.

Caesars Pocono Resorts *(800-432-9322; www.caesarspoconoresorts.com)* See their Web site for locations and directions to all of their resorts throughout the Pocono Mountains region.

Thankfully the honeymoon resorts of the Poconos still exist. In fact there are three Caesars resorts in the Poconos—all of which offer amenities that couples might enjoy, like the heart-shaped pools and fantasy suites. If you're a fan of kitsch and want a fun weekend, head to these resorts for your romantic escape.

The resort closest to the city is the Pocono Palace in Marshall's Creek. This resort has suites available where you can bathe in a seven-foot-high champagne glass for two in a room decorated with Roman columns. You can also book the Fantasy Apple suite where you can enjoy a private pool and a heart-shaped whirlpool bath for two in your own room. If you want to feel secluded from the world, try booking a room at the Garden of Eden suite that offers no windows but bright red carpets and a red-trimmed heart-shaped tub. If you're at a loss for fun Valentine's Day plans or have an upcoming anniversary, you can't beat this unique experience. Check the Web site for online virtual tours of all the suites, so you can choose the one that suits you and your partner.

Side trips:

Located off Exit 298 near the Deerfield Spa and the Pocono Palace at Caesars is the **Pocono Bazaar** *(Route 209 North, Marshall's Creek, PA; 570-223-8640; www.poconobazaar.com)*, a 30-acre flea market open year-round on Saturdays and Sundays. Both the indoor and outdoor areas of this enormous flea market sell everything from pickles to antiques. You can easily spend an entire morning walking around and sifting through old comics and new merchandise at this larger-than-life flea market. There are over one thousand vendor spaces at this market. We've visited this flea market throughout the year; it is quieter in the colder months, but due to the ample indoor space, it still attracts many vendors.

If you love candy, then you must take a ride down Route 209 to the largest candy store I've ever seen. The **Country Kettle** *(2523 Milford Road,*

East Stroudsburg; 877-553-8853; www.country- kettle.com) has aisles of wooden barrels filled with every candy you could think of. Choose from this large variety of sweets as you fill up your plastic bag with goodies. The Country Kettle calls itself one of the largest shopping attractions in the Poconos, filled with loads of candy and a good selection of candles and other gift items. When I'm in the Poconos, I always stop by this candy store to fill up a bag of treats for the ride home. If you're heading to or returning from Great Wolf, this candy haven is just off of Exit 298 and is a must-stop if you have kids in tow.

If you need to work off all the extra energy from the sugar at the Country Kettle, drive along 209 North until you'll see signs for **Bushkill Falls** *(Bushkill Falls Road; 570-588-6682; www.visitbushkillfalls.com)*, called the "Niagara of Pennsylvania." You can take a short walk to view the 100-foot main falls or enjoy more extensive trails throughout the woods to see even more falls. There are other activities to do at the falls like play a game of miniature golf, view an exhibit on Native Americans, ride a paddleboat, or buy yummy fudge.

Ride the Track at the Pocono Raceway

If you ever wanted to drive a race car on an actual racetrack that holds annual NASCAR races, head over to the **Stock Car Racing Experience at Pocono Raceway** *(877-786-2522; www.877stockcar.com)*, which offers lessons on stock car racing. They offer a variety of stock car driving programs that allow you to choose the number of laps and provide personal coaching, and also instruction in ProKart racing. If you want to ride in a race car but don't want to drive, you can take laps around the raceway with an instructor and enjoy the fast ride without the responsibility.

Seasonal Events

APRIL
Earth Day at Bushkill Falls
Bushkill, PA
570-588-6682
www.visitbushkillfalls.com

AUGUST
Pocono Garlic Festival
Shawnee on Delaware, PA
610-381-3303
www.poconogarlic.com

Pocono State Craft Festival
Stroudsburg, PA
570-476-4460
www.poconocrafts.com

OCTOBER
Pocono Timber & Balloon Festival
Shawnee on Delaware, PA
570-421-7231
www.shawneemt.com

Chapter Twenty

Kitsch and Antiquing in the Country:

New Hope, Pennsylvania, and Lambertville, New Jersey

Travel time from NYC: 2 hours

Driving directions: For New Hope, take New Jersey Turnpike South to Exit 14 and merge onto I-78 West. Take Exit 29 to I-287 South. Take Exit 17 to merge onto US-206 South toward Flemington. Make a left onto Route 31 (US-202 South). Exit onto PA-32 South toward New Hope.

For Lambertsville, from Route 31 (US 202 South), exit onto Route 29 toward Stockton/Lambertsville and make a left onto Alexauken Creek Road.

Public Transportation: Take Transbridge Bus from Port Authority (610-868-6001; www.transbridgebus.com) to New Hope, PA.

New Hope and Lambertville are neighboring towns. Despite being located in different states, you can easily get from New Hope to Lambertville by simply walking across the bridge that connects the two. Although they are located next to each other they have completely opposite vibes. New Hope's Main Street is a flavorful mixture of historic restaurants, cool cafés, and shops with a hippie feel. Lambertville's streets are lined with antique shops, high-end home-goods stores and galleries. New Hope hosts events like the annual Miss Gay Pennsylvania USofA pageant, a beauty pageant for drag queens (www.missgaypausofa.com) at the Eagle Firehouse Ballroom, while Lambertville hosts the annual family-friendly and stroller crowded Shad Fest on their cobble-stoned side streets to celebrate their local fish. New Hope is loud, and Lambertville is much quieter. Together these towns complement each other quite nicely. Neither is overwhelming and combined together, there is something that will appeal to every type of city folk looking for a fun getaway.

Places to see:

Start your Saturday morning at **Rice's Market** *(6326 Greenhill Road, New Hope; 215-297-599; www.ricesmarket.com)*, a 30-acre outdoor market that dates back to 1860. Located on an old country field that was originally a farm owned by Mr. A. L. Rice, Rice's is filled with everything from Amish goods to discounted brand-name clothes to pets. On our trip, we had to drag my daughter away from the vendor who was selling bunnies. The grounds are gorgeous and you feel as if you're in a timeless country market.

Although the market is outdoors, there are bathrooms on the premise. Rice's is open on Tuesdays from 7 a.m. to 1:30 p.m. and Saturdays from 7 a.m. to 1 p.m., from March until December. Get to Rice's early since many vendors leave by 1 p.m. Rice's is a bit hard to find since it's off a quiet country road, so just watch for the signs, which are small but posted near the site. Located about ten minutes from the heart of New Hope's Main Street, it's a worthwhile excursion.

If you want to visit a flea market that specializes in antiques, head over to the **Golden Nugget Market** *(1850 River Road, Lambertville; 609-397-0811; www.gnmarket.com)*, held on Wednesdays and weekends from 6 a.m. to 4 p.m. This market has a totally different vibe than the Rice Market. Bustling with tables of antique dealers, it has everything from furniture to comic books. Although the Golden Nugget is open year-round, it's much quieter off-season. The market is in its prime in the summer, with hundreds of vendors outside as well as an indoor area of permanent vendors.

A new addition to the Golden Nugget is a green market, where you can get fresh produce, flowers, poultry, and baked goods. If you're hungry and want to sit down for a meal, there are two restaurants at the market, which is convenient since the Golden Nugget is about two miles from town and a bit removed from the main shopping areas of New Hope and Lambertville.

Once you head back to New Hope, you can fill a day window-shopping and browsing the galleries of New Hope, as well as Lambertville. Although the towns are separated by a bridge, it's an easy walk across. You can easily explore both towns in an afternoon. You can start by shopping on New Hope's Main Street at the local independently owned shops. While there are many places where you can pick up a bobble-head doll or a funny T-shirt, there are also a great number of boutiques that sell tasteful home goods.

A favorite shop of mine is **Heart of the Home** *(28 South Main Street, New Hope; 215-862-1880; www.heartofthehome.com)*, carrying fine American crafts from jewelry to stunning pottery. I can also get lost in the aisles of

Farley's Bookshop *(44 South Main Street, New Hope; 215-862-2452; www.farleysbookshop.com)*. Dotted with restaurants and funky shops, I always like to refer to New Hope's Main Street as "Manhattan's Christopher Street in the country." In short, shopping in New Hope is fun.

For antiques and a quieter shopping experience, walk over the bridge to New Jersey. Lambertville, filled with historic brick row houses and cobblestone streets, is very reminiscent of Greenwich Village or brownstone-lined Brooklyn. On my last trip to Lambertville, they were celebrating Shad Fest and the streets were filled with vendors. It gave this small town a carnival-like atmosphere.

Stroll down Bridge Street, which is the street you'll reach when you walk across the bridge from New Hope, and stop by the many galleries that give this town its arty edge. On Bridge Street, you'll find **Hass Gallery** *(71 Bridge Street, Lambertville; 609-397-7988; www.haasgallery.com)* that offers paintings of Buck's County, France, and other original oil paintings. There are tons of galleries around Lambertville; visit the website for the Lambertville Area Chamber of Commerce for a complete list at *(www.lambertville.org)*.

Sneak down Klines Court, a side street off Bridge Street, where you'll find **Buck's County Dry Goods** *(5 Klines Court, Lambertville; 609-397-1288)* selling an eclectic selection of clothes, furniture, and hip pieces for the home. You can always score a deal on cute dresses or sweaters for men. I've picked up everything from bags to prints for my apartment at this store over the years. If you are a fan of board games, you must walk a few doors down to the **Missing Piece** *(15 Klines Court, Lambertville; 609-397-3999; www.tmppuzzles.com)*; this shop is crammed full of board games and puzzles for all ages.

Head back to Bridge Street and visit the interesting shops like the **Lime Boutique** *(49 Bridge Street, Lambertville; 609-397-3100)* for gorgeous lingerie and other women's wear in this historic-home-turned-boutique. If you'd like to find a retro-cool handbag, stop by the **Mix Gallery** *(17 South Main Street, Lambertville; 609-773-0777)*, where you can get a vintage bag. The owner is an expert on vintage bags and is fascinating to talk to.

There are other ways to spend your weekend in New Hope besides shopping; you can rent a bike at **New Hope Cyclery** *(404 York Road, New Hope; 215-862-6888; www.newhopecyclery.com)* and cycle on the **Delaware and Raritan Canal and Towpath** *(609-924-5705; www.dandrcanal.com)* along the Delaware Canal. You can access the path in Lambertville on Bridge Street past the **Lambertville Station Restaurant** *(11 Bridge Street; 609-397-8300; www.lambertvillestation.com)*. Lining this 70-mile park that runs through scenic towns like Frenchtown, N.J., are various locations where you can launch small boats, canoes, and kayaks. Check the Web site for a list of launch locations as some include moderately priced canoe rentals.

For those who want to sit back and enjoy a ride on the Delaware River, **Coryell's Ferry Historic Boat Rides** (*22 South Main Street, New Hope; 215-862-2050*) offers a forty-five-minute ride in a paddlewheel boat, available from May until September. Pick up tickets at **Gerenser's Exotic Ice Cream** on Main Street.

You can also take a scenic steam or diesel locomotive trip through the countryside on the **New Hope and Ivyland Railroad** (*32 West Bridge Street, New Hope; 215-862-2332; www.newhoperailroad.com*). They offer a fifty-minute trip in either first class or coach on these fully restored historic trains. They also have holiday-themed trips and a dinner ride. This is a great family excursion.

Right across the tracks from the New Hope and Ivyland Railroad station is the new **James Michener Art Museum** in New Hope (*Union Square at Bridge Street; 215-862-7633; www.michenermuseum.org*). This 5,000-square-foot satellite facility of the popular Doylestown museum has revolving exhibits as well as a permanent exhibit on "The Artist Among Us" that pays tribute to the artists of New Hope and its cultural past.

To absorb the beauty of the region, you should spend an afternoon at **Bowman's Hill Wildflower Preserve** (*1635 River Road, New Hope; 215-862-2924; www.bhwp.org*), located a couple of miles south of New Hope on the scenic Route 32. In fact if you have time, you should take a longer drive along Route 32 which is an extremely picturesque ride parallel to the Delaware River. Bowman's has over a hundred acres of more than a thousand species of trees, plants, flowers, and wildlife. You can pick up a trail map and a birding checklist at the visitor center. Birders will love both the Sinkler Bird Observatory in the auditorium of the visitor center where there are windows overlooking bird feeders that attract many species of birds. The Platt collection of birds, eggs, and nests is also located in the lower level of the visitor center. The preserve is open year round. Daily guided one hour long tours take place at 2 p.m. from mid-March through October.

If you're still in the mood to shop, then visit **Peddler's Village** (*Routes 202 and 263; 215-794-4000; www.peddlersvillage.com*) in Lahaska, about a ten-minute drive from downtown New Hope. This colonial-themed shopping center has restaurants, an inn, and a carousel. They also host various events throughout the year and I'll admit that my husband and I signed up for their pumpkin-pie-eating contest at the Scarecrow Festival. The specialty shops at Peddler's Village are filled with unique items for your home and are a great place to pick up holiday gifts. If you have kids in tow, you must visit Giggleberry, a Chuck E. Cheese–style restaurant, play space, and game room that houses a gorgeous, fully restored 1922 carousel. For those in need of upscale dining, check out Earl's Prime. Fans of kitsch should book a table at the Peddler's Village Dinner Theater at the Peddler's Pub in the Cock 'n' Bull Restaurant.

For even more shopping on the way back home from your getaway, discount shoppers are drawn to **Liberty Premium Outlets** *(1 Church Street; 908-782-8550; www.premiumoutlets.com)* in Flemington, New Jersey. These outlets maintain over sixty shops including Izod and the Gap, among other name brand stores.

You could also spend the day outside of New Hope and Lambertville by taking advantage of gorgeous Buck's County. For the adventurous who have dreamt of riding in a hot-air balloon at sunrise, head to **Balloon's Aloft** just a half hour from New Hope in Pittstown, New York, at the Sky Manor Airport *(48 Sky Manor Road; 866-800-4FUN / 908-996-3333; www.njballoon.com).*

If you would like to escape the summer heat, try tubing just eight miles north of New Hope at **River Country** *(2 Walters Lane, Point Pleasant; 215-297-5000; www.rivercountry.net).* Here you can rent kayaks, tubes, canoes, or rafts to spend the day on the Delaware River. River Country advises that you make reservations in advance, since they are often busy and cannot guarantee space for walk-ins.

If you're in the mood for a spooky night, then join the **Ghost Tours of New Hope** *(215-343-5564; www.ghosttoursofnewhope.com)*—a nighttime walking tour led by a guide carrying a lantern that takes you to New Hope's most haunted spots. The tour meets on Main and Ferry Street at 8 p.m. on Saturdays from June through November. In the month of October the tour also meets on Fridays, and, of course, on Halloween. There are no tours on the 4th of July or over Labor Day weekend.

For fans of the theater, a trip to New Hope wouldn't be complete without taking in a play at the well-respected **Buck's County Playhouse** *(70 South Main Street; 215-862-2041; www.buckscountyplayhouse.com).* Transformed from a gristmill to a theater in the 1930s, the playhouse shows plays and musicals. They also have a children's theater with a line of kid-friendly productions shown during the mornings and afternoons. It's interesting to note that many famous actors have performed on their stage, from Grace Kelly to Merv Griffin. After the theater stop in for a drink at **Havana** *(105 South Main Street, New Hope; 215-862-9897; www.havananewhope.com).* Havana also host concerts with performers like Loudon Wainwright.

Places to eat:

Karla's *(5 West Mechanic Street, New Hope; 215-862-2612; www.karlas-newhope.com)* Dine outside in this European-style restaurant with a full menu of options for both meat lovers and vegetarians. They offer a yummy Sunday brunch, but that doesn't mean you have to wait to grab a delicious frittata from their lunch menu.

Martine's Restaurant *(14 East Ferry Street, New Hope; 215-862-2966)* Enjoy the view of the river or dine near the fireplace at this New Hope staple.

Wildflowers *(8 West Mechanic Street, New Hope; 215-862-2241; www.wild-flowersnewhope.com)* This is the place I keep returning to when I head to New Hope. They specialize in Thai, Mexican, and American food including a few pesto-flavored options on the menu. Beyond pesto, I'm a sucker for any menu that has fondue and they have both on their eclectic menu. In the warmer months, you can even dine by the stream. Although the ambiance is romantic and quiet, they are extremely kid-friendly.

The Full Moon Cafe *(23 Bridge Street, Lambertville; 609-397-1096; www.cafe-fullmoon.com)* Dinner at the Full Moon Cafe is only served when there is a full moon, and if your birthday also happens to fall on one, you get a free meal. The lunch menu serves up everything from cheese fries to smoked turkey Reubens. They also have a good selection of salads.

Places to stay:

New Hope's 1870 Wedgwood Inn *(111 West Bridge Street, New Hope; 215-862-2570; www.wedgwoodinn.com)* The Wedgwood Inn is housed in a re-stored Victorian "painted lady." This historic inn is romantic, charming, and immaculate. The scrumptious breakfast can be eaten in the dining room or it can be served to your room. This is a well-run bed-and-breakfast; in fact, the owners run a bed-and-breakfast school for those who are interested in start-ing their own B and B. For an additional fee, there is available access to the pool and tennis club, just a mile from the inn. The inn is in walking distance of New Hope's Main Street.

Side trips:

Cool places to bring the kids

Just because New Hope is filled with tons of things adults find fun and relaxing like fine restaurants and shopping, doesn't mean you can't plan a kid-friendly excursion to the area. Of course you can spend the day at **Giggleberry's** in Peddler's Village, but here are some other family side trips.

Sesame Place (100 Sesame Road, Langhorne, PA; 215-752-7070; www.sesameplace.com) Located less than thirty minutes from New Hope, Sesame Place is a wonderful option for the under-six set. With tons of amazing shows, water rides, and a daily parade of your favorite costumed characters, it's a wonderful day trip from New Hope. I will admit that lines do get long here, so come prepared with items to keep your little ones entertained. Try to attend any of the available shows, all of which are very entertaining. The Elmo's World show fills up quickly, so get on line for that one early and you won't regret it. My children were amazed to see Elmo in the flesh. Since the majority of the rides and activities at Sesame Place are water-related, you should plan your visit during the summer months. You can have meals with your favorite Sesame characters, but again, book the event in advance. There are kid-friendly chain hotels near Sesame Place, although lodgings are a bit hard to find in and around New Hope and Lambertville.

Crayola Factory (30 Centre Square, Easton, PA; 610-515-8000; www.crayola.com) A little less than an hour from New Hope is the Crayola Factory where kids can spend the day engaged with interactive exhibits and art projects. Although this isn't the actual plant that manufactures the crayons and markers, kids get to learn how they are made through their educational exhibits.

Pine Creek Golf (394 Route 31, West Amwell, NJ; 606-466-3803; www.pinecreekgolf.com) Just fifteen minutes from New Hope is one of America's largest miniature golf courses. They have two eighteen-hole courses on a gorgeous landscaped property. Relax and absorb the beautiful scenery as you play golf. This isn't the type of miniature golf course that's filled with tacky figurines; instead it is almost like playing in a garden or a real golf course. City kids will love being surrounded by nature while they golf.

Local Events in New Hope and Lambertville

JANUARY
Lambertville-New Hope
Winter Festival
www.winterfestival.net

APRIL
Shad Fest in Lambertville
609-397-0055
www.lambertville.org

MAY
Strawberry Festival at
Peddler's Village
215-794-4000
www.peddlersvillage.com

AUGUST
The New Hope
Automobile Show
215-862-5665
www.newhopeautoshow.com

SEPTEMBER
Scarecrow Festival at
Peddler's Village
215-794-4000
www.peddlersvillage.com

NOVEMBER
Apple Festival at
Peddler's Village
215-794-4000
www.peddlersvillage.com

DECEMBER
Christmas Festival at
Peddler's Village
215-794-4000
www.peddlersvillage.com

Chapter Twenty-One

Seasonal Festivals and Great Hikes:

Great Barrington and Lenox, Massachusetts

Travel time from NYC: 2 hours

Driving directions: For Great Barrington, take I-87 (New York State Thruway) North to Exit 5 onto Central Park Avenue towards White Plains. Make left to merge onto Sprain Brook Parkway North. Continue onto Taconic State Parkway North and make right onto CR-10. Make a left onto CR-27 and a right onto CR-11 and finally a right onto Route 23. For Lenox, take I-87 (New York State Thruway) North to Exit 21A toward I-90 East. Take Exit B3 and make right onto Route 22 toward New Lebanon. Make left onto Route 958, which becomes Route 102 (State Line Road). Make left at Swamp Road and a slight right onto Lenox Road.

Public transportation: Peter Pan Bus Lines (888-751-8800; www.peterpanbus.com) to Main Street in Great Barrington.

Every summer, music fans flock to the Southern Berkshires to visit Tanglewood, the summer home of the Boston Symphony Orchestra. But there is a lot more to do and see in Lenox and Great Barrington than summer concerts. The area is home to scenic hikes, skiing, a yoga retreat, world class spas, farms, notable restaurants, great shopping, and is mired in literary history. You can easily fill up any weekend enjoying the Berkshires or you can relax and soak in the mountainous views that surround you in these picturesque towns. The Southern Berkshires is an all-season getaway that will refresh city folk.

Places to see:

If you want to spend your weekend outdoors, there are many great hikes and walks in the area. For some creative inspiration, writers and artists might like to hike up **Monument Mountain** (*Route 7 between Great Barrington and Stockbridge*). The three-mile hike is immersed in literary history: At the start of the hike is a sign that tells the story of when Herman Melville and Nathaniel Hawthorne hiked up the mountain to have a picnic. On the way they were caught in a rainstorm and had to hide out in a cave, and their talk while waiting out the storm inspired Melville to write *Moby Dick*. There is a trail map at the start on the hike, as well as a picnic table and parking area.

If you don't want to go uphill or want a gentle hike or walk, consider spending the day at the **Pleasant Valley Wildlife Sanctuary** *(472 West Mountain Road, Lenox; 421-637-0320; www.massaudubon.org)*, which has trails for all levels of hikers. Those who usually spend their weekends on pavement as I do will enjoy the thirty-minute walk to Pike's Pond where they can observe otters in their natural habitat. You must register when you enter the main building and there is a nominal charge to hike around the grounds.

There are great hiking trails in Lenox at **John Drummond Kennedy Park**, right off of Lenox's Main Street. You can hike, ski, or bike in the park. I obtained a map of the trails at the wildlife sanctuary. If you want to rent a bike or skis, stop by the **Arcadian Shop** *(91 Pittsfield Road, Lenox; 413- 637-3010; www.arcadian.com)*, an outdoor specialty shop that rents everything from tents to GPS equipment. Their Web site also has a map of Kennedy Park's trails.

If you want to be a part of nature, but aren't a fan of hiking in the woods, head to Stockbridge and spend the day at the gorgeous **Berkshire Botanical Garden** *(Routes 102 and 183; Stockbridge; 413-298-3926; www.berkshirebotanical.org)*, which has lovely grounds and a wonderful children's garden. They also host various events throughout the year.

For those who just want to relax and shop, there is much to see in Great Barrington, Stockbridge, and Lenox. These are quaint towns with a timeless appeal where you can very easily spend an afternoon exploring, whether it's leafing through books at their independent bookstores or sipping tea in their cafés. Also, don't miss Lenox's Housatonic and Church Streets, which are filled with galleries that sell everything from jewelry to antiques.

Great Barrington is the largest of the three picturesque villages. Main Street is filled with toy shops, cool boutiques, and great restaurants. If the Monument Mountain hike inspires you to start your first novel, you might want to set up shop at the **Fuel Coffee Shop** *(286 Main Street, Great Barrington; 413-528-5505)* and grab a coffee while taking advantage of their free Wi-Fi. If you'd like to hike, but came unprepared, head to **Barrington Outfitters** *(289 Main Street, Great Barrington; 413-528-0021; www.barringtonoutfitters.com)*. They have a great collection of hiking boots, sturdy walking shoes, and outdoor attire. My personal favorite is the **Soco Creamery** *(5 Railroad Street; 413-528-9420; Great Barrington / 26 Housatonic Street; Lenox; 413-637-9192; www.sococreamery.com)*, which serves up exceptional homemade ice cream.

If you'd like to spend the weekend museum-hopping or if you need to seek refuge from bad weather as we did, head to the **Norman Rockwell Museum** *(9 Glendale Road, Stockbridge; 413-298-4100; www.nrm.org)*. This impressive museum has the world's largest collection of Norman Rockwell paintings. Rockwell lived and painted in Stockbridge from 1953 to 1978. When you enter you can see the Rockwell's painting of Stockbridge. From the painting you can see how Stockbridge's Main Street has remained incredibly unchanged from a half century ago. Younger visitors like myself might also be shocked to see how influential Rockwell was in American politics. When I was there, they had an exhibit of correspondence between Rockwell and Kennedy, Eisenhower, and Nixon. Looking at Rockwell's *Saturday Evening Post* covers will make you feel as if you stepped back in time. I left the museum with a better appreciation of Rockwell's work.

If you have children, you must stop at the exceptional **Berkshire Museum** *(39 South Street; 413-443-7171; www.berkshiremuseum.org)* in Pittsfield, which is a five-minute drive from Lenox. This interactive museum allows kids to explore touch pools, dig for dinosaur fossils, create conceptual art, and learn about the environment and wildlife of the Berkshires. The museum's extra large gift shop is located down the block from the museum and has an extensive collection of educational toys and unique gifts for all ages. When it was time to leave, I had to literally drag my kids from the museum.

Parents and American history fans might also want to visit **Hancock Shaker Village** *(1843 West Housatonic Street, Pittsfield; 413-443 0188; www.hancockshakervillage.org)* about ten minutes from the Berkshire Museum. This restored Shaker village allows a glimpse into the life of the Shakers. At the village, you can do many things like tour a traditional home or school. You can even see a demonstration of Shaker crafts. Kids will love the discovery room where they can try using a kid-sized loom or have their picture taken in Shaker clothes. The grounds are quite lovely and I was just taken with the idea of being on a farm and seeing the cows mooing in the pasture.

In the summer, fans of Herman Melville can tour his house, **Arrowhead** *(780 Holmes Road, Pittsfield; 413-442-1793; www.mobydick.org)*, in Pittsfield, where he wrote *Moby Dick*. Although the museum is open until 4 p.m., the last tour is given at 3 p.m. For the near future, you can tour the **Mount** *(2 Plunkett Street, Lenox; 413-551-5111; www.edithwharton.org)*, which was the summer home of Edith Wharton. The stunning home and gardens were designed by the author and reflect her impeccable taste. Since the museum has had some financial concerns, they may be forced to close. Yet there is a huge campaign to save the Mount, so it may be open for visits after all. Call the museum or check the Web site before visiting.

Two historic homes to tour in Stockbridge are the **Naumkeag** and the **Mission House** *(978-921-1944; www.thetrustees.org)*. Both homes are open from Memorial Day until Columbus Day. Naumkeag was built in 1885 and was the summer cottage for the Choate family. Stroll their Chinese Garden and the eight acres of landscaped gardens. The Mission House was built in 1740 and is decorated with colonial-era furniture.

The reason so many spend the summer weekends in the Southern Berkshires is for **Tanglewood** *(297 West Street; 617-266-1200; www.tanglewood.org)*, the summer music festival, and the summer home to the Boston Symphony Orchestra. From late June until the end of August, you can listen to music and picnic on the lawn at Tanglewood. You can opt for tickets inside the Koussevitzky Music Shed or you can purchase lawn tickets, which are considerably cheaper.

Tanglewood hosts classical, jazz, and pop festivals throughout the summer, as well as a program for children called Tanglewood for Kids, offering free lawn tickets for kids under twelve and a Kid's Corner on Sundays at noon before afternoon concerts and during open rehearsals on Saturdays. In the Kid's Corner, children can try their hand at musical arts and crafts projects.

Fans of theater will enjoy the year-round **Shakespeare and Company** *(70 Kemble Street, Lenox; 413-637-3353; www.shakespeare.org)*, which performs both Shakespearean plays as well as other theatrical productions. In the summer months they have outdoor performances at their Bankside festival. They also offer a popular children's series for kids ages five and up.

In addition to music and theater, you can enjoy a summer-long dance festival in Becket, Massachusetts, about thirty minutes from Tanglewood at **Jacob's Pillow** *(358 George Carter Road, Becket; 413-243-9919; www.jacobspillow.org)*. Various dance companies perform each year at this festival, which had its first showing in 1933. In addition to watching dance performances, you can dine at the Pillow Café, the Pillow Pub, the Tea Garden, or you can picnic at the festival. They also offer a family-friendly dance series. Check the site for their eclectic dance lineup.

For other nightlife you can head to **Club Helsinki** *(284 Main Street, Great Barrington; 413-528-3394; www.clubhelsinkiweb.com)* to listen to bands or spend the evening listening to a concert at **The Lion's Den** *(30 Main Street; 413-298-5545; www.redlioninn.com)* at the historic Red Lion Inn located in Stockbridge.

If you'd like to take in a day of yoga or have a massage, you should drive over to **Kripalu Center for Yoga and Health** *(West Street, Stockbridge; 413-*

448-2400 / 800-741-7335; www.kripalu.org), which offers a day pass for $100 to their Retreat and Renewal workshop. The Retreat and Renewal workshop focuses on yoga and on health and wellness. The program runs from 8 a.m. to 8 p.m, although you'd get the most benefit out of Kripalu if you visit for an entire weekend. The Kripalu Center offers various weekend workshops from women's retreats to writing weekends; look up upcoming workshops and events on their Web site. The overnight accommodations range from a dorm room to a private room with a bath. When I was there I learned that the Kripalu Center is in the process of building more housing with rooms that have private baths. But in the meantime, if you'd like your own room, you should book early. The weekend rates include all activities and food, including yummy vegetarian options offered in their dining hall.

I wasn't quite expecting the institutional feel of Kripalu, but the grounds and views from the rooms make up for the center's lack of charm. There is hiking available around the grounds and Kripalu also offers healing services, like the Ayurvedic sinus treatment and the Kripalu deep-tissue massage. You can sign up for a treatment without having to attend any of the Kripalu events. It's also the perfect place to cure yourself of a cell-phone addiction, as Kripalu discourages the use of mobile devices.

For those who would like to indulge, book a long weekend at **Canyon Ranch** (165 Kemble Street; 800-742-0900; www.canyonranch.com) in Lenox. There is a three-night minimum to stay at this well-respected luxury spa. The spa is extremely high-end and the services are limited to folks staying at the spa. If you want to be pampered, splurging at the ranch is well worth it.

Cranwell Resort Spa and Golf Club (5 Lee Road, Lenox; 800-272-6935; www.cranwell.com) offers overnight accommodations, including full use of their spa. The golf course is open to the public, so even if you don't stay there you can take advantage of playing eighteen holes on their picturesque course. They also host a golf school. If you decide to spend a weekend at Cranwell, you can sign up for their bike tours and hikes. They have rental bikes on their grounds. Those who just want to spend the day at the spa can indulge in their day spa packages, but note that the packages aren't available on Saturdays, although individual treatments are still available off the spa menu.

Skiers love coming to Great Barrington for **Ski Butternut** (380 State Road; 413-528-2000; www.skibutternut.com). This ski resort offers twenty-two downhill ski trails, one hundred and ten skiable acres, ten lifts, and a professional ski school. They also offer five lanes for tubing.

During the fall you can go apple-picking at **Windy Hill Farm** (686 Stock-

bridge Road; 413-298-3217) in Great Barrington. You can also take advantage of the **Great Barrington Farmer's Market** from mid-May until the end of October on Saturdays from 9 a.m. to 1 p.m., at the corner of Taconic Avenue and Castle Street, at the historic railroad station.

Train lovers shouldn't miss the **Berkshire Scenic Railroad** *(413-637-2210; www.berkshirescenicrailroad.org)* in Lenox, open from Memorial Day to Columbus Day. At the museum, you can get tickets to ride a diesel locomotive to either Lee or Stockbridge. Both trips offer narrated tours from a uniformed conductor.

Places to eat:

Baba Louies *(286 Main Street, Great Barrington; 413-528-8100; www.babalouiespizza.com)* With locations in Great Barrington and Hudson, New York, Baba Louies's wood-fired pizza can be made on sourdough or wheat-free spelt bread. I opted for the sourdough and was not disappointed. This place is quite popular, so you should get there at 5 p.m. when they open to avoid long lines—although I'll admit the wait is well worth it.

Bizen Sushi Bar and Japanese Restaurant *(17 Railroad Street, Great Barrington; 413- 528-4343)* If you're looking for Manhattan-quality sushi in the Berkshires, this is the place. Make a reservation on the weekends, as it gets crowded.

Chocolate Springs Café *(55 Pittsfield Lenox Road, Lenox; 413-637-9820; www.chocolatesprings.com)* Just thinking about this place makes me salivate. They have high-quality chocolates and many chocolate-dipped goodies like biscotti and cinnamon sticks. They also have an extensive tea menu, but you might want to opt for the extremely rich hot chocolate. If you're a fan of chocolate, you will think you are in heaven.

Main Street Café *(40 Main Street, Stockbridge; 413-298-3915)* A casual restaurant in Stockbridge with an American-fare menu, the Main Street Café is probably the best place to get a meal if you have your kids with you. I was impressed with the quality of food and the great service.

Martin's Restaurant *(49 Railroad Street, Great Barrington; 413-528-5455)* This is the place to have breakfast in Great Barrington. Sip some coffee and order one of their scrumptious omelets. They also have lunch and serve homemade soup.

Once Upon a Table *(34 Main Street, Stockbridge; 413-298-3870; www.once-uponatablebistro.com)* Located on a mews, this intimate restaurant has a menu that will satisfy all diners, with lunch entrees that include a delicious grilled Alaskan salmon burger and gnocchi. They serve both lunch and dinner.

Xicoh Ten Catl *(50 Stockbridge Road, Great Barrington; 413-528-2002)* This Mexican restaurant's name is pronounced "Shi-koh-ten-cat." Great-tasting food with nice outdoor seating makes a great combo. According to the menu, their Especial Mole Poblano was featured on the Food Network's *Emeril Live*. They offer tons of vegetarian options, and the food was extremely flavorful. I was also taken by the inexpensive kid's meal.

Places to stay:

There are many chain hotels in Lenox and Great Barrington that offer good rates. I stayed at a chain hotel, which was cost effective and adequate. However, if you want more of a romantic weekend, you can book a weekend at one of the places below.

The Old Inn on the Green *(Route 57, New Marlborough; 413-229-7924; www.oldinn.com)* I can understand why a certain friend who happens to be a chef has been coming to this inn in New Marlborough for years. The grounds are stunning, the rooms are decorated with antiques, and the inn is perfectly charming. If you'd like to be in the center of things, this probably isn't the place for you since you can't walk to any of the shops and it's about six miles from Great Barrington.

However, if you love historic elegance and superb food you'll enjoy your weekend at what was once an old stagecoach relay station. You have the option of staying in one of the five rooms at the Old Inn, which houses the restaurant, or you can stay in one of the six spacious rooms the in Thayer House, a few steps from the Inn facing the Green. In the summertime you can have your dinner on the outdoor terrace. Foodies will truly enjoy dining at their well-respected restaurant.

The Red Lion Inn *(30 Main Street, Stockbridge; 413-298-5545; www.redlion-inn.com)* Stay in a place that was in one of Norman Rockwell's paintings. The Red Lion Inn is a Stockbridge institution and is over two hundred years old. Even if you don't stay the night, it's worth a visit to dine in their restaurant and relax on their front porch. They also offer great off-season rates.

Stonover Farm Bed and Breakfast *(169 Under Mountain Road: 413-637-9100; www.stonoverfarm.com)* When I told a friend I was writing this book, she told me I must include this luxurious B and B. In fact you can walk to Tanglewood from the Stonover Farm Bed and Breakfast, a 100-year-old Berkshire "cottage" turned quaint bed-and-breakfast with three suites. If you don't want to stay at the bed-and-breakfast, they also have two other properties available to rent on the grounds' 10 acre property, a restored Schoolhouse Suite and the four room Rock Cottage. The schoolhouse is a restored 1850 schoolhouse perfect for a romantic weekend with a fireplace and a Jacuzzi for two. The Rock House is ideal for families since it has a master suite and twin beds for the kids.

Side trips:
Millerton, NY: The Scenic Way Home

This town was picked as one of the "Top Ten Coolest Small Towns in America" by *Budget Traveler* in 2007. On the border of Connecticut and Massachusetts, Millerton *(www.millertonny.com)* is a great stop on a leisurely way home from the Berkshires. The ride from Great Barrington to Millerton is quite scenic and takes on you on many roads that offer various antiquing opportunities. While in Millerton, stroll Main Street and grab a bite to eat at the retro, silver-paneled **Millerton Diner** *(19 Main Street; 518-789-3480)*. Walk down Main Street and browse through the large selection of books and CDs at **Oblong Books and Music** *(26 Main Street; 518-789-3739; www.oblongbooks.com)*. You should also visit the many unique shops, some of which offer hand-blown glass and jewelry.

If you have your bike easily accessible, you can cycle to the town of Wassaic on the **Harlem Valley Rail Trail** *(518-789-9591; www.hvrt.org)*; the 10.7 mile ride can be accessed from the trailhead on Main Street. You can actually see the trailhead from the Millerton Diner since it's across the street. The uninterrupted trail ends at the Wassaic train station. There you can catch the MetroNorth train to Grand Central Station making it a convenient day trip for city goers. At the moment the trail runs from Wassaic to Millerton, but they are expanding the trail to a 46-mile bike trail that goes from Dutchess to Columbia counties. The expansion of this trail housed on the abandoned Upper Harlem train line is currently in development.

Chapter Twenty-Two

Beaches, Part 1: Long Island, New York

Travel time from NYC: Varies according to location on Long Island

Driving directions: For the Hamptons, follow Long Island Expressway or Southern State Parkway to their ends and then follow signs. Long Beach is off the Loop Parkway, which can be reached from the Meadowbrook Parkway. Jones Beach is located at the end of the Meadowbrook Parkway.

Public transportation: All locations are accessible by Long Island Railroad (718-217-5477; www.lirr.org). Hamptons entries are also easily reached by the Hampton Jitney (212-362-8400; www.hamptonjitney.com).

From surfing to celebrity stalking, it can all be done on Long Island. Plan a weekend escape to Montauk and feast on fresh lobster from Gosman's Pier or take a day trip to Long Beach for a surf lesson. There is much fun to be had on this beautiful stretch of land with its gorgeous pristine beaches. Since you can take either a day trip or weekend excursion to Long Island, it works within everybody's budget and time constraints. Many parts of the island are accessible by public transportation and in fact on Fire Island you can't even bring a car, so this is a great trip for those who want to be eco-friendly.

Long Beach

In less than an hour's train ride from Penn Station, you can be dropped off in the middle of Long Beach and only a few blocks from their amazing surf and immaculate sandy beaches. I must admit that I do favor Long Beach over other beaches since my parents have been living here for over fifteen years and I've spent countless weekends on the beach and the boardwalk.

Long Beach is a public beach, but you do have to pay a $10 daily rate to get on the sand. If you take the LIRR to the beach, they offer discounted beach passes with the purchase of a train ticket. Walk east from the train station through the suburban streets filled with eclectic old homes and apartment buildings, and you might think you're in Brooklyn, since the area has an urban layout. Once you hit the boardwalk, you'll enter your summer escape. If you brought a bike, take a ride along the two-mile long board-walk or just simply enjoy a leisurely walk stopping at the many available benches to admire the view from the water. You can bring food onto this beach, which is a must since the boardwalk doesn't offer much in the way of food and libations. There is only one place to get food on the entire two-mile stretch, and although there are the occasional folks selling ice cream and bottles of water around the beach, it's best to pack a lunch.

If you'd like to take a break from the beach and head to Park Avenue for lunch, you can grab a slice at the extremely popular **Gino's Restaurant and Pizzeria** (16 West Park Avenue; 516-432-8193). If you want to stay for dinner and dine from a menu filled with everything from pistachio-encrusted salmon to pot stickers, I'd recommend **Duke Falcon's Global Grill** (36 West Park Avenue; 516-897-7000), located directly across from the LIRR station. For those in search of breakfast food like a bagel or a sandwich for your beach visit, stop by **Max Bialystok & Co.** (159 East Park Avenue; 516-432-5300)

On the west side of Long Beach at the end of the boardwalk, there is a small town offering some nightlife. Most people in the bars are locals since Long Beach isn't an overnight destination and doesn't offer any real accommodations, although a hotel is in the process of being built, the **Allegria Hotel and Spa** (80 West Broadway; 516-889-1300; www.allegriahotel.com), slated to open in the summer of 2009. But for now, most city people just enjoy the beach and then head back on the Long Island Railroad. If you do opt to drive to Long Beach, get there early since parking fills up quickly. There is no designated parking lot for the beach, but you can park on the many free parking spaces on the blocks bordering the beach.

If you always wanted to know how to surf, you can take a lesson at the popular Long Beach surfing school, **Surf 2 Live** (516-432-9211; www.surf2live.com). You can take a private lesson for $115 (or $125 with master surf instructor Elliot Zuckerman) or on weekends, as part of a group, take a group lesson for $65, both of which include the gear for the lesson like the wetsuit and board. Please note that you will still have to pay the $10 admission to the beach. All lessons take place on Long Beach. If you want to purchase some surf equipment, head to **Unsound Surf** (359 East Park Avenue; 516-889-1112; www.unsoundsurf.com), a large surf shop on the main road.

You can also spend the day at **Jones Beach** (516-785-1600; www.nysparks.state.ny.us), which is about fifteen minutes from Long Beach. Jones Beach is a bit harder to get to without a car. You must take the railroad to Freeport and then get a connecting bus from the Freeport Train Station. If you have a car, this beach is easily accessible and less than an hour from the city. The beach is six and a half miles long and offers amenities like a snack bar, a pool, and miniature golf. There is also a popular amphitheater at the beach complex that hosts a summer concert series; the Jones Beach Web site has the current schedule (www.jonesbeach.com).

Fire Island

Ditch your car and hop aboard a thirty-minute ferry (99 Maple Avenue, Bayshore; 631-665-3600; www.fireislandferries.com) from Bayshore to **Fire Island** (www.fireisland.com), where weekenders pack up coolers with food from home and fill red wagons for their time on the beach. The island is made up of many sections, from Ocean Beach, attracting NYC singles to areas like Fair Harbor and Dunewood attracting a more family friendly crowd, to Cherry Grove, a popular gay community. Most restaurants, shops, bars and clubs are located in Ocean Beach or Cherry Grove.

The draw of Fire Island is the immaculate beaches. Walkers will enjoy an outing to the Sunken Forest, a maritime forest on the island, where the tree branches are twisted due to wind and salt spray. Explore the forty-acre forest on the boardwalk that runs through it. The forest is a great place for bird-watching. There are also a lot of deer on Fire Island, especially in the Sunken Forest, so you should take proper precautions to avoid ticks that may carry Lyme disease. The Sunken Forest is easily accessible from both Cherry Grove and Ocean Beach.

There aren't many hotel accommodations on Fire Island since most people rent homes for the weekend, and the few hotels book up quickly. You can find house rentals for all sections of Fire Island on Fire Island's official Web site (www.fireisland.com), (www.cyberrentals.com) or check Craigslist (www.craigslist.org).

Looking for a hotel on Ocean Beach? Try the **Palms Hotel** (168 Cottage Walk; 631-583-8870; www.thepalmsatoceanbeach.com). This boutique hotel is located in the center of Ocean Beach, but it's quite popular and books up fast. Folks also enjoy staying at the **Clegg's Hotel** (Bayberry Walk; 631-583-5399; www.cleggshotel.com) conveniently located across from the ferry dock in Ocean Beach.

If you want to spend the weekend in Cherry Grove, check out the rooms at **Grove Hotel** (631-597-6600; www.grovehotel.com). This hotel is also home to the Miss Fire Island contest.

If you like to camp, **Watch Hill** *(631-567-6664; www.watchhillfi.com)* is the only camping facility on the island. They have twenty-six sandy sites, with running water, bathrooms, showers, and grills. They don't take phone reservations, and you must download the application and send it to them before you arrive. They do accept walk-ins, but they book up fast so it's hard to count on getting a space. When I called their number to get camping information, there was a helpful recording of all the weekends they were fully booked.

To get to the campgrounds at Fire Island, you should take the Long Island Railroad to Patchogue, where just a short walk from the train station you will be able to access the **Davis Ferry Park** *(631-475-1665; www.davispark-ferry.com)* for ferry service to Watch Hill. Come prepared with all the essentials since this part of Fire Island is a bit removed from the other sections and it will be a long walk to Cherry Grove or Ocean Beach if you've forgotten anything. It also tends to get very buggy in this area, so pack lots of bug spray and citronella candles.

Southampton and East Hampton

Filled with celebrities and Manhattan's elite, the Hamptons are not only beach towns but also define a certain way of living. Of course when I think of the Hamptons, the first thing that comes to mind is the intense traffic and how much time I wasted just trying to get a few blocks in my car. The Hamptons are accessible by both the Long Island Railroad and the Hampton Jitney, a bus that runs from various points in NYC to the Hamptons.

Spend the day in Southampton, where you can either worship the sun at the beach or go shopping on their Main Street, stopping in at **Hildreth's** *(51-55 Main Street; 631-283-2300; www.hildreths.com)* to browse their classic home goods. I'm somewhat fascinated by this place since it's so classic and seems so fitting on Main Street. At Hildreth's, they sell everything from furniture to children's toys and clothes. I also always like to stop by **BookHampton** *(91 Main Street; 631-283-0270; www.bookhampton.com)*. This is one of my favorite independent bookstores, which also has locations in East Hampton, Amagansett, and Sag Harbor.

Head over to East Hampton and grab a bite at **Babette's** *(66 Newtown Lane; 631-329-5377; www.babetteseasthampton.com)*, where vegetarians will love the yummy lentil-walnut burger. Meat lovers will be happy too with their selection of non-veggie dishes. Perhaps you might also like to dine on fabulous Italian food at the East Hampton staple **Nick and Toni's** *(136 North Main*

Street; 631-324-3550; www.nickandtonis.com). This restaurant has been a local favorite for years and the owners of Nick and Toni's also own **Rowdy Hall** (10 Main Street; 631-324-8555), where you can get classic pub fare. It is also open for lunch.

If you'd like to visit a calm beach on the Long Island Sound, head to **Cooper's Beach** (268 Meadow Lane; 631-283-0247). At this beach, nonresidents must pay $35 on weekends for parking but it has the benefit of being patrolled by lifeguards and having restrooms and a snack bar.

If you have kids along for the weekend, you might want to stay at the extremely kid-friendly **Southampton Inn** (91 Hill Street, Southampton; 631-283-6500; www.southamptoninn.com), which has a playroom with art supplies and ride-on toys. The ninety-room inn also offers free shuttles to Cooper's Beach in the summer. It's a short walk to town from Southampton Inn and is also near a playground.

Kids might also enjoy a visit to the **Children's Museum of the East End** (376 Bridgehampton Turnpike; 631-537-8250; www.cmee.org) in Bridge-hampton, just a few minutes from Southampton. The museum has exhibits on the East End, exposing kids to local East End farm stands and sea-faring ships. They also have a drop-in art center. This museum is the ideal place to spend the day with the family if the weather isn't in your favor, or if you visit off-season.

Sag Harbor and Amagansett

The neighboring towns of Sag Harbor and Amagansett are my favorite places to spend the weekend while in the Hamptons. If you want the feel of a New England whaling village, then you should spend the weekend in Sag Harbor. This quaint town has tons of shopping, a ferry to Shelter Island, and its own theater. Amagansett has a lot of offer too, with nightlife and two public beaches. Nestled between the Hamptons and Montauk, these two towns should not be overlooked.

Bibliophiles will love Sag Harbor's Main Street, which houses many book-stores and other independently-owned shops. Main Street is filled with great home-goods shops including one that I always make a point of visiting. **Flash-backs** (69B Main Street, Sag Harbor; 631-725-9355) is known for their diverse selection of interesting Indonesian furniture and home accessories. Flash-backs, until recently, was known as Back to Bali, but it still offers the same merchandise in the same location, as it has for over twenty years.

Looking for a fresh seafood lunch? Take a ride on the ferry from Sag Harbor to Shelter Island and have lunch at **Bob's Fish Market and Restaurant** *(87 North Ferry Road; 631-749-0830)*, about a ten-minute drive from the ferry terminal. A local suggested this place and although it's just a fish market with a few tables, everything they cook is fresh. It's definitely worth the ferry ride over from Sag Harbor. After lunch, head back to Sag Harbor, to **Big Olaf** *(Long Wharf, Sag Harbor; 631-725-7505)* for a scoop of freshly made ice cream and to take a walk along the pier.

If you're in Sag Harbor for dinner, make reservations for the restaurant at the **American Hotel** *(49 Main Street; 631-725-3535; www.theamerican-hotel.com)* or have a meal while staring at the views of the water at the **Dockside Bar and Grill** *(26 Bay Street; 631-725-7100)*. For nightlife, have at drink and see a band in Amagansett at the **Stephen Talkhouse** *(161 Main Street; 631-267-3117; www.stephentalkhouse.com)* or stay in Sag Harbor to see a show at the **Bay Street Theater** *(631-725-9500; www.baystreet.org)*, open from March through December.

You can spend the day at **Atlantic Beach** *(Atlantic Avenue; 631-324-2417)*, a public beach in Amagansett that has concession stands and a lifeguard. Unfortunately, the beautiful Indian Wells Beach is off limits to nonresidents. If you stay in an area hotel, they often provide transportation to the beaches.

For a nice weekend on a private beach, book a room at the **Ocean Dunes** *(379 Bluff Road, Amagansett; 631-267-8121; www.oceandunes.net)* in Amagansett. The resort doesn't allow anyone under fourteen to stay there, so leave the kids at home. The rooms, ranging from studios to two bedroom apartments, are equipped with kitchens and decks. They also have a private beach located a few hundred yards from Indian Wells Beach and an outdoor pool and pond.

Another Amagansett resort is the **White Sands Resort** *(18 Shore Road; 631-267-3350; www.whitesands-resort.com)*. This resort has a private beach and doesn't allow kids under thirteen years of age, although they said they are flexible in the off-season. The rooms range from small efficiencies to suites.

Montauk

En route to Montauk from Amagansett, I always stop for lunch at the **Clam Bar** *(Montauk Highway, Amagansett; 631-267-6348)*, a little roadside restaurant that has some of the best fresh seafood and baked clams in town. Across the road from the Clam Bar is the **Lobster Roll** *(1980 Montauk Highway, Amagansett; 631-267-3740; www.lobsterroll.com)*, which is another roadside joint that is quite popular. Since there is a large LUNCH sign outside, the Lobster Roll is also referred to as "Lunch" by the locals. Both are excellent and are great places to stop for a casual roadside lunch.

Located at the tip of Long Island, past the glitz of the Hamptons, is the town of Montauk. This is the very end of Long Island and in fact, you can purchase MONTAUK: THE END bumper stickers and T-shirts in various tourist shops in the area. Montauk might be the end of the island, but it's a great place to begin a weekend getaway. Montauk's main street is quite small and isn't posh and overwhelming like the main drags of the other Hamptons. I find the laid-back vibe of Montauk quite refreshing and every time we plan a getaway out east, we stay in Montauk for this very reason. Although Montauk was once home to the famous Andy Warhol, there isn't much of a celebrity presence.

The town's vibe is changing a bit in Montauk; recently the **Surf Lodge** *(183 Edgemere Street; 631-238-5190; www.thesurflodge.com)* opened. This new boutique hotel features a restaurant with executive chef Sam Talbot, who was once featured on Bravo's *Top Chef*. The thirty-two-room hotel offers surfing lessons and an all-day cocktail bar, although I don't recommend taking a surfing lesson after a day at the bar.

Besides the Surf Lodge, there is another boutique hotel in town, the **Solé East** *(90 Second House Road; 631-688-2105; www.soleeast.com)*, a renovated historic Montauk hotel once known as the Shepherds Neck Inn that now offers bungalow-style rooms with amenities like iPod docks and a poolside DJ. Despite attracting a hip clientele, the Solé East also caters to families and has a playroom on the premises. The hotel is about a mile from town and is not located on the water. If you want to stay closer to the beach, they also run the **Solé East Beach,** a motel (in the process of being renovated), located only yards from the surf and the main street.

For a visit to old-school Montauk, which I fell in love with years ago, grab a bite at **Gosman's Dock** *(500 West Lake Drive, Montauk; 631-668-5330; www.gosmans.com)*, which has a seafood menu that never disappoints. You can even watch the fishermen returning to shore in their boats with their catches of the day. There is no finer getaway moment than watching the sunset while dining on the deck overlooking the water. If you have access to a grill, pick up some fresh fish at **Gosman's Fish Market**. Gosman's pier also houses some shops.

You can also grab a dinner by the docks at **Dave's Grill** *(Montauk Harbor Docks; 631-668-9190; www.davesgrill.com)* for fun atmosphere, fresh food, and waterfront views. They also have a nice selection of pastas and steak. This is a great place to spend your Saturday evening in Montauk. Reservations are suggested.

A few blocks down from the dock is the **Viking Fleet Ferry Terminal** *(www.vikingfleet.com)*, which provides ferry service to Block Island, Rhode Island. In season, they operate a high-speed ferry, cutting the trip to Block Island to an hour. During the summer, the ferry leaves daily at 10 a.m. and departs Block Island at 5 p.m. We love to take our bikes on the ferry and ride around Block Island. You can also rent a bike at the ferry stop in Block Island. If you aren't a fan of cycling uphill, this might not be for you. The ferry leaves you off at the opposite side of the island from all the shopping, where the New London ferries dock, so you must find your way to the other side if you're in search of food and drink. You can rent bikes at the ferry terminal or you can take a taxi into the center of Block Island. This is a great day trip from Montauk if you are there for an extended weekend.

You can easily spend a week relaxing on Montauk's beaches, which have great surf, and although the nightlife is slim, we like to splurge on ocean-view rooms so we can simply sit on the deck and look at the ocean while drinking some wine. For the best ocean view in town, you should book a room at the **Royal Atlantic Motel** *(South Edgemere Street; 631-668-5103; www.royalatlantic.com)*. The Royal Atlantic isn't fancy, but the views, the pool with beach access, and the free breakfast make up for any shortcomings some might find. In the spring and fall, it's quite a deal. The motel is also kid-friendly, which is hard to find in many of the surrounding areas. The Royal Atlantic has a bit more upscale apartments across the street, but none are directly on the ocean.

If you're there to surf, you should stay near Ditch Plains beach, which has the best surf. Book a room and meet other surfers at the **East Deck Motel** *(40 Deforest Road; 631-668-2334; www.eastdeckmotel.com)* a surfer haven located right near the popular Ditch Plains beach.

If you want something a bit more fancy, stay at the stunning and historic **Montauk Manor** *(236 Edgemere Street, Montauk; 631-668-4400; www.montaukmanor.com)*, which has been around since 1927 and has the timeless appeal of an old-fashioned vacation resort. We always spend long weekends here taking advantage of their outdoor and indoor pools and gorgeous property. The Montauk Manor offers a variety of rooms that are actually individually owned condominiums that the resort manages and rents. The only caveat is the lack of waterfront property as this hotel is located on a hill overlooking Montauk. The rooms don't come with breakfast, although there is a nice restaurant at the hotel.

If you're looking for a satisfying breakfast, drive down to the main street and wait on line for some of the best pancakes I've ever tasted, at Montauk's famous **Mr. John's Pancake House** *(Main Street, Montauk; 631-668-2328)*. If you want to indulge, order the *E.T.* pancakes, which are filled with chocolate and peanut butter. You might want to wait awhile before hitting the surf as the food here is rich and heavy—and extremely tasty.

Another fun way to spend the afternoon is getting a massage at **Seawater Spa at Gurney's** *(200 Old Montauk Highway; 631-668-2345; www.gurneysinn.com)*. This spa menu includes everything from loofah scrubs to massages. Please note that if you aren't staying at Gurney's Inn, there is a $28 facility fee added on to the cost of your treatment, but which provides access to their sauna, fitness room, and Roman bath. If you want to spend the day at the spa, but aren't interested in a specific treatment, you can just pay the facility fee and take advantage of the wonderful amenities Gurney's has to offer. This might entice you to spend an entire weekend at the resort, which has over a hundred deluxe ocean suites as well as cottages, if you are looking for a bit more privacy.

For those who want an afternoon away from the sand, take a trip to the **Montauk Lighthouse** *(Turtle Hill, Montauk; 631-668-2524; www.montauklighthouse.com)*, which sits at the very tip of Long Island. If you drive all the way to the end of Montauk Highway, you'll arrive at the lighthouse. The lighthouse is the oldest one in New York State, dating back to 1796. If you don't mind the steep spiral staircase, it's fun to climb to the top. The lighthouse is still active and it's interesting to tour the museum and the grounds that overlook the ocean beyond the end of Long Island.

Tips for Planning Your Hamptons Getaway

If you want a peaceful weekend away that won't cost a ton, head to the Hamptons during the off-season. We always spend a long weekend in Montauk in either May or September because the beaches aren't crowded and you have access to private beaches. They also don't check beach passes in the off-season and it's easier to get reservations at our favorite restaurants. Keep in mind that lifeguards aren't on duty during the off-season, so be cautious in the water. The benefits of the days before Memorial Day or after Labor Day are plentiful, such as escaping the summer traffic and getting great rates at area hotels and bed-and-breakfasts.

Chapter Twenty-three

Beaches, Part 2:

The Jersey Shore

Travel time from NYC: Varies according to location on the Shore

Driving directions: Most shore towns are accessible by the Garden State Parkway.

Public transportation: All shore towns are accessible by New Jersey Transit (973-275-5555; www.njtransit.com). Academy Bus (201-420-7000; www.academybus.com) and Greyhound (800-231-2222; www.greyhound.com) run buses to the shore from the Port Authority.

From high rollers to beachgoers, there is always something happening at the shore. The Jersey Shore is a great destination for a weekend getaway because of the many towns that offer diverse experiences. You can spend the weekend sunbathing and enjoying the boardwalk rides at Point Pleasant or relax in Spring Lake at a Victorian B and B that has the feel of an 18th-century seaside resort. You can also embrace the miles of boardwalks filled with endless amusements and caramel corn in Ocean City. From dry towns that forbid the sale of alcohol to all-night parties, you can find it down at the Shore. So put on some Springsteen and head to the sunny shores of Jersey.

I've listed the towns on the Jersey Shore by proximity to New York City. Some of the Jersey towns are only an hour from the city, giving you the option of spending the day at the beach or a weekend soaking in the sun and the sights.

Asbury Park

When most people think about Asbury Park, they think of Bruce Springsteen and the Stone Pony. Yes, the Stone Pony is still there, but the landscape of this beach metropolis has changed. Similar to New York City's Coney Island, for years the neighborhood was disrepair, but a recent surge in development at Asbury Park (www.theasburyparkboardwalk.com) has brought a second life to this now hip beach town.

In 2008 the city revamped the boardwalk area and brought miniature golf back to the boardwalk at **Asbury Park Boardwalk Miniature Golf** (Boardwalk, Third and Fourth Avenues; 732-897-6500). The building that once housed the carousel at the end of the boardwalk is now a performance space that is home to the local **ReVision Theatre** *(700 Ocean Avenue; 732-455-3059; www.revisiontheatre.org)*, which produces everything from classic Broadway shows like *Hair* to productions by new playwrights.

Across from the Revision Theatre is the gay-friendly **Empress Hotel** *(101 Asbury Avenue; 732-774-0100; www.asburyempress.com)*, a chic South Beach–flavored ocean-side hotel with 101 rooms, and a large pool with pool-side tiki huts. The Empress is also home to the popular gay club **Club Paradise** *(732-988-6663 www.paradisenj.com)* as well as the **Ketchup Grill** *(732-988-6663)*, which opened in the hotel in 2008.

The once boarded-up main street, Cookman Avenue, is now flourishing with cool restaurants and home-goods stores like **Shelter Home** *(704 Cookman Avenue; 732-774-7790; www.shelterhome.com)* and pet specialty shops like **Asbury Bark** *(611 Cookman Avenue; 732-775-4801; www.asburybark.com)*. Art abounds on Cookman Avenue at the **Cry Baby Gallery** *(717 Cookman Avenue; 732-869-0606; www.crybabyartgallery.com)*, which features artists from around the country.

Stop in for dinner at **Old Man Rafferty's** *(541 Cookman Avenue; 732-774-1600; www.oldmanraffertys.com)* for delicious American fare. Cookman Avenue is undergoing a major transformation and every summer we visit, there are lots of new restaurants and shops to visit.

For the folks in search of signs of the Bruce, you can spend a night listening to bands at the **Stone Pony** *(913 Ocean Avenue; 732-502-0600; www.stoneponyonline.com)* and hoping he'll stop in and jam. Although Madame Marie, the famed fortuneteller that Bruce Springsteen immortalized in the song "4th of July, Asbury Park," passed away in 2008, the sign for her booth, the Temple of Knowledge, is still on the boardwalk.

Other parts of Asbury's past are still alive, like the famous **Wonder Bar** *(1213 Ocean Avenue; 732-502-8886; www.wonderbarasburypark.com)*, which reopened in 2008 and is the perfect place to have a drink or see a band. Don't forget to bring your dog along to their fun doggie happy hour. The **Paramount Theater** *(1300 Ocean Avenue; 732-897-8810; www.theasburyparkboardwalk.com)* has been immersed in Asbury Park's lavish past for decades and at one time held shows featuring the Marx Brothers. The theater has been fully restored and is now a popular concert venue.

Ocean Grove

Next to rocking Asbury Park sits the gorgeous Victorian town of **Ocean Grove** (www.oceangrovenj.com), which is on the National Register of Historic Places. Methodist ministers who wanted a seaside resort with religious values created Ocean Grove in 1869. The town still hosts the Ocean Grove Camp Meeting Association (www.ogcma.org), offering folks the chance to connect with their spiritual side through church services. There are still remnants of ties to the religious background of this neighborhood, as the town is "dry"—alcohol consumption and beach activities are not allowed on Sunday mornings.

Very similar to the Victorian style of Cape May, but only a little over an hour from the city, Ocean Grove has a small-town feel, with a quaint main street and a plethora of bed-and-breakfasts to choose from, some of which are located across from the beach. Main Avenue, Ocean Grove's main street, is filled with high-end antique dealers and home-goods shops. Stop in for an egg cream at **Nagle's Apothecary Café** (43 Main Avenue; 732-776-9797). This classic ice cream parlor looks like it's straight from the 1950s. Most restaurants allow you to bring your own alcohol, which you can pick up in neighboring Asbury Park. Ocean Grove a great place to spend the day with the family or for a romantic escape to a bed-and-breakfast.

Spring Lake

Spring Lake is another gorgeous Victorian town that will make you feel as if you're at a classic beach resort. This quiet town is the perfect getaway for over-stressed New Yorkers. Book a room or just enjoy a nice meal in their dining room with views of the ocean at the **Breakers on the Ocean** (1507 Ocean Avenue; 732-449-7700; www.breakershotel.com) located directly across from the boardwalk. Or you can choose to spend your days strolling the one-and-a-half-mile boardwalk. The beach is open to the public, with just a small fee to enter. There are two beach houses on the boardwalk for changing. A few blocks from the ocean is Spring Lake's main street, Third Avenue, which is filled with independently owned shops providing everything from chocolates to books. Third Avenue certainly has character and also offers folks some casual dining.

Spring Lake has tons of charming places to stay—from old Victorian summer homes turned into bed-and-breakfasts to larger inns. Places tend to book up fast, so reserve early. Make sure to arrange for a table at **Whispers** (200 Monmouth Avenue; 732-974-9755; www.whispersrestaurant.com), which is housed in the **Hewitt-Wellington Hotel** (732-974-1212; www.hewittwellington.com), where you can dine overlooking Spring Lake in an elegant Victorian setting.

Spring Lake is ideal for folks without a car, because the quiet beach, the lush park with a lake in the center of town, as well as all of the shopping, are all easily accessible by foot. There isn't much by way of nightlife, but if you are looking for some casual waterfront dining and bars, visit neighboring Belmar Beach, which borders Spring Lake.

Cycle, walk, or drive to Belmar, which is also extremely kid-friendly. Have some seafood at **Annie's Ocean Grill** *(732-245-3122)* on the boardwalk at the 8th Avenue Pavilion overlooking a playground—a great place to grab quick food with the kids. There is also a mix of Jersey nightlife. For a taste of the classic Jersey club scene, you can dance the night away at **D'jais** *(1801 Ocean Avenue; 732-681-5055; www.djais.com)*, which first opened in 1979. They also have an outdoor grill. Since the surf is amazing at both Spring Lake and Belmar, book a lesson with **Summer Time Surf** *(732-599-2700; www.summertimesurf.com)*, housed at the 2nd Avenue Beach in Belmar. Their private lessons for all levels start at $60, and they offer a "Surf Skills" class on Saturdays for adults who already know how to surf and want to improve their technique.

Point Pleasant Beach

As this destination is located just a little more than an hour from the city, you can either plan a day trip or a weekend getaway to Point Pleasant Beach. Either way, you'll definitely get a taste of the spirit of the Jersey Shore in this beach haven. Point Pleasant is home to Jenkinson's Boardwalk, which houses an amusement park, a nightclub, an aquarium, a band shell, and tons of eateries and shops, as well as being a prime viewing spot for fireworks displays, this kitschy beach town never fails to amuse.

We love to head down to Point Pleasant *(www.pointpleasantbeach.com)* to enjoy the clean public beaches. For a small fee, you get a day pass to the beach, and kids under the age of five are free. After a morning of sunning yourself at the beach and surfing the waves, check out what lives under the water at **Jenkinson's Aquarium** *(300 Ocean Avenue; 732-892-0600; www.jenkinsons.com/aquarium)*, where you can see penguins, seals, sharks, and alligators having their daily meals. The aquarium is housed indoors so you can visit even in the heart of the winter.

After learning about the wonders of the sea, try your luck at the many classic games that line the boardwalk where you can win everything from stuffed animals to video game consoles. Kids and tots alike will love **Jenkinson's South Amusement Park** located directly on the boardwalk. Here you can buy tickets for the kiddie ferris wheel as well as the many rides that appeal to the under-

48-inches set. The amusement park is well maintained and Jenkinson's does a great job of providing specialized family entertainment, including weekly fireworks shows and kid-friendly Sunday night movies on the beach.

There is a great selection of good eats (or should I say bad-for-your-waistband eats), ranging from pizza to fried fish. Kitschy vendor stands shaped like large lemons, where you get fresh lemonade, line the boardwalk and add to the beach vibe. The boardwalk also has the famous **Kohrs** *(732-899-9444; www.kohrbros.com)* frozen custard stand.

What could be more fun than having a cocktail and hearing the waves of the ocean splashing ashore? Enjoy a night out on the boardwalk at **Martell's Tiki Bar** *(732-892-0131; www.tikibar.com)* where you can hang out both day and night. They often host live music, and they have a great raw bar and patio where you can have cocktails on the beach with friends. If you want to dine off the boardwalk, head to **Spike's Fish Market** *(415 Broadway; 732-295-9400)* for some fresh seafood or to **Red's Lobster Pot** *(57 Inlet Drive; 732-295-6622; www.redslobsterpot.com)* for either indoor or dockside dining.

Point Pleasant is another great escape for New Yorkers who do not wish to travel as far as Wildwood or Ocean City, but who want a similar atmosphere. If you would like to spend the night, there are a bunch of motels in the area, like the popular **Point Pleasant Manor** *(310 Sea Avenue; 800-756-7717; www.pleasantmanor.com)*, which is equipped with a pool and a free shuttle to the beach.

Atlantic City and Surrounding Areas

Probably the most famous town of the Jersey Shore, this year-round resort town is the East Coast version of Vegas. Stay at one of the many hotel-casinos that line the boardwalk and you'll be in the center of Atlantic City's famed beachfront strip. From the Trump Taj to Bally's, luxury hotels offer great nightlife—some with concert venues—and top-rated restaurants and luxurious spas. It's no wonder that New Yorkers flock to this weekend destination to have fun at the casino, indulge in amazing buffets, and spend time at the beach. Although I've been to Atlantic City many times, I've never felt sand on my feet, and I'm sure that most folks will agree that although this is a shore town, you don't go there for the beach.

Step into the casinos that line the boardwalk, including the Wild West–themed **Bally's** *(609-340-2000)* with the popular Virginia City Buffet, a lunchtime stop for many casino patrons. Of course, not all folks come to Atlantic City to gamble and spend their days casino-hopping; some take in the amusements at the **Steel Pier** *(www.steelpier.com)*, which has classic seaside rides like the carousel and the flume. Others might enjoy shopping at the **Piers Shops at Caesar's** *(www.thepiershopsatcaesars.com)*, a mall on the boardwalk that has everything from an Apple Store to a Louis Vuitton boutique and includes my personal favorite, **It'Sugar**, a candy shop where you can actually design your own chocolate bar.

For years the only place to try your luck was at the casinos along the boardwalk, and of course they are still a great option for your weekend getaway, but for the past few years the casinos around the marina, like the **Trump Marina** and **Harrah's,** have branched out, attracting many weekenders who are looking for a little luxury with their Atlantic City staples.

For New Yorkers who yearn for lodgings with a more cosmopolitan feel rather than a kitschy casino atmosphere, the **Borgata Hotel Casino and Spa** *(1 Borgata Way; 866-MY-BORGATA; www.theborgata.com)*, which opened in 2003, is an excellent option. The Borgata attracts a hip, younger crowd and plays host to many popular bands and comedians at their two venues, the Event Center and the Music Box.

If you're like me and enjoy the amenities of a nice hotel but don't want to stay in a casino, book a room at the **Water Club at the Borgata** *(800-800-8817; www.thewaterclubatborgata.com)*. This 800-room hotel, located next to the Borgata, doesn't have a casino on premises, but offers five-star amenities like indoor and outdoor pools, and the phenomenal Immersion Spa, which has a full menu of massages, facials, and other treatments. At this spa, all treatments are at least eighty minutes long. I indulged in a hot stone massage during my stay at the Water Club and highly recommend it. Since there are a limited number of treatment rooms, it's best to book your appointment in advance. If you do stay at the Water Club, don't forget to pack your bathing suit and pool-hop around the hotel's five pools. In the summer months the outdoor pools tend to get crowded, but as long as you book in advance you can reserve a poolside cabana. Also don't bring the kids since you have to be eighteen or older to use the Water Club pools.

The best thing about staying at the Water Club is that their guests can also use all of the facilities at the neighboring Borgata Casino. Guests at the Water Club can enjoy the Borgata's spa as well as their large pool and outdoor sunning area. The Borgata also has a first-rate barbershop where men can get a good shave. Women can enjoy a relaxing manicure and pedicure treatment at the salon. You can easily reach the Borgata through the lobby at the Water Club; both hotels are connected through an indoor walkway filled with upscale retail shops like La Perla and Just Cavalli. I loved my stay at the Water Club, because while I could enjoy the casino, the restaurants, and clubs at the Borgata, I could also sneak back to the Water Club for some peace and quiet. Having the option of escaping the often-overwhelming energy of the casino really helps folks get the most out of their Atlantic City escape. The rooms at the Water Club are spacious. I had a club room, which is their standard option. I loved staring at the view of the ocean from the large windows. At the Water Club, you have the choice of a view of the ocean or the scenic New Jersey wetlands. If you choose the ocean view room, you can see the lights in the distance from the boardwalk strip as well as the purple lights of the Borgata at night.

If you like to stay where all the action is, however, I would encourage you to book a room at the Borgata. Stripped of any Atlantic City cheesiness, this tasteful casino doesn't overwhelm with kitsch and is outfitted with dramatic colorful glass chandeliers by the artist Dale Chihuly, as well as upscale shopping, nightclubs, and wine bars.

In addition to luxury hotels, boardwalk haunts, and gambling, there are other attractions in Atlantic City. You can see the **Atlantic City Surf** (*Bernie Robbins Stadium, 545 North Albany Avenue; 609-344-7873; www.acsurf.com*), Atlantic City's minor league team, play at the Bernie Robbins Stadium.

Another option is to head over to Margate, about fifteen minutes from Atlantic City, to see **Lucy the Margate Elephant** (*9200 Atlantic Avenue, Margate; 609-823-6473; www.lucytheelephant.org*), a shore attraction that is a personal favorite of mine. This sixty-five-foot-high wooden elephant was built in 1881 to lure people to purchase real estate in the area. You can explore the inside of the elephant and climb to the top on a guided tour where you will find out interesting historical facts about its origin and the development of the region.

About thirty minutes from Atlantic City are the popular Jersey Shore beach towns of **Ocean City** (*www.ocnj.us*) and **Wildwood** (*www.wildwoodsnj.com*). With their vibrant boardwalks and amusement parks, water parks, and miniature golf courses, these towns are great fun for everyone. Both destinations are excellent weekend getaways, although you might want to book an extended weekend since even with light traffic they are almost three hours travel outside the city. Although Ocean City and Wildwood both have bustling boardwalks, Ocean City tends to be a bit more family-friendly, possibly due the fact that it's a "dry" town. Wildwood has a retro 1950s feel, with many motor lodges that show the architecture of the era. If you head to Ocean City, stop by a great eatery called **Ikes Famous Crab Cakes** (*1344 Boardwalk Avenue; 609-814-1700*) for nothing but the finest crab cakes.

The hotels and bed-and-breakfasts in both Ocean City and Wildwood fill up quickly during the summer season, and many charge additional fees if you don't book a room within fourteen days of your stay. It's also important to note that many will refuse to refund your deposit if you cancel within fourteen days of your stay. Be mindful of each hotel's and B and B's rules. Off-season, even well into mid-June, the hotels are quite flexible and offer lower rates that don't require a minimum two-night or one-week stay.

Ferry to Sandy Hook

The pristine beaches of the Jersey Shore are closer than you think and you don't have to sit in traffic to get there. Hop aboard the **Sea Streak ferry** (www.seastreak.com) from either the pier at East 35th Street or Pier 11 on Wall Street, to Sandy Hook, New Jersey (www.sandy-hook.com). Ferries depart daily in the summer and on weekends throughout June and September and the trip takes roughly thirty to forty minutes. Sandy Hook is known for its great five-mile bike trail, so remember to bring your bike on the ferry. There is an additional charge for bicycles.

Sandy Hook isn't a beach town but a national park, which is a part of the **Gateway National Recreation Center** (www.nps.gov/gate). When you get off the Sea Streak ferry you'll pass through the once-operational Fort Hancock, and the historic Sandy Hook lighthouse that was built in 1764. History buffs should take the time to tour the Fort Hancock Museum, the Battery Potter, and the History House. Or simply climb the steps of the lighthouse to see the views of the water.

Sandy Hook has both ocean and bay beaches with changing areas and showers. In addition to extremely tidy beaches, it also is home to the **Sandy Hook Bird Observatory** (20 Hartshorne Drive; 732- 872-2500; www.njaudubon.org/centers/shbo), run by the New Jersey Audubon Society.

It would be smart to pack a picnic lunch for your excursion since there aren't many dining options aside from a few concession stands at areas B, C, D, and E of the beach as well as the Seagull's Nest restaurant, which is located in beach area D. If you are interested in some fresh seafood, take the Sea Streak ferry or cycle over the drawbridge to the town of Highlands, where you will have your pick of seafood restaurants. If you'd like to stay for the weekend, Highlands offers bungalows or house rentals, including some bed-and-breakfasts. They advertise on the region's community Web site (www.sandy-hook.com).

The Best Excuses to Head out of NYC

From drive-in movies to pick-your-own farms, there is always a reason to plan a weekend getaway or to pick up a Zipcar. Here is a list of cool places to see within a couple hours from the city. Whenever possible I've mentioned weekend getaway locations near the places listed below so you can add them on to one of your weekend day trips or even create your own trip around these activities.

Drive-in Movie Theaters:

If you like to smoke, or you have kids that don't know the meaning of volume control, or you want to take your dog along to the movies, you'll feel welcome at the drive-in. For over seventy-five years, drive-in movie theaters have let folks watch flicks in the comfort of their own car or lawn chair. Just don't forget the portable radio if you want to watch the film outside your car!

Fair Oaks Drive-In *(Route 17, Middletown, NY; 845-361-5774; www.fairoaksdrivein.info)* Located about an hour and half from New York City, this drive-in has two screens and is so close to Route 17 that you can see the screens from road. There is also a concession stand on the grounds with video games. The drive-in is also located en route to or from Livingston Manor and Roscoe, so you can take in a flick on your fly-fishing weekend. The drive-in gets buggy, so pack the bug spray if you want to sit outside.

Hi-Way Drive-In *(10769 State Route 9W; 518-731-8672; www.hiwaydrivein.com)* Hi-Way Drive-In is located between Catskill and Coxsackie, about two-and-a-half hours from the city. It's an ideal spot to catch a flick if you are on a getaway to Hudson, New York, since it's only twenty minutes away from that town. We trek over here from Woodstock, too, since we are such fans of the drive-in. This is a rather large drive-in with four screens and they presently offer double features on three of the four screens.

Hollywood Drive-In *(Route 66, Averill Park, NY; 518-283-4425; www.holly-wooddrivein.com)* The Hollywood is only twenty minutes away from Hancock, Massachusetts, in the Berkshires, and a little less than an hour from Hudson, New York. It's been in operation since 1952. The family-run drive-in has one screen and a recently renovated concession stand where you can order homemade pizza.

The Hyde Park Drive-In *(510 Albany Post Road, Hyde Park, NY; 845-229-4738 www.hydeparkdrivein.com)* (See Hyde Park, page 113.)

The Overlook Drive-In *(Overlook Road; Poughkeepsie, NY; 845-452-3445; www.overlookdrivein.com)* Located off of Route 44 near the Poughkeepsie/Millbrook Exit on the Taconic, roughly two hours from New York City, the Overlook has one screen and a concession stand. The Overlook is open from May until October and they show double features. This drive-in is easily accessible from Hyde Park, Rhinebeck, Rosendale, and New Paltz.

The Warwick Drive-In *(9 Warwick Turnpike, Warwick, NY; 845-986-4440; www.webusers.warwick.net)* The Warwick has three screens and is located about an hour and a half from New York City in Warwick, New York. This drive-in is the perfect place to visit after spending the day at Mountain Creek Water Park, which is fifteen minutes away in neighboring New Jersey. We usually visit the Warwick every September after a day picking apples at the many local orchards. The Warwick is open until the end of October.

Drive-in Restaurants:

These drive-in restaurants offer a retro dining experience. You can feel as if you've stepped back into the 1950s as you eat burgers and sip shakes at A-frame restaurants with outdoor seating or inside your own car at the drive-ins that still offer carhop service.

All American Drive-In *(4286 Merrick Road, Massapequa, NY; 516-798-9574; www.allamericanhamburger.us)* This classic restaurant has been serving hamburgers and franks to folks on Long Island's South Shore since 1963. Despite the lack of indoor seating, the All American is open year round. In the warmer months folks sit at the few picnic tables outside the restaurant or opt to eat in their cars. Although they don't have carhop service, All American calls itself a Drive-In and is a classic example of the restaurants of a bygone era.

Circus Drive-In *(State Highway 35, North Belmar, NJ; 732-449-2650; www.circusdrivein.com)* Since 1954, this classic Jersey Shore drive-in has been one great reason to hit the beach. Open from March until mid-October, the restaurant dishes all-American staples like hamburgers, and because it's at the shore, the seafood menu is chockfull of goodies like their famous stuffed Maryland soft-shell crabs. Oh, and don't forget to order the onion rings and a milk shake; you won't regret it. You can opt for carhop service or enjoy sitting at their casual dining area at this fun drive-in that was featured on a Food Network special. Throughout the beach-going season the drive-in hosts family-friendly events like visits from clowns. They also sell cool red Circus Drive-In T-shirts.

Red Rooster *(1566 Route 22, Brewster, NY; 914-279-8046)* If you're en route to the Berkshires, just a little over an hour from the city on Route 22 you should plan a stop at this A-frame drive-in restaurant that sells tasty burgers in a truly retro setting. The glass exterior of the Red Rooster is filled with all the press this little restaurant has gotten over the years, and it deserves the attention. You can sit on a picnic bench on their landscaped lawn behind the restaurant and chow down on their burgers and fries, and wash it down with an egg cream. After your meal, walk next door and play a game of miniature golf.

Sycamore Drive-In *(282 Greenwood Avenue, Bethel, CT; 203-748-2716; www.sycamoredrivein.com)* The Sycamore has been in continuous operation since 1948. This drive-in, which seems as if it's come straight off the set of *Happy Days*, still has carhop service as well as Elvis Nights and Cruise Nights, where people meet up in their antique cars. This drive-in has also been featured on the Food Network and people often make pilgrimages just to eat their famous burgers and drink their delicious homemade root beer. If you'd like to do a tour of drive-in restaurants, the Sycamore is less than half an hour from the Red Rooster. It's approximately an hour and a half from New York City, near Danbury, Connecticut.

Stewart's Drive-In *(938 Passaic Avenue; Kearny, NJ; 201-998-0600; www.stewartsfood.com)* The closest drive-in to New York City, only twenty minutes from downtown Manhattan and a few miles from the Holland Tunnel, is Stewart's. You'll be able to eat a hot dog here without even having to get out of your car as they still offer carhop service. This particular outpost of Stewart's Drive-In was featured on an episode of HBO's *The Sopranos*. The menu not only serves up hamburgers and fries, but also offers side orders of perogies. There are various locations of Stewart's Drive-Ins through-out New Jersey and each offers a slightly different menu. This location is open from March through October.

Weber's Famous Drive-In *(6019 Lexington Avenue, Pennsauken, NJ; 856-662-6632)* Weber's Famous struck my eye as I was driving to Philadelphia. Sitting in New Jersey right outside the outskirts of Philly, the once-national chain still offers carhop service. The carhop clips the tray to your car window and you can dine in the privacy of your car. At Weber's you can chow away on their famous Taylor pork roll sandwiches and yummy root beer floats. The drive-in is open from March through October.

Local Farms:

There is nothing like picking your pumpkin straight from the patch or making an apple pie with apples you chose from lush orchards. Personally, these days I love to know exactly where my fruit and vegetables come from. It's also a per-fect way to escape from the urban environment and to enjoy the scenic coun-tryside. Don't just buy your produce from a bodega this year; embrace the local farms and pick your own.

Apples, Pumpkins, Peaches, Pears, and Plums

Apple Hill Farm *(124 Route 32 South, New Paltz, NY; 845-255-1605; www.ap-plehillfarm.com)* After Labor Day, you can start picking many varieties of ap-ples, from Red Delicious to Rome Beauty, at this popular orchard in New Paltz. This is a great stop if you're in town for the language immersion weekend or it can easily become a day trip from the city. You don't need kids to enjoy a hayride around the orchard. Although, if you do have them with you, in addi-tion to the hayride, there are also fire truck rides available.

Applewood Orchards *(82 Four Corners Road, Warwick, NY; 845-986-1684; www.applewoodorchards.com)* Warwick is known for its many orchards, and my husband and I have been to most, but Applewood is a particularly quiet orchard that offers a petting zoo, puppet shows, and other kid-friendly activ-ities. For the adults, there is also a winery on the premises, so you can do a flight tasting of their tasty Hudson Valley wine. We like to combine a trip here with a visit to the Warwick Drive-In and also my personal favorite, **Bellvale**

Farms *(385 Route 17A, Warwick, NY; 845-988-1818; www.bellvalefarms.com)*, located just ten minutes away from the orchards, which sells the best home-made ice cream around. Atop Mount Peter, we like to hang out here and enjoy the view after a day picking apples, before we hit the flicks.

Lawrence Farms *(39 Colandrea Road, Newburgh, NY; 845-562-4268)* You can pick a lot more than apples at this Newburgh Farm. In the summer, you can pick strawberries, apricots, and peaches. You can even pick vegetables like broccoli and eggplant, along with many other fruits and vegetables. In the fall, you can try to escape from their fun corn maze, and I have to admit that it took me longer than I thought it would. They also have a little kid-sized village set up, where my kids love playing in the little homes, the small church, and jail.

Terhune Orchards *(330 Cold Soil Road, Princeton, NJ; 609-924-2310; www.terhuneorchards.com)* Heading to New Hope and Lambertville? This would be an easy stop since it's located in nearby Princeton, New Jersey. Ter-hune Orchards lets folks pick their own apples and pumpkins. They also offer hayrides and a petting zoo. The reason this is a great orchard is that the ap-ples are grown on dwarf trees, which makes them very easy to pick. Many orchards grow the apples on large trees, which require sticks for removing the apples from the high branches. This orchard requires very little work and is a great place to bring the little ones. In addition to apples, you can pick a variety of fruit including strawberries and cherries. Don't forget to grab some cider and tasty doughnuts for the ride home.

Love Apple Farm *(1421 Route 9H, Ghent, NY; 518-828-5048; www.loveap-plefarm.com)* Pick your own pears, plums, peaches, nectarines, and apples at this Columbia County farm. You can get to the farm easily from Hudson or on the way home from the Berkshires. You can also stock up on homemade jel-lies and jams at their farm store. They even have a petting zoo, where you can bottle-feed the baby animals on the farm or opt to buy a bag of feed for the adult animals.

Davis Peach Farm *(Hulse Landing Road, Wading River, NY; 631-929-1115; www.davispeachfarm.com)* If you're on your way to the North Fork, the Hamp-tons, or Montauk, you should make a detour to the Davis Peach Farm, where starting in July you can pick peaches and plums. Davis has over seventy vari-eties of peaches and over fifty varieties of plums. They also have "plumcots," a cross between a plum and an apricot. So stop by on your way east and stock up on fresh peaches and plums for your weekend at the beach.

Berries

Alstede Farms *(84 Route 513, Chester, NJ; 908-879-7189; www.alstede-farms.com)* Pick strawberries and cut your own flowers at this New Jersey Farm. Alstede offers pony rides and a bouncy castle on weekends, which is quite a hit with the kids. I like the idea of going out and cutting your own flowers. You can also pick red, black, and purple raspberries, currants, black-berries, peaches, peppers, tomatoes, eggplants, and apples. They also have events throughout the year. You can enjoy feeding the animals at farm or in the autumn crawling through their hay tunnel. We like to combine a straw-berry picking trip at Alstede Farms with a visit to either the Valley Shepherd Creamery or Wild West City. On the way home, we often stop at Stewart's Drive-In at Kearny before we head back through the Holland Tunnel.

Hodgson Farm *(2290 Albany Post Road, Walden, NY; 845-778-1432; www.hodgsonfarm.com)* Pick strawberries, blueberries, and raspberries from this Orange County farm that's been open for over sixty-two years. You might want to combine a trip to this farm with a visit to Middletown's Fair Oaks Drive-In or a day at the Orange County Fair, which is held at the end of July in Middletown. You can pick tomatoes, peppers, and eggplant at the farm. If you're lucky enough to have outdoor space in the city, you should visit their enormous gar-den center to pick up some flowers for your terrace or yard. In the fall you can pick pumpkins and they have a spooky haunted house and corn maze.

Johnson's Corner Farm *(133 Church Road, Medford, NJ; 609-654-8643; www.johnsonsfarm.com)* Just thirty minutes outside of Philadelphia, this is a great farm to visit if you're traveling to Philly for the weekend and would like to experience a country setting on your urban getaway. You can also com-bine it with a trip to the Adventure Aquarium since it's not very far from Cam-den, New Jersey. We've also taken a day trip to the Johnson Corner Farm. They have tasty strawberries for the picking, as well as cherries, peas, and blueberries. There is a great farm store and a petting zoo. You can also pick sweet corn, peaches, apples, popcorn, sweet potatoes, and cotton at various times throughout the year. Check their Web site for the picking schedule. From Thanksgiving to Christmas you can make your own wreaths at the farm.

Grieg Farms *(223 Pitcher Lane, Red Hook, NY; 845-758-1234; www.greig-farm.com)* Pick blueberries, raspberries, apples, and pumpkins at this laid-back farm in Red Hook, where there aren't any bouncy castles or hayrides, just orchards and fields where you can pick fresh fruit. Take your picked berries next door and wash them down with a glass of wine at the neighboring Alison Vineyard. The tasting room is downstairs in a room that was comfortably chilly on the blistering summer day that we were in Red Hook. If you do a tasting you get a free wine glass, which of course I had to have since it had my name imprinted on it. It was hard to bring my son down to the wine cellar since he didn't want to leave the baby goats outside the vineyard behind Gigi's Market, where you can grab some fresh food. This is a great place to visit if you're in Rhinebeck since it's just a few miles from downtown Rhinebeck and even closer to the Old Rhinebeck Aerodrome.

Cheese

Sprout Creek Farm *(34 Lauer Road, Poughkeepsie, NY; 845-485-8438; www.sproutcreekfarm.org)* Stop by the Sprout Creek Farm to buy cheese and peer through the window of the market to see cheese being made or into the barn to see the animals. They offer cheese-making classes for adults on Saturdays, so call ahead for their schedule. The farm offers educational workshops for kids, too.

The farm also has a three-bedroom cottage that is available for rent if you'd like to spend the weekend on an actual farm, where you can participate in farm chores like milking cows and feeding chickens. You have to be over twelve to participate in farm chores. This would be a fun getaway for couples as the farm offers coupons for the Millbrook Winery. This is a great place to visit or stay if you are on a getaway to Hyde Park or Rhinebeck or on the way to Lenox and Great Barrington.

Valley Shepherd Creamery *(50 Fairmount Road, Long Valley, NJ; 908-876-3200; www.valleyshepherd.com)* Take a tour of the farm and creamery at Valley Shepherd Creamery located an hour from New York City. They have a popular cheese-making class, where you get to make your own cheese wheel, but you must leave the wheel in a cave at the creamery for aging. You also get a farm tour, a cheese tasting, and lunch included in the class price. They host many events throughout the year including a shearing festival in May and a fall festival. You can tour the farm on weekends in the spring and summer. The Valley

Shepherd Creamery is located near both Alstede Farms and Wild West City, so you can combine a trip to the creamery with a visit to either of those attractions. If you want lunch, the **Long Valley Pub and Brewery** *(One Fairmount Road, Long Valley, NJ; 908-876-1122; www.longvalleypubandbrewery.com)* is on the same road as Valley Shepherd, and has good eats and a nice selection of brews.

Eggs

Stone Barns Center *(630 Bedford Road, Pocantico, NY; 914-366-6200; www.stonebarnscenter.org)* Stone Barns Center for Food and Agriculture offers a farm education program on the weekends. One of their family programs allows families to feed chickens and then gather their own eggs. They also house Blue Hill, a high-end restaurant that features local food. The tasting menu is roughly $95. For more casual fare, you can dine on a panini at the Blue Hill Café. Stone Barns offers many educational programs for adults including a popular "insider's tour" of the farm.

Amusement Parks:

You don't have to be a kid to enjoy a day at an amusement park. There is no better way to relieve tension from the week than by riding a roller coaster and screaming your head off. Here are a bunch of great amusement parks within a couple hours of the city. From water parks to enormous theme parks, there is a type of park to please any thrill seeker. Of course, I didn't mention the Cyclone in Coney Island since it's not out of town, but you can't beat a ride on that historic wooden roller coaster, which always leaves me slightly bruised but refreshed.

Adventureland *(2245 Route 110, Farmingdale, NY; 631-694-6868; www.adventureland.us)* I'm partial to this amusement park because my husband grew up ten minutes from it and it played a large part in his childhood. I also remember begging my parents to take me here when I was growing up in Queens. The park, which opened in 1962, is recently renovated with three water rides and an enormous section for the little park-goers. You don't have to pay admission to the park and instead can purchase single tickets for the rides. It's less than an hour from the city and is a great detour if you are heading out east to the beach or towards the North Fork.

Dorney Park and Wildwater Kingdom *(3830 Dorney Park Road, Allentown, PA; 610-395-3724; www.dorneypark.com)* Visit Charlie Brown and Snoopy at Camp Snoopy at this oversized amusement park in Pennsylvania. This is a great excursion to add on to your weekend getaway to Philadelphia, but it's also accessible as a day trip from the city since it's only ninety minutes from city limits. The park includes live shows, a water theme park, and tons of engaging rides for all ages. You can purchase tickets online at their Web site. You only have to pay one all-inclusive price and can spend the day seeing shows and riding on all the rides both at Dorney Park and the Wildwater Kingdom. There are discounts available if you purchase a two-day pass. Honestly, this park is so large that you might need two days to enjoy it properly. I'm a sucker for any Peanuts-related activities, so I'm a big fan of Dorney Park.

Great Adventure *(1 Six Flags Boulevard, Jackson, NJ; 732-928-1821; www.sixflags.com)* This is probably the most famous park in the tri-state area, but there is a reason for it. The popular park offers you the chance to drive through a 350-acre safari at an additional charge, where you can see giraffes and bears from the comfort of your own car. Great Adventure also has a large number of high-speed rides. If you have little ones, they can enjoy Wiggles World or the Bugs Bunny National Park. If you want to spend the day in the water, head next door to Six Flags Hurricane Harbor, the Six Flags water park. This is a great day trip from the city, or you can combine it with a trip to the Jersey Shore or Philadelphia. Buy discounted tickets online and peruse their Web site to plan your day around this large park.

Lake Compounce *(822 Lake Avenue, Bristol, CT; 860-583-3300; www.lakecompounce.com)* One of the oldest amusement parks in North America, this park grew from a pre–Civil War picnic park to an amusement park over the last two centuries. It was also the site of 1980's famed Milli Vanilli's lip-synching scandal, since they apparently lip synched at a show at Lamp Compunce. Fans of wooden roller coasters will be pleased with the two woodies on site at Lake Compounce. Soda addicts, like my husband, will get their fix because the park offers free Pepsi to all their guests. With a mix of classic rides and a nice water park, it's a great place to cool off in the summer. If you have the wee ones with you, they offer tons of family-friendly rides from kiddie bumper cars to a caterpillar train. Located two hours outside the city in picturesque Bristol, Connecticut, you can enjoy either a day trip or stay overnight at the many local accommodations.

Land of Make Believe *(354 Great Meadows Road, Hope, NJ; 908-459-9000; www.lomb.com)* Located a little more than an hour from the city and only twenty minutes from Wild West City and Alstede Farms, this amusement park caters to the under-twelve set and has been entertaining folks for over fifty years. This is an old-school park that really brings you back to the fifties idea of an amusement park and good old-fashioned fun. Ride on a historic carousel, a tilt-a-wheel, and don't forget your bathing suits because you can splash away on the Pirate Peak's water slide. This is also a good place to visit en route to the Poconos.

Mountain Creek Water Park *(200 Route 94, Vernon, NJ; 973-864-8444; www.mountaincreekwaterpark.com)* At the Mountain Creek Water Park you can ride a water slide that ends with an 18-foot drop into a quarry. This is a water park that will appeal to both adults and kids. It's filled with slides, wave pools, and an assortment of tubing slides. If you have toddlers, they can soak in the fun at the L'il Dippers section with gentle water play. This is a great day trip since it's little more than an hour from the city and is also located fifteen minutes from the Warwick Drive-In.

Quassy *(2132 Middlebury Road, Middlebury, CT; 800-FOR-PARK; www.quassy.com)* Enjoy a picnic at this lakeside amusement park that has been open since 1908. The park has tons of rides and a water play area called the "saturation center," where you can cool off after a day of rides or after relaxing at their beach at Lake Quassapaug. The amusement park has classic rides like a tilt-a-whirl and bumper cars.

Rye Playland *(Playland Parkway, Rye, NY; 914-813-7010, www.ryeplayland.org)* To me, the summer isn't complete without riding on my favorite wooden roller coaster, the Dragon Coaster. This park is located within thirty minutes of New York City in Rye. Bring your bathing suit since it's on the beach and they also have a pool on the premises. There is a nice selection of both kiddie and adult rides. They also have a miniature golf course. The park admission is free; you buy tickets for individual rides. You can also rent pedal boats for fun on Playland lake. I always have fun playing old-school video games in the arcade and riding the Log Flume. You can also spend the day soaking in the rays at the beach on the Long Island Sound at Rye Playland. They have a nice boardwalk and a public pool right near the beach and boardwalk. This is an easy day trip, but is also right off I-95 if you're on your way to Mystic or any other destination off the interstate.

Sesame Place *(100 Sesame Road, Langhorne, PA; 215-752-7070; www.sesameplace.com)* See New Hope and Lambertville, page 147.

Splish Splash *(2549 Splish Splash Drive, Riverhead, NY; 631-727-3600; www.splishsplashlongisland.com)* If you want to get wet on your way to the Hamptons, stop by this popular Long Island water park, located right off the Long Island Expressway, that was rated one of the top water parks by the Travel Channel. Explore Monsoon Lagoon with your little ones or go on a movie inspired adventure on the family raft ride, the Hollywood Stunt Rider. Slip and slide as you cool down at this water park that is fun for all ages.

Storybook Land *(6415 Black Horse Pike, Egg Harbor Township, NJ; 609-641-7847; www.storybookland.com)* This theme park based on children's fairy tales is a great place to spend the day if you're away for the weekend at the Jersey Shore. You might feel as if you are stepping back in time to your childhood, since little has changed in this park from the last twenty years. In fact, I have pictures of a visit to this park in the seventies and most of the buildings, like the large Humpty Dumpty, still exist. Storybook Land provides a gentle introduction to the world of children's literature and park rides. Kids can visit the house of the three little pigs or Cinderella's pumpkin chariot. This is a park for the under-six set; a child's height only has to be between 36 and 42 inches to ride most of the rides. The park is very conveniently accessed from Atlantic City, Ocean City, Wildwood, and Cape May.

Wild West City *(50 Lackawanna Drive, Stanhope, NJ; 973-347-8900; www.wildwestcity.com)* For over fifty years this Wild West heritage park has been holding up stagecoaches and hosting live music at the Golden Nugget Saloon. If you're a fan of fifties kitsch, this theatrical park is a must-visit. They offer twenty-two live action shows daily and have shops with western-themed merchandise. Since the Wild West City is modeled after Dodge City in the 1800s, the roads aren't paved, so wear comfortable and casual clothes. They also have miniature golf and a petting zoo on their grounds. Wild West City is located near Alstede Farms and the Valley Shepherd Creamery.

Web Resources

Here is a list of handy Web sites that were helpful in planning the excursions for the book.

New York City

www.nycvisit.com
NYC Tourism site

www.flavorpill.com
Cool things to do in NYC

www.gocitykids.parentsconnect.com
Cool kid-friendly activities in NYC

www.gonyc.about.com
About.com guide to NYC

www.hopstop.com
Guide to subway directions around NYC

www.iloveny.com
Official tourism site for NYC

www.manhattanusersguide.com
Online guide to city living

www.mta.info/nyct
Transit information for NYC

www.newyork.citysearch.com
Activities in NYC

www.notfortourists.com/newyork.aspx
Tourism site for NYC

www.nyc.gov
Official NYC site

www.nycgovparks.org
NYC Department of Parks and Recreation

sitewww.brooklyn-usa.org
Brooklyn Borough President's site

www.heartofbrooklyn.org
Organization that promotes tourism in Brooklyn

www.newyorkled.com
Website featuring activities in NYC

www.nymag.com
New York magazine

www.gothamist.com
New York City Daily Weblog

www.nytimes.com
New York Times Travel section on-line

www.newsday.com/travel
Local paper's travel section

www.nycvisit.com
Tourism site for NYC

www.queens.about.com
About.com guide to Queens

www.statenislandusa.com
Staten Island Borough President's site

www.timeout.com/newyork/kids
Time Out New York Kids

www.visitbrooklyn.org
Brooklyn tourism site

Weekends Away

www.discoverlongisland.com
Guide to Long Island, NY

www.longisland.com
Guide to Long Island, NY

www.eastofnyc.com
Web guide to events on Long Island, NY

www.mystic.org
Tourism site for Mystic, Connecticut

www.state.nj.us/travel
Tourism site for New Jersey

www.thebrandywine.com
Tourism guide to the Brandywine Valley

General Travel

www.chowhound.com
Food lovers posting about good eats

www.driveinmovie.com
Guide to U.S. drive-in movie theaters

www.foodcandy.com
Food lovers discussing new restaurants

www.tripadvisor.com
Site for hotel reviews and links to other sites (good for finding reasonable rates)

Index

city weekends